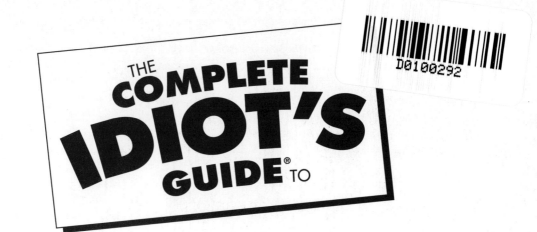

THE COMPLETE IDIOT'S GUIDE® TO

Cover and Bake Meals

by Ellen Brown

ALPHA

A member of Penguin Group (USA) Inc.

This book is dedicated to the generations of inspirational women food writers such as Marion Cunningham and my mentor Julia Child, who have shown us how to share the pleasures of food with those we love.

ALPHA BOOKS

Published by the Penguin Group

Penguin Group (USA) Inc., 375 Hudson Street, New York, New York 10014, U.S.A.

Penguin Group (Canada), 10 Alcorn Avenue, Toronto, Ontario, Canada M4V 3B2 (a division of Pearson Penguin Canada Inc.)

Penguin Books Ltd, 80 Strand, London WC2R 0RL, England

Penguin Ireland, 25 St Stephen's Green, Dublin 2, Ireland (a division of Penguin Books Ltd)

Penguin Group (Australia), 250 Camberwell Road, Camberwell, Victoria 3124, Australia (a division of Pearson Australia Group Pty Ltd)

Penguin Books India Pvt Ltd, 11 Community Centre, Panchsheel Park, New Delhi—10 017, India

Penguin Group (NZ), cnr Airborne and Rosedale Roads, Albany, Auckland 1310, New Zealand (a division of Pearson New Zealand Ltd)

Penguin Books (South Africa) (Pty) Ltd, 24 Sturdee Avenue, Rosebank, Johannesburg 2196, South Africa

Penguin Books Ltd, Registered Offices: 80 Strand, London WC2R 0RL, England

International Standard Book Number: 1-59257-371-1
Library of Congress Catalog Card Number: 2005926958

07 06 05   8 7 6 5 4 3 2 1

Interpretation of the printing code: The rightmost number of the first series of numbers is the year of the book's printing; the rightmost number of the second series of numbers is the number of the book's printing. For example, a printing code of 05-1 shows that the first printing occurred in 2005.

Printed in the United States of America

Note: This publication contains the opinions and ideas of its author. It is intended to provide helpful and informative material on the subject matter covered. It is sold with the understanding that the author and publisher are not engaged in rendering professional services in the book. If the reader requires personal assistance or advice, a competent professional should be consulted.

The author and publisher specifically disclaim any responsibility for any liability, loss, or risk, personal or otherwise, which is incurred as a consequence, directly or indirectly, of the use and application of any of the contents of this book.

Most Alpha books are available at special quantity discounts for bulk purchases for sales promotions, premiums, fundraising, or educational use. Special books, or book excerpts, can also be created to fit specific needs.

For details, write: Special Markets, Alpha Books, 375 Hudson Street, New York, NY 10014.

Publisher: *Marie Butler-Knight*
Product Manager: *Phil Kitchel*
Senior Managing Editor: *Jennifer Bowles*
Senior Acquisitions Editor: *Renee Wilmeth*
Development Editor: *Christy Wagner*
Production Editor: *Megan Douglass*

Copy Editor: *Nancy Wagner*
Cartoonist: *Shannon Wheeler*
Cover/Book Designer: *Trina Wurst*
Indexer: *Angie Bess*
Layout: *Becky Harmon*
Proofreading: *Donna Martin*

Contents at a Glance

Contents

What the recipe symbols mean:

- ▲ Fast
- ● Healthy
- ■ Make-ahead

Introduction

Casseroles, the well-known subset of cover and bake meals, are part of American life. Think about a potluck dinner or church social, and a vision of a lasagna or some other layered dish with meat and pasta comes to mind. Picture a summer cook-out, and right next to the platter of burgers are casseroles of baked beans along with macaroni and cheese.

Casseroles have been part of American cooking since the country's inception, but they didn't begin here. The actual word *casserole* comes from the French and refers to a *casse*, which was a medieval cooking vessel.

Some international casseroles have fancy names, such as French *coq au vin*, which is just chicken cooked in wine with various vegetables, or Greek *moussaka*, which is ground meat and eggplant topped with a custard sauce. In classical Chinese cooking, casseroles are assembled and eaten from pottery casseroles called sand-pots, also the name of the genre of food.

In a world that increasingly judges success by the efficient use of time, many of these meals might seem like a bother. Many recipes do require more than 15 minutes to prepare. But they are the whole dinner, perhaps augmented with a simple tossed salad. The preparation time for the entrée is the preparation time for the entire meal!

The initial benefit of preparing a cover and bake one-dish dinner is that you don't have to worry about whether or not different recipes work well together when joined on a plate. It's all right there in the same pan; the dish is everything you need for a complete, nutritious, and well-balanced meal.

Cover and bake is the overall term, but many of these recipes are prepared on top of the stove and are really *cover and simmer*. This is a boon during warm months when the heat generated by the oven is not exactly welcome.

The dishes in this book are "real food." They're not made with convenience products that list more chemicals on their labels than words recognizable as foods. It's a reliance on convenience products that led to the pejorative connotation that cover and bake meals have developed in this country over the past 40 years. In Chapter 1, you'll read about the pantry staples that simplify preparation, but none of them is a can of cream of anything soup or a cheese that is anything other than a cheese.

In addition to being made up of real foods, these meals are also economical. The less expensive cuts of meat perform the best when gently braised in liquid. Inexpensive pastas, rice, and beans also play a role in many of these recipes and are but pennies a serving.

Cover and bake recipes are also tolerant. Most can be at least partially prepared in advance, and the recipes are annotated with that information. Unlike a soufflé that must be eaten immediately from the oven, these dishes can wait or be served at different times. This aspect of cover and bake meals gives you such flexibility. This is a bonus when you're serving a buffet supper or on nights when family members might be eating at different times. Servings can be portioned out or reheated as necessary.

Cover and bake meals create a delicious aroma in the house that comes from the blending of innate flavors as dishes cook for a long time. This aroma creates anticipatory enthusiasm for the meal that will follow.

George Bernard Shaw wrote that "there is no love sincerer than the love of food." I would like to add that there are few more powerful ways to show love than by cooking for family and friends. I hope you enjoy these dishes in that context.

How This Book Is Organized

The book is divided into seven parts:

Part 1, "Fundamentals to Follow," gives you some basic knowledge concerning both equipment and ingredients. Each recipe chapter contains introductory material concerning the foods that serve as the foundation for the recipes, but the useful information in Part 1 concerns cover and bake cooking in general.

Part 2, "Rise and Shine," extends the cover and bake concept to the morning. Here you'll find recipes for a wide range of egg dishes, and a chapter of savory bread puddings perfect as side dishes as well as breakfast fare. Some recipes in Part 2 are vegetarian, while others are breakfast and brunch recipes that include various meats and seafood. There are also some new recipes for old favorites like grits.

Part 3, "From the Seas," begins with a chapter of recipes that rely on that pantry staple—canned tuna fish. Then we move to the ever-growing number of species of fresh fish available in supermarkets. There's one chapter for fin fish fillets and steaks and another chapter of recipes glorifying shrimp and other shellfish.

Part 4, "From the Coops," presents new options for poultry, both uncooked and cooked. One chapter is dedicated to whole parts of chicken, while another focuses on popular, lean boneless, skinless breasts. Part 4 ends with a chapter that provides ways to transform leftover cooked chicken or turkey into exciting options for other meals.

Part 5, "From the Butcher Shop," tells you not only where the beef is, but also where you'll find the pork, lamb, and veal. One chapter gives you recipes to add to your repertoire for ground meats, and other chapters focus on ways to cook stews and other dishes. One chapter features beef, another pork and its related foods such as ham, and Part 5 ends with a chapter devoted to lamb and veal.

Part 6, "Vegetable Patch Panache," is comprised exclusively of vegetarian recipes. An added bonus: the recipes can serve double-duty as exciting options for the side of the plate as well as the meal centerpiece. The chapters in Part 6 are devoted to pasta, beans and legumes, and vegetables from around the world. Part 6 ends with a chapter on rice and other nutritious grains.

Part 7, "Just Desserts," is full of easy recipes for sweets that are made quickly and served right from the pan with little or no further embellishment. One chapter is a must for chocoholics, and the other two chapters are primarily for fruit desserts. The recipes are divided by dishes appropriate for warm and cold months.

After the dessert chapters you'll find some useful appendixes. There's a glossary to add to your knowledge of cooking lingo and tables to aid in converting measurements to the metric system and common measures for ingredients.

Extras

In every chapter you'll find boxes that give you extra information that is either helpful, interesting, or both.

Half Baked

It's always a good idea to be alerted to potential problems in advance. Half Baked boxes provide just such a warning, either about cooking in general or the recipe in particular.

Bake Lore

Check out these boxes for amusing tidbits of food history. They're fun to read and share with friends, and they'll make you sound like a real gourmet.

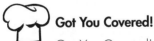

Got You Covered!

Got You Covered! boxes are full of cooking tips. Some are specific to the recipes they accompany; others will boost your general cooking skills or give you ideas for food presentation. These tips are meant to make your life easier and your time in the kitchen more pleasurable.

Ellen on Edibles

Cooking has a language all its own, and some of the terms and ingredients can be intimidating if you don't know what they mean. Look to these boxes for technique and ingredient definitions if you don't want to flip to the glossary.

Acknowledgments

Writing a book is a solitary endeavor, but its publication is always a team effort. My thanks go to …

Renee Wilmeth of Alpha Books and Gene Brissie of James Peters Associates for proposing the project.

Christy Wagner, Megan Douglass, and Nancy Wagner for their expert and eagle-eyed editing.

Karen Berman for her expert critique and guidance as a technical editor.

Grace Skinger Lefrancois for her valuable editorial contributions.

Many friends who participated in endless tasting sessions for lending their palates.

Tigger-Cat Brown, my furry companion, who kept me company for endless hours at the computer and approved all fish and seafood recipes.

Special Thanks to the Technical Reviewer

The technical reviewer for *The Complete Idiot's Guide to Cover and Bake Meals* was Karen Berman, a Connecticut-based writer and editor who specializes in food and culture. She is a contributing editor to *Wine Enthusiast* magazine, and her work has appeared in magazines, newspapers, and newsletters. She is the author of an illustrated history book, *American Indian Traditions and Ceremonies*, and she has worked in various editorial capacities on numerous cookbooks.

Trademarks

Part 1

Fundamentals to Follow

Luckily, making casseroles—the old-fashioned word for what we now term "cover and bake meals"—requires no advanced cooking skills. If you can boil water, dice an onion, and brown a piece of meat, you can successfully make almost all the recipes in this book.

Part 1 could be titled "Everything You Ever Wanted to Know About Casseroles but Were Afraid to Ask." This part contains information on the categories of foods and rudimentary kitchen equipment that play a key role in these recipes. You learn to stock your pantry, so you're always in the express lane at the supermarket.

Casserole Cunning

In This Chapter

- Basic kitchen equipment to make almost everything
- Ingredients to keep on hand
- Tips for cover and bake success
- Rules for food safety

This chapter is your one-stop guide to cover and bake dishes. The information is general and details the basics of what you need to know to successfully make any recipe in this book.

Information pertaining to specific foods introduce the chapters in which they are featured. This first chapter is intended to give you a foundation upon which to build. Once you've mastered these fundamentals, you can start to improvise your own creations.

A Panoply of Pots and Pans

Cover and bake meals are easy to create because both the cooking techniques and the equipment are pretty basic. There are no surprises here, so the best thing to do is to read through the recipe and gather all the equipment you'll need as you gather the ingredients. That leads to a seamless transition from initial preparation to readying a dish for the oven.

You'll see these pans called for in the recipes in this book:

- **Dutch oven.** These are heavy, squat pots that usually hold between 6 and 8 quarts. Because they have a large surface area that sits on the burner, Dutch ovens can be used for frying and sautéing as well as for simmering. It's important that they are sturdy and that the cover fits tightly. A pan with a cover that doesn't create a tight seal can allow too much moisture to escape, thus making the food dry.

  Cast-iron pots are less expensive than heavy stainless-steel or enameled steel, but they can react to acids in foods and give dishes an off-taste. Consider a durable Dutch oven a once-in-a-lifetime purchase, and splurge on a good one. Dutch ovens are used both on top of the stove and in the oven, so choose one without plastic handles or cover knobs that could melt in the oven.

- **Skillets.** Ideally, you should have a 10-inch cast-iron skillet; it's great for cooking as well as baking upside-down cakes. Then you also need a 12-inch skillet with a tight-fitting cover and sloping sides to cook all the recipes referred to as "skillet meals."

  Skillets now come with nonstick coatings, and should you choose one of these, it's important to use only plastic utensils. Metal utensils can scratch off the nonstick coating. As is true with Dutch ovens, cast iron holds heat well but should not be used with acidic ingredients.

- **Saucepans.** You'll need a small, 1-quart pan for making white sauces and a 3-quart pan for simmering and boiling. As with the other pots detailed in this section, a key to performance is a tight-fitting lid, especially when cooking foods such as rice. When it comes to nonstick coating, the same cautions apply as to skillets.

- **Baking pans.** Almost all the recipes in this book are baked in either a 9×13-inch baking pan or its first cousin, a 10×14-inch baking pan because, according to recent surveys, these pans are in almost all American kitchens.

Bake Lore

The Pennsylvania Dutch developed Dutch ovens in the early 1700s. Originally made from cast iron, they were used both for stewing and baking and were either hung over the fire or buried in the hot ashes. Now they can be made of any durable metal.

Half Baked

Using the correct size pan is vital to the success of these recipes. If a pan is too small, it might boil over in the oven; if a pan is too large, the food will be spread out too much and might become dry.

My choice for baking pans is Pyrex, not metal or ceramic. The downside of metal pans is that they cannot be scrubbed with abrasive steel-wool pads or the food will catch in the scratches and stick. Ceramic pans work well, but they chip more easily than Pyrex.

You do have to be careful when handling any glass or ceramic pan. Never place one on a hot stove burner, and when you remove one from the oven, place it on a dry surface, such as a cooling rack. Any moisture on a counter can cause the dishes to crack, at which time you've lost the food, as well as the pan.

Bake Lore

Pyrex glass was developed by the Corning Glass Works and was introduced to the scientific community for laboratory beakers in 1915. It's made from borosilicate glass, a formulation developed in Europe in the late 1800s. It can be heated and reheated to high temperatures without melting.

Gadgets Galore

Every cook has a number of favorite kitchen gadgets. Here are my can't-live-withouts:

- **Food processor.** My food processor has a dedicated spot in the dishwasher because I use it every day and it always needs a thorough washing. Get one that holds at least 2 quarts, or you'll be wasting time with multiple batches. Although most accessories are superfluous, I use the shredding disc for cheeses and the slicing disc for vegetables as often as the steel blade. Except for when I'm making smoothies, I haven't had a blender on my counter in more than 20 years, when I bought my first food processor.

Ellen on Edibles

Zest is the outermost layer of the skin of citrus fruits, where all the aromatic oils are located. It's important to remove only the colored portion because the white pith beneath it is very bitter.

- **Zester.** This gizmo, which resembles a vegetable peeler with small holes in the top, makes removing the *zest* from citrus fruits an effortless task.

- **Instant-read thermometer.** This does just what it promises, and it's a sure-fire way to ensure that chicken is cooked sufficiently or that a roast remains rare. Once inserted into food, an instant-read thermometer produces an accurate reading in about 5 seconds.

- **Flat-bottom whisk.** This makes cooking flour for a roux a dream job. It has an angled handle and covers the entire surface of the saucepan. Rounded balloon whisks are great for whisking, but a flat-bottom whisk is what you want for sauces.

- **Gravy separator.** These look like measuring cups, but the spigot comes from the bottom. Because fat rises (as you'll see when you look at a bottle of salad dressing), the gravy separator pours from the bottom, so you can stop pouring when the fat starts coming through.

- **Sturdy colander.** I like mesh colanders because some metal ones with small holes do not drain foods as effectively. Look for one with a ring on the bottom that you can place over the drain in your sink.

Larder Largesse

Very few folks list grocery shopping as one of the ways they like to spend their time. If you have already packed your pantry with cans, packages, and bottles of things you use frequently, you can keep the trips to the store to just the Express Lane when you get the perishable items for these easy recipes.

It's a good idea to start a master shopping list for these staples. Tape the list up in your kitchen or pantry so you can check off items as you deplete them. A small chalkboard or dry-erase board mounted in the kitchen can serve the same purpose.

What Every Cook Needs

Let's start with the basics:

- All-purpose flour
- Granulated sugar
- Brown sugar
- Salt
- Black pepper

Got You Covered!

Common table salt is finely ground and made with additives that keep it from clumping, and iodized salt is table salt with added iodine (sodium iodide), which prevents hypothyroidism. Kosher salt contains no additives and is coarse-grained; many cooks prefer its texture and flavor. Sea salt is the result of the evaporation of sea water. Some of the most prized sea salt comes from southern France.

I urge you to buy a pepper mill and grind your black pepper from whole peppercorns as you need it or purchase the small bottles of peppercorns that come with built-in grinders. The difference grinding makes in the flavor of the finished dish is amazing.

In the canned section, keep on hand a few cans of the following:

- Diced tomatoes
- Whole peeled tomatoes
- Tomato sauce
- Tomato paste
- A few different canned beans (like black beans and kidney beans)

- Chicken stock
- Beef stock
- Tuna packed in water or pouches
- Coconut milk

If you like Asian flavors, also stock the following:

- Soy sauce
- Hoisin sauce

- Oyster sauce
- Thai fish sauce (*nam pla*)

Half Baked _____

Certain foods can be stored for months in the pantry before they are opened but should be refrigerated after opening. Although many of them are marked with that instruction, others frequently are not. Refrigerate after opening mustard, maple syrup, barbecue sauce, Asian condiments such as oyster sauce and hoisin sauce, tortillas, and bottled lemon and lime juice. I also refrigerate expensive olive and nut oils after they've been opened, to retard rancidity.

Shelf-stable grains and grain-based products are always a quick-cooking lifesaver:

- Long-grain rice
- Arborio rice (for risotto)
- Fragrant jasmine rice (a Southeast Asian variety great with Asian meals and other foods as well)
- Basmati rice (a South Asian variety great for Indian meals as well as other foods)

- Spaghetti or linguine
- Orzo
- Macaroni or small shells
- Couscous
- Larger tube pasta, such as penne

Also stock other dried foods such as plain breadcrumbs, Italian breadcrumbs, and herbed stuffing cubes. Another pantry-friendly food that can help round out a meal is dried beans:

- Garbanzo beans (chickpeas)
- Black beans

- White beans
- Red kidney beans

A flavorless vegetable oil, plus olive oil and Asian sesame oil are the basics in the oil department. Vinegars, although not called for very often in this book, are also good to add to your inventory. Balsamic, cider, rice wine, white wine, or red wine are the basics. Don't waste money on fancy flavored vinegars. You can always add a pinch of dried tarragon to wine vinegar to replicate tarragon vinegar.

Other foods to stock include the following:

- Small capers
- Worcestershire sauce
- Hot red pepper sauce (such as Tabasco)
- Barbecue sauce

- Maple syrup (be sure it's pure maple and not an imitation maple pancake syrup)
- Dijon and whole-grain mustard

Got You Covered!

Markets today are drowning in olive oils. They range in price from a few dollars to the equivalent of the gross national product of a third-world nation. The expensive stuff is a condiment and is meant to be drizzled on salads. The cheap stuff is for cooking foods. Not only is it a waste of money to use expensive oil in cooking, but it also doesn't work as well.

Got You Covered!

A display rack with pretty glass bottles over the stove is about the worst place to put dried herbs and spices because both heat and light are foes of these foods. Keep them in a cool, dark place to preserve their potency. The best test for freshness and potency is to smell the contents. If you don't smell a strong aroma, you need a new bottle.

Your Flavorful Friend Herb

A collection of basic herbs and spices is essential for all cooking. Although the tally for stocking a larder from scratch can be high, the good news is that rarely do you have to replenish more than one jar at any one time.

I prefer whole leaves rather than ground for herbs such as oregano and basil. The smaller the particles, the sooner the flavor and aroma dissipates. The ground form of spices like cinnamon and cumin work fine. Keep these basic herbs and spices on hand:

- Basil
- Bay leaves
- Cinnamon (ground)
- Coriander (ground)
- Cumin (ground)
- Dry mustard
- Ginger (ground)

- Nutmeg (ground)
- Oregano
- Rosemary
- Sage
- Tarragon
- Thyme

Also include these spice blends and seeds as a part of your spice rack:

- Curry powder
- Chili powder
- Herbes de Provence
- Sesame seeds
- Poppy seeds

- Caraway seeds
- Cardamom pods
- Crushed red pepper flakes
- White peppercorns
- Paprika

Fresh Favorites

It's great to use fresh herbs for most dishes, although there are exceptions to the rule. That's why the recipes in this book list amounts for both fresh and dried herbs. Parsley is the only "must" on the fresh herbs list; dried parsley has no flavor. Other herbs that suffer from dehydration are cilantro and dill. Both of these are far more flavorful in fresh form.

Fresh herbs should be refrigerated and can be stored in a number of ways. Wrap leafy herbs such as parsley, cilantro, and dill in paper towels and then plastic bags to protect from moisture. Treat herbs with sturdy stems, including basil, oregano, and rosemary, like cut flowers. Trim the stems and refrigerate the herbs with the stems in a glass of cold water to prolong their life.

Got You Covered!

You can rinse bunches of parsley, cilantro, and dill, trim off the stems, and then wrap in small bundles and freeze them. When you need some, you can "chop" it with the blunt side of a knife. It will chop easily when frozen, and this method produces far better flavor than dried.

The Chilled Collection

In addition to stocking your pantry shelves, you should also stock your refrigerator with some basics. You probably have most of these on hand most of the time anyway:

- A quart of milk
- A pint of half-and-half
- A half-pint of heavy cream
- A pint of sour cream (or plain nonfat yogurt if you're watching your fat grams)

- A dozen eggs
- A pound of butter (If you don't use butter that often, freeze three of the four sticks to keep them fresh.)

In addition, stock some cheeses in your refrigerator:

- Parmesan
- Cheddar

- Gruyère
- Swiss

Half Baked

Onions can be stored in the refrigerator, but they're usually the first food to go if space is at a premium. You can always store them in a cool, dry place on the counter, but don't store them near potatoes. The gas given off by onions will cause potatoes to sprout and rot faster.

Some of these are available preshredded, but keep in mind that the flavor of cheese dissipates once it's grated, especially Parmesan, so it's better to grate it as you need it. I have included feta and goat's milk cheese in some of these recipes, but because they spoil more quickly than hard cheeses, buy them as you need them.

In your vegetable drawer, stock the following:

- Carrots
- Celery
- Garlic
- Onions

These all are sturdy and will keep for up to 2 weeks refrigerated. Leafy vegetables cannot be kept as long and should be purchased only for use in special recipes. If you don't eat salad every night, buy greens in small bags when you need them. Salad greens spoil within a few days.

To save time, purchase already sliced mushrooms in 8-ounce packages. I list them this way in the recipes. Should you buy whole mushrooms, the gross weight should be 9 ounces, to account for the trimming.

Fresh from the Freezer

Let's not overlook the freezer for quick food fast. Stock your freezer with such foods as the following:

- Packages of mixed vegetables
- Chopped broccoli
- Cut green beans
- Peas
- Chopped spinach
- Pearl onions
- Corn
- Peach slices
- Blueberries
- Strawberries
- Raspberries

These fruits and vegetables come in handy for any number of recipes, especially the fruit for baking some of the easy recipes in Part 7. Sheets of puff pastry and a few premade pie crusts are other essentials.

Incidentals

Red wine, white wine, dry sherry, and marsala are all used in these recipes. Although you don't have to buy vintage wines for cooking, my rule is that I'd never use a wine in a pot that I wouldn't drink from a glass.

Got You Covered!

Sherry and vermouth can be stored for months at room temperature after they're opened, but red and white wine soon turn to vinegar, even if refrigerated. You can preserve them for future use in either of two ways: either freeze them right out of the bottle or reduce them and then freeze them. Freezing right out of the bottle is a great way to use them for marinades later on. But if you're adding them to sauces, you might as well take the time to reduce them in advance. Boil the wine until it's reduced by half, then freeze it in a plastic bag or an ice cube tray. Note on the package that the wine has been reduced.

Foods for Sweet Sensations

I split this part of the pantry list up from the other list because, except for a few spices, the foods are very different. And if you're not into making desserts, even the ones in this book that are so incredibly easy, there's no need to stock most of these items.

In addition to the all-purpose flour, granulated sugar, brown sugar, and salt listed previously, add:

- Confectioners' sugar
- Light brown sugar
- Buttermilk powder
- Pure vanilla extract
- Pure almond extract

Fruits and nuts are added to many recipes. It's best to buy whole nuts and chop them yourself, and store nuts in the freezer to extend their shelf life. Walnuts, pecans, and blanched almonds are the best all-purpose baking nuts. You might also want to include skinned hazelnuts and unsalted roasted peanuts in your nut inventory.

Raisins are essential to baking, so if you're only going to stock one dried fruit, make it golden raisins. Other dried fruits give desserts a more exotic flavor. Dried currants, dried apricots, dried cranberries, and dried cherries are all easy to find. Store dried fruits in airtight plastic bags after the bag has been opened.

Got You Covered!

It's sometimes difficult to find skinned hazelnuts. If this is the case, toast your hazelnuts, skin on, in a 350°F oven for 5 to 7 minutes or until the skins are browned. Then place them in a linen tea towel and cover them. Rub them back and forth on the counter inside the towel, and the skins should slide right off.

Another ingredient that is called for frequently for both cooking and baking is grated coconut. If possible, buy frozen grated coconut. It's unsweetened, so it can do double duty in Asian recipes as well. If you can't find frozen, you can always find sweetened coconut in the baking aisle.

Reaching the Finish Line

A frequent complaint about many cover and bake meals is that the dishes are all soft and lack real texture. That's because too often they were assembled and placed in the oven without regard to the time each individual ingredient requires to cook—but not overcook.

That's not true for the recipes in this book. You can take some liberties when you're cooking meals in a slow cooker, but you shouldn't leave the house while dishes are either baking in the oven or simmering on the stove. It's just not safe.

But you can add ingredients to the mix at various stages of the cooking process, and you'll see that this is the procedure for many recipes. The goal with cover and bake meals is that all ingredients are properly cooked at the end of the cooking time, and often this involves adding them to the pan in stages.

Skillet Savvy

Although the official title for these recipes is "cover and bake," a number of recipes can be more accurately defined as "cover and simmer." They're made on top of the stove from beginning to end and usually contain the word *skillet* in the recipe title. The same rules apply regarding adding ingredients, but there are a few other tricks for success in this genre.

Be sure to set the heat correctly. If the recipe calls for reducing the heat to a simmer, the liquid should be barely bubbling and not looking like a rolling boil. This is easier to control with a gas rather than electric range, because the heat reduction is instant. If using an electric range, reduce the heat and then remove the pan from the burner until the liquid stops boiling entirely. Then return it to the burner and judge how rapidly it is boiling.

The second strategy for success is to stir the pan often. The heat of the oven surrounds a pan on all sides. But food on a stovetop burner is cooking from the bottom only, with some heat retained if the pan is covered. The less liquid in the pan, the more often it should be stirred. So a stew can go for far longer than a stovetop casserole with little liquid.

What to Add When

The addition process is logical when you think about how long it takes foods to cook. At the longest end of the cooking-time spectrum are inexpensive cuts of meat; they can take up to a few hours to *braise* to a state of true tenderness. Amongst animal foods, whole pieces of chicken are next in time sequence, while dishes made with boneless, skinless chicken breasts and any sort of seafood are relatively fast.

Sturdy root vegetables, such as potatoes and carrots, cook in approximately the same time as meats, so they're added to stews at the beginning. But tender green beans or peas are added within moments of serving a dish.

Some foods cook at about the same rate, such as long-grain rice with pieces of chicken breast or fish. In those cases, the recipes call for starting them at the same time. In many cases, however, it's best to stir already-cooked rice or pasta into a dish at the end of the cooking time.

Ellen on Edibles

Braise is the term for cooking meats or vegetables in liquid at a low temperature for a long period of time to make them tender. Braising is always done covered and usually in the oven.

Top Tips

Here are some general tips to make great cover and bake meals:

- **Slightly undercook pasta and rice.** I discuss this at length in the appropriate chapters, but the idea is to allow these foods to absorb flavor from sauce in the finished dish but not become mushy.

- **Pay attention to size.** Follow the directions in the recipes, because pieces larger than those specified will take longer to cook.

- **Use the size and shape pan specified.** There's no chart in this or any chapter giving volume equivalents for different baking pans, such as a soufflé dish versus a 9×13-inch because the shape of the dish makes a difference. Use the pan specified.

- **Check the temperature of your oven.** An inexpensive oven thermometer could save many a cook from disaster. It doesn't matter if your stove is old or new, gas or electric. The fact is that many ovens need re-calibration and do not have accurate settings. Even if you adjust the temperature manually, know what your oven is actually producing.

◆ **Allow cover and bake meals to cool, if instructed.** I know you're hungry and have eager folks waiting at the table, but certain dishes need a few minutes of "resting" after baking so the layers will hold together and the sauce will be absorbed. Don't skip this step if it's listed. If it's not necessary, the step is not given.

Safety First

The first—and most important—requirement for good cooking is knowing the basic rules of food safety. This begins with trips to the supermarket and ends after leftovers are refrigerated or frozen at the end of a meal.

The sections that follow may seem like common sense, but after many decades as a food writer who has heard horror stories about very sick people, please believe me, they're not.

Safe Shopping

Most supermarkets are designed to funnel you into the produce section first. But that's not the best place to start. Begin your shopping with the shelf-stable items from the center, then go to produce, and end with the other refrigerated and frozen sections.

Never buy meat or poultry in a package that is torn and leaking, and it's a good idea to place all meats and poultry in the disposable plastic bags available in the produce department.

Check the "sell-by" and "use-by" dates, and never purchase food that exceeds them. For the trip home, carry an insulated cooler in the back of your car if it's hot outside or if the perishable items will be out of refrigeration for more than 1 hour. In hot weather, many seafood departments will provide some crushed ice in a separate bag for the fish.

> **Got You Covered!**
> If you have any questions about food safety, the U.S. Department of Agriculture is the place to go. The Food Safety Inspection Service was designed to help you. The website, www.fsis.usda.gov, provides a wealth of information in a very user-friendly format.

Banishing Bacteria

Fruits and vegetables can contain some bacteria, but it's far more likely that the culprits will grow on meat, poultry, and seafood. Store these foods on the bottom shelves of your refrigerator so their juices cannot accidentally drip on other foods. And keep these foods refrigerated until just before they go into the dish.

Bacteria multiply at room temperature. The so-called "danger zone" is between 40°F and 140°F. As food cooks, it's important for it to pass through this zone as quickly as possible.

If you want to get a jump-start on dinner by browning meats or poultry or cutting up vegetables in advance, that's fine. Just refrigerate all foods separately until it's time to combine them and cook the finished dish. Like all rules, this one has exceptions. Raw eggs can come into contact with other foods, such as with the strata recipes in Chapter 3.

Don't Cross-Contaminate

Cleanliness is not only next to godliness, it's also the key to food safety. Wash your hands often while you're cooking, and never touch cooked food if you haven't washed your hands after handling raw food.

The cooked food and raw food shall never meet precept extends beyond the cook's hands. Clean cutting boards, knives, and kitchen counters often. Or if you have the space, section off your countertops for raw foods and cooked foods, as many restaurant kitchens do. Don't place cooked foods or raw foods that will remain uncooked (such as salad) on cutting boards that have been used to cut raw meat, poultry, or fish. Bacteria from raw animal proteins can contaminate the other foods.

 **Got You Covered!**

Wooden cutting boards might be attractive, but you can never get them as clean as plastic boards that can be run through the dishwasher. Even with plastic boards, use one for only cooked food and foods such as vegetables that are not prone to containing bacteria, and another for raw meats, poultry, and fish.

The Least You Need to Know

♦ Cast-iron pots and pans can react to acidic ingredients in recipes and give foods an off-flavor.

♦ Keep dried herbs and spices in cool, dark cabinets to preserve their color and flavor.

♦ Add ingredients to cover and bake meals at different times according to how long they take to cook, so all ingredients are properly cooked when a dish is completed.

♦ To ensure food safety, never allow cooked food or food that will remain uncooked (such as salad) to come into contact with raw food that may harbor bacteria. This includes on hands and on cutting boards or platters.

Part 2

Rise and Shine

In all candor, Part 2 is my favorite part of the book because I've often said that I would rather cook dinner for 20 than breakfast for 2. The recipes in Part 2 will make mornings much easier and more pleasurable for you, as they have for me.

One chapter is devoted to various egg preparations, all of which you can do for a group in a matter of minutes without the individual attention it takes to make dishes like omelets. Some are vegetarian, while others pair the eggs with breakfast meats and even some luxurious smoked salmon.

The other chapter is all about stratas. Stratas are basically savory bread puddings and are even better if they're assembled the night before they're baked.

Chapter 2

Egg-Cetera: One-Dish Breakfasts and Brunches

In This Chapter

♦ Frittatas: Italian baked omelets

♦ Baked casseroles bound together by egg custards

♦ New dishes to make with old-fashioned Southern grits

Many cooks feel overwhelmed—and understaffed—when preparing breakfast or brunch for a crowd, as they contemplate the number of individual omelets, stacks of pancakes, and rashers of bacon they need to prepare. But this need not be the case, as you'll discover when cooking the recipes in this chapter.

Although the cover and bake concept begins at sunrise, you can partially prepare many of these dishes a day in advance to further ease morning stress. These one-pot dishes need only simple accompaniments. A bowl of fruit salad and/or a basket of fresh bread, rolls, muffins, or croissants will serve the purpose. Neither will add to the stress of the morning, as the fruit salad can be done ahead of time and the breads can be purchased. Add some juice and coffee or milk, and you're good to go.

Easy on the Eggs, Please!

The size of eggs (jumbo, extra large, large, medium, and small) is determined by how much the eggs weigh per dozen. All the recipes in this book, and in most cookbooks, specify large eggs. It's important to use the correct size egg when preparing batters for baked goods.

If you're using small eggs, increase the number by 1 for every 4 large eggs specified in a recipe. If you're using medium eggs, increase the number by 1 for every 6 large eggs. On the other side, decrease the number of eggs called for by 1 for every 4 jumbo eggs used and by 1 for every 8 extra large eggs used.

Egg Chemistry 101

It's a misnomer that something is "as easy as boiling an egg." Although anyone can cook eggs, achieving a light, velvety texture takes some care. The basic principle for cooking all egg dishes is to use gentle, low heat so the eggs do not toughen. Typically, cover and bake egg recipes call for adding milk or other liquids to the eggs to create a thin batter. Heat causes the proteins in this batter to coagulate, or solidify, usually at a relatively low temperature. At high temperatures, the proteins don't just solidify; they toughen. That's why the baking temperature given for scrambled eggs is lower than that given for eggs that are baked whole. Also, covering egg dishes produces a lighter texture, because covering a pan creates a more even heat inside the pan.

Fancy Frittatas

Frittatas are Italian-style omelets which are becoming increasingly popular here. Unlike their French counterparts, which are cooked in single portions entirely on the stove, frittatas start on the stovetop and finish in the oven and can be made in a big pan to serve a crowd.

The easy part is that frittatas use one pan from start to finish. However, that also creates a potential problem if you only have skillets with plastic handles. If this applies to you, wrap the handle in a double layer of aluminum foil before you place the skillet into the oven to prevent the plastic from cracking or even melting.

Easy Oven-Baked Perfect Scrambled Eggs

4 TB. (½ stick) butter, sliced

12 to 16 large eggs

½ cup light cream

Salt and freshly ground black pepper to taste

Optional ingredients:

1 cup grated Swiss or cheddar cheese

¼ cup chopped fresh herbs (chives, parsley, or marjoram)

1 cup cooked, crumbled bacon, sausage, or ham

¾ cup sautéed onion and bell pepper

½ cup diced smoked salmon

1 cup diced stir-fried asparagus

1 cup sautéed sliced mushrooms or wild mushrooms

Serves: 6 to 8
Prep time: 5 minutes
Cook time: 25 minutes

1. Preheat the oven to 300°F. Place butter in a 10×14-inch baking pan. Place the pan in the oven and heat for 3 to 5 minutes or until butter is melted.

2. Whisk eggs in a large mixing bowl until frothy. Add cream, salt, and pepper and whisk again. Tilt the pan so butter coats sides and pour egg mixture into the pan.

3. Cover the pan with aluminum foil and bake for 15 minutes. Remove the pan from the oven and scrape the sides and bottom with a wooden spoon to dislodge cooked portion of eggs, breaking up any clumps. Recover the pan, bake for an additional 10 minutes, and then scrape the sides and bottom again with a wooden spoon. Break up lumps with the spoon and add any optional ingredients, if using.

4. Return pan to oven for 5 minutes, remove from oven, and stir. Serve immediately.

 Got You Covered!

This recipe can be multiplied for up to 3 dozen eggs; however, the baking time and pan will be different. For 2 dozen eggs, use the same pan but increase the baking time to 40 minutes. For 3 dozen eggs, use a large roasting pan and increase the baking time to 40 minutes.

Vegetable Frittata with Pasta

Serves: 6 to 8
Prep time: 20 minutes
Cook time: 15 minutes

1 (6-oz.) pkg. fresh angel hair pasta (found in the supermarket refrigerated case), cut into 2-inch sections

3 TB. olive oil

2 small zucchini, trimmed and thinly sliced

4 scallions, trimmed with all but 2 inches of green tops discarded, thinly sliced

1 garlic clove, peeled and minced

2 ripe medium tomatoes, cored, seeded, and finely chopped

3 TB. chopped fresh basil or 2 tsp. dried

1 TB. chopped fresh oregano or ½ tsp. dried

¼ cup sliced green olives

Salt and freshly ground black pepper to taste

8 large eggs

¾ cup grated Parmesan cheese

3 TB. butter

1. Cook pasta according to package directions until al dente. Drain and set aside to cool.

2. Heat olive oil in a large skillet over medium-high heat. Add zucchini, scallions, and garlic. Cook, stirring constantly, for 3 minutes or until zucchini is tender. Add tomatoes, basil, oregano, and olives. Cook for 5 minutes, stirring occasionally, or until liquid from tomatoes has evaporated. Season to taste with salt and pepper and let cool for 10 minutes. (Do this a day in advance and refrigerate, tightly covered, if you want. Before baking, reheat vegetables to room temperature in a microwave-safe dish or over low heat.)

3. Preheat the oven to 350°F. Whisk eggs well, stir in Parmesan cheese, and season to taste with salt and pepper. Stir cooled vegetable mixture and cooled pasta into eggs. Heat butter in a large, ovenproof skillet over medium heat. Add egg mixture and cook for 4 minutes or until bottom of frittata is lightly browned. Cover the skillet, transfer it to the oven, and bake for 10 minutes. Uncover the skillet and bake for 5 to 7 minutes or until top is browned.

4. Run a rubber spatula around the sides of the skillet and under bottom of frittata to release it. Slide it gently onto a serving platter and cut it into wedges. Serve immediately.

 **Got You Covered!**

If you're not sure how fresh your eggs are, place them in a mixing bowl filled with cold water. As eggs age, they develop air pockets, so older eggs float while fresher ones sink. If the eggs are floating high on the surface of the water, it's best to get a fresh dozen.

Leek, Tomato, and Goat's Milk Cheese Frittata

8 TB. (1 stick) butter

4 leeks, white part only, trimmed, thinly sliced, and well rinsed

½ cup heavy cream

1 cup small cherry tomatoes, rinsed

8 large eggs

¼ lb. crumbled goat's milk cheese

Salt and freshly ground black pepper to taste

Serves: 6 to 8
Prep time: 20 minutes
Cook time: 15 minutes

1. Melt 5 tablespoons butter in a large skillet over medium heat. Add leeks, toss to coat with butter, and cover the pan. Reduce heat to low and cook leeks for 5 minutes. Remove cover, increase heat to medium, and stir in cream. Cook, stirring occasionally, for 10 minutes. Stir in cherry tomatoes and remove the pan from heat.

2. Preheat the oven to 350°F. Whisk eggs well, stir in goat's milk cheese, and season with salt and pepper. Stir cooled leek mixture into eggs. Heat remaining 3 tablespoons butter in a large, ovenproof skillet over medium heat. Add egg mixture and cook for 4 minutes or until bottom of frittata is lightly browned. Cover the skillet, transfer it to the oven, and bake for 10 minutes. Uncover the skillet and bake for 5 to 7 minutes or until top is browned.

3. Run a rubber spatula around the sides of the skillet and under bottom of frittata to release it. Slide it gently onto a serving platter and cut it into wedges. Serve immediately.

Half Baked

It's important that the cherry tomatoes *not* be halved or diced for this recipe. They will be cooked and juicy if whole, but they will release too much liquid into the eggs if they're cut, which can create a watery dish.

Spanish Tortilla

Serves: 6 to 8
Prep time: 30 minutes
Cook time: 15 minutes

2 TB. olive oil

1 large Russet or Idaho potato, peeled and cut into ½-inch dice

1 red bell pepper, seeds and ribs removed, thinly sliced

1 sweet onion, such as Vidalia or Bermuda, peeled and thinly sliced

1 cup chopped serrano ham or prosciutto

2 garlic cloves, peeled and minced

1 TB. fresh thyme or 1 tsp. dried

Salt and freshly ground black pepper to taste

10 large eggs

¼ cup grated Parmesan cheese

¼ cup shredded mozzarella cheese

2 TB. (¼ stick) butter

1. Heat olive oil in a large skillet over medium-high heat. Add potatoes and cook, stirring occasionally, for 5 minutes or until potatoes are browned. Add red bell pepper, onion, ham, garlic, and thyme to the skillet. Cook, stirring constantly, for 3 minutes or until onion is translucent. Reduce the heat to low, cover the pan, and cook vegetable mixture for 15 minutes or until vegetables are tender. Season to taste with salt and pepper and let cool for 10 minutes. (You can do this a day in advance and refrigerate, tightly covered. Before baking, reheat vegetables to room temperature in a microwave-safe dish or over low heat.)

2. Preheat the oven to 350°F. Whisk eggs well, stir in Parmesan and mozzarella cheeses, and season to taste with salt and pepper. Stir cooled vegetable mixture into eggs. Heat butter in a large, ovenproof skillet over medium heat. Add egg mixture and cook for 4 minutes or until bottom of tortilla is lightly browned. Cover the skillet, transfer it to the oven, and bake for 10 minutes. Uncover the skillet and bake for 5 minutes or until top is browned.

3. Run a rubber spatula around the sides of the skillet and under bottom of tortilla to release it. Slide it gently onto a serving platter and cut it into wedges. Serve immediately.

 **Got You Covered!**

Unlike the plate of leftover poached eggs that should be destined for the trash, save and refrigerate leftover slices of frittatas or this Spanish tortilla, which is a first cousin. Tortillas are served in small pieces as tapas. Take them on picnics or cut the leftovers into small squares as an hors d'oeuvre.

Ham and Cheese Grits Casserole

3½ cups water

1 cup quick-cooking white *grits*

2 tsp. fresh thyme or ½ tsp. dried

Salt and freshly ground black pepper to taste

1½ cups grated sharp cheddar cheese

2 TB. (¼ stick) butter

¾ lb. ham steak, trimmed of all fat and cut into ½-inch dice

⅓ cup sliced pimientos, drained and rinsed

½ cup milk

3 large eggs, lightly beaten

Serves: 6 to 8
Prep time: 25 minutes
Cook time: 45 minutes

1. Grease a 9×13-inch baking pan. Bring water to a boil in a heavy saucepan over high heat. Stir in grits, thyme, salt, and pepper. Reduce heat to medium-low, cover pan, and cook, stirring occasionally, for 15 minutes or until very thick. Remove pan from heat and stir in ¾ cup cheddar cheese and butter.

2. Cool 10 minutes, then stir in ham, pimientos, milk, and eggs. Spoon mixture into prepared pan. (This can be done up to 1 day in advance and refrigerated, tightly covered. Add 15 minutes to initial covered baking time.)

3. Preheat the oven to 350°F. Cover pan with aluminum foil and bake for 30 minutes. Uncover pan, sprinkle with remaining ¾ cup cheddar cheese, and bake for an additional 15 minutes or until set and top is browned. Let stand for 5 minutes and serve.

Ellen on Edibles

Grits nowadays means hominy grits made from ground corn that's ground with steel rollers that, in essence, partially cook the corn. This makes it quicker to cook. However, grits can also be made from wheat or rice. The term refers to any coarsely ground grain.

Southwest Vegetarian Grits Casserole

Serves: 6 to 8
Prep time: 20 minutes
Cook time: 45 minutes

3½ cups water

1 cup quick-cooking grits

Salt and freshly ground black pepper to taste

1½ cups grated jalapeño Jack cheese

2 TB. (¼ stick) butter

1 (15-oz.) can red kidney beans, drained and rinsed

2 ears fresh corn, kernels cut off, or 1 cup frozen corn, thawed

½ cup fresh tomato salsa from the produce section (do not use jarred salsa), drained

½ cup milk

3 large eggs, lightly beaten

1. Grease a 9×13-inch baking pan. Bring water to a boil in a heavy saucepan over high heat. Stir in grits, salt, and pepper. Reduce heat to medium-low, cover pan, and cook, stirring occasionally, for 15 minutes or until very thick. Remove the pan from heat and stir in ¾ cup jalapeño Jack cheese and butter.

2. Cool 10 minutes; then stir in beans, corn, salsa, milk, and eggs. Spoon mixture into prepared baking pan. (You can do this a day in advance and refrigerate, tightly covered. Add 15 minutes to initial covered bake time.)

3. Preheat the oven to 350°F. Cover pan with aluminum foil and bake for 30 minutes. Uncover the pan, sprinkle with remaining ¾ cup jalapeño Jack cheese, and bake for an additional 15 minutes or until set and top is browned. Let stand for 5 minutes and serve.

Got You Covered!

If an egg falls and breaks on the floor, cover the mess with lots of salt and let it stand for 20 minutes. After that time, it should be solid enough to sweep into a dust pan.

Summer Vegetable Flan

1 (1-lb.) eggplant, trimmed and cut into ½-inch dice

Salt

¼ cup olive oil

3 onions, peeled and diced

2 garlic cloves, peeled and minced

1 red bell pepper, seeds and ribs removed, cut into ½-inch dice

2 small zucchini, trimmed and cut into ½-inch dice

4 plum tomatoes, cored, seeded, and cut into ½-inch dice

2 TB. chopped fresh basil or 1 tsp. dried

1 TB. fresh thyme or ½ tsp. dried

Freshly ground black pepper to taste

6 large eggs

¼ cup sour cream

Serves: 6 to 8
Prep time: 55 minutes
Cook time: 45 minutes

1. Place eggplant in a colander and sprinkle liberally with salt. Place a plate on top of eggplant cubes and weight the plate with cans. Place the colander in the sink or on a plate and allow eggplant to drain for 30 minutes. Rinse eggplant cubes and squeeze hard to remove water. Wring out remaining water with a cloth tea towel.

2. Heat olive oil in a large skillet over medium heat. Add onions and garlic. Cook, stirring frequently, for 3 minutes or until onions are translucent. Add eggplant, red bell pepper, zucchini, tomatoes, basil, and thyme to the skillet. Cook, stirring frequently, for 5 minutes or until vegetables begin to soften.

3. Reduce heat to low, cover the skillet, and cook vegetables for 20 minutes or until they are soft and liquid has almost evaporated. Season with salt and pepper and let cool 10 minutes. (You can do this a day in advance and refrigerate, tightly covered. Reheat in a microwave-safe dish or over low heat until room temperature before continuing.)

4. Preheat the oven to 350°F. Grease a 9×13-inch baking pan. Whisk eggs with sour cream and season with salt and pepper. Stir vegetables into eggs and pour mixture into the prepared pan. Bake flan for 45 minutes or until set and the top is lightly browned. Allow to sit for 5 minutes. Serve hot, at room temperature, or chilled.

Bake Lore

In botany, eggplants, like tomatoes, are classified as fruits; however, when cooking them, they are always vegetables. The flesh has a rich, earthy, almost nutlike flavor, and the skin retains its vibrant color even when cooked. Eggplants have male and female gender, and the males are preferable because they have fewer seeds and are generally less bitter. To tell a male from a female, look at the stem end. The male is rounded and has a more even hole while the female hole is indented.

Tomato and Egg Cobbler

Serves: 6 to 8
Prep time: 10 minutes
Cook time: 50 minutes

2½ cups herb-seasoned bread stuffing cubes

3 lb. ripe tomatoes, cored, seeded, and cut into ½-inch dice

6 large eggs, hard-boiled, peeled, and cut into ½-inch dice

1 TB. chopped fresh oregano or ½ tsp. dried

2 tsp. fresh thyme or ½ tsp. dried

⅔ cup light cream

½ cup chicken stock

Salt and freshly ground black pepper to taste

½ cup grated Parmesan cheese

1. Preheat the oven to 375°F. Grease a 9×13-inch baking pan.

2. Combine stuffing cubes, tomatoes, eggs, oregano, thyme, cream, chicken stock, salt, and pepper in a mixing bowl. Toss to combine. Spread mixture in the prepared pan and sprinkle with Parmesan cheese. Cover the pan with aluminum foil and bake for 30 minutes. Remove the foil and bake for an additional 20 to 30 minutes or until almost no liquid remains in the pan. Serve immediately.

Got You Covered!

I don't believe it's worth the time to peel tomatoes. If you are a purist and insist on peeling, cut an X into the root end of each tomato and plunge the tomatoes into boiling water for 30 seconds, and the skins will slip off from the root end. To seed tomatoes, cut them in half and squeeze them gently over a sink or mixing bowl. I frequently save the seeds and juice and use them in stocks.

Sun-Dried Tomato, Porcini, and Potato Flan

½ oz. dried porcini mush-rooms

¼ cup sun-dried tomatoes (not packed in olive oil)

½ cup boiling water

2 TB. (¼ stick) butter

1 TB. olive oil

½ lb. white mushrooms, trimmed, wiped with a damp paper towel, and sliced

6 scallions, trimmed with all but 2 inches of green tops discarded, thinly sliced

6 large eggs

2 TB. all-purpose flour

1 (3-oz.) pkg. cream cheese

⅓ cup light cream

1 tsp. dried oregano

Salt and freshly ground black pepper to taste

¾ cup grated Parmesan cheese

1½ lb. frozen hash brown potatoes, thawed

Serves: 6 to 8
Prep time: 15 minutes
Cook time: 60 minutes

1. Preheat the oven to 350°F. Grease a 10×14-inch baking pan. Place dried porcini and sun-dried tomatoes in a small bowl. Add boiling water and stir. Allow to sit for 10 minutes.

2. Heat butter and oil in a large skillet over medium-high heat. Add mushrooms and cook, stirring frequently, for 3 minutes. Add scallions and cook an additional 3 minutes, stirring fre-quently, until mushrooms are soft and liquid has evaporated. Set aside.

3. Combine eggs, flour, cream cheese, cream, oregano, salt, pepper, and ½ cup Parmesan in a food processor fitted with a steel blade or in a blender. Purée until smooth.

4. Drain porcini and sun-dried tomatoes, reserving ¼ cup soaking liquid. Add porcini and tomatoes along with reserved liquid to the food processor and chop finely, using on-and-off pulsing action. Scrape mixture into a mixing bowl and stir in mushroom mixture and potatoes. Pour mix-ture into the prepared pan.

5. Cover the pan with aluminum foil and bake for 30 minutes. Remove the foil, sprinkle with remaining cheese, and bake for an additional 30 minutes or until set and top is browned. Allow to sit for 5 minutes and serve.

Half Baked

Eggs are fairly sturdy and age well, even if not refrig-erated. Never buy cracked eggs because the cracks can allow bacteria to enter. Also store eggs in their pro-tective carton, not in the indented egg tray in many refrigerator doors. The constant opening and closing of the refrigerator can cause cracks.

Dilled Smoked Salmon, Scallion, and Asparagus Cheesecake

Serves: 8 to 10
Prep time: 20 minutes
Cook time: 50 minutes

5 TB. butter

¾ cup breadcrumbs

½ cup grated Parmesan cheese

2 TB. olive oil

6 scallions, trimmed with all but 2 inches of green tops discarded, thinly sliced

½ lb. fresh asparagus, woody ends discarded, thinly sliced

3 (8-oz.) pkg. cream cheese, softened

3 large eggs

⅓ cup heavy cream

¾ cup grated Swiss cheese

¾ lb. smoked salmon, finely diced

¼ cup chopped fresh dill or 2 TB. dried

Salt and freshly ground black pepper to taste

Half Baked

When dealing with foods like smoked salmon, ham, bacon, or prosciutto, go lightly on the salt or use none at all. These are all inherently salty foods, and that salt escapes into other foods during the cooking process. You might not taste it at the beginning, but you will at the end. And it's nearly impossible to delete salt.

1. Preheat the oven to 325°F. Melt 3 tablespoons butter in a microwave-safe mixing bowl. Add breadcrumbs and Parmesan cheese. Mix well and pat mixture evenly into the bottom of a 9×13-inch baking pan. Set aside.

2. Melt remaining 2 tablespoons butter and oil in a skillet over medium heat. Add scallions and asparagus. Cook, stirring frequently, for 4 to 6 minutes or until vegetables are soft. Set aside to cool.

3. Place cream cheese in a food processor fitted with a steel blade. Add eggs, one at a time, processing well between each addition and scraping down the sides of the bowl. Pour in cream and process again. (This can also be done with an electric mixer on medium speed.)

4. Scrape mixture into a mixing bowl and stir in cooked vegetables, Swiss cheese, smoked salmon, and dill. Season to taste with salt and pepper. Pour cheese mixture over breadcrumb crust, smoothing top with a rubber spatula. (You can do this a day in advance and refrigerate, tightly covered. Add 15 minutes to initial baking time.)

5. Cover the pan with aluminum foil and bake for 20 minutes. Remove the foil and bake for an additional 30 to 40 minutes or until a toothpick inserted in the center comes out clean and the top is browned. Serve immediately.

Smoked Salmon, Shallot, and Potato Hash

3 TB. butter

2 TB. olive oil

1½ lb. frozen hash-brown potatoes, not thawed

3 large shallots, peeled and finely chopped

½ lb. smoked salmon, cut into thin strips

¼ cup *capers,* drained and rinsed

⅓ cup sour cream

2 TB. bottled horseradish

2 TB. Dijon mustard

Salt and freshly ground black pepper to taste

Serves: 6 to 8	
Prep time: 10 minutes	
Cook time: 20 minutes	

 Ellen on Edibles

Capers are the flower buds of a bush native to the Mediterranean, ranging in size from tiny nonpareil to ones the size of your thumbnail. They are dried and then usually packed in brine, which makes them quite salty. Be sure to rinse them before using.

1. Heat butter and olive oil in a large skillet over medium-high heat. Add potatoes and shallots, cover the pan, and cook for 5 minutes. Uncover the pan, turn potatoes and shallots with a metal spatula, and cook for an additional 5 to 10 minutes or until golden brown. While potatoes are cooking, combine smoked salmon, capers, sour cream, horseradish, and Dijon mustard in a small mixing bowl.

2. Reduce heat to low and stir in salmon mixture. Cook, stirring gently, for 2 minutes or until heated through. Season with salt and pepper.

Spicy Chorizo, Corn, and Egg Enchilada Casserole

Serves: 6 to 8
Prep time: 10 minutes
Cook time: 60 minutes

½ lb. chorizo sausage, thinly sliced

6 scallions, trimmed with all but 2 inches of green tops discarded, thinly sliced

2 (10-oz.) pkg. frozen corn, thawed

1 (8-oz.) pkg. cream cheese

½ cup yellow cornmeal

6 large eggs

2 TB. granulated sugar

1 cup grated mild cheddar cheese

1½ tsp. dried oregano, preferably Mexican

Salt and cayenne to taste

¾ cup milk

1 (4-oz.) can diced mild green chilies, drained

8 (6-in.) corn tortillas

1 cup grated Monterey Jack cheese

1. Preheat the oven to 350°F. Grease a shallow, 2-quart casserole and set aside.

2. Place a medium skillet over medium-high heat. Add chorizo and cook for 3 minutes, stirring occasionally, until chorizo is lightly browned. Add scallions and cook for 2 minutes, stirring occasionally. Set aside.

3. Combine 1 package corn, cream cheese, cornmeal, eggs, sugar, cheddar cheese, oregano, salt, cayenne, and milk in a food processor fitted with a steel blade or in a blender. Purée until smooth.

4. Transfer mixture to a mixing bowl and stir in remaining corn, chilies, and chorizo mixture. Place 4 tortillas in the bottom of the prepared pan. Layer ½ corn mixture on top of tortillas and sprinkle top with ½ cup Monterey Jack cheese. Repeat with remaining tortillas, corn mixture, and Monterey Jack cheese.

5. Cover the pan with aluminum foil and bake for 30 minutes. Remove the foil and bake for an additional 30 minutes or until casserole is set and top is browned. Let stand for 5 minutes and serve.

 **Got You Covered!**

To layer or not to layer, that is the question, with all apologies to Shakespeare. For casseroles like this one, the custard fills in between the cracks of the other ingredients, and the layers look attractive. A good general rule is not to layer unless instructed to do so in a recipe.

Corned Beef Hash with Baked Eggs

1 TB. butter

2 TB. vegetable oil

1 large sweet onion such as Bermuda or Vidalia, peeled and diced

1 red bell pepper, seeds and ribs removed, chopped

2 garlic cloves, peeled and minced

1 lb. cooked corned beef, coarsely chopped

2 cups mashed potatoes (homemade or purchased from the supermarket's refrigerated aisle)

1 tsp. fresh thyme or ½ tsp. dried

Salt and freshly ground black pepper to taste

6 to 8 large eggs

Serves: 6 to 8	
Prep time: 15 minutes	
Cook time: 30 minutes	

1. Preheat the oven to 400°F. Grease a 9×13-inch baking pan. Heat butter and oil in a large skillet over medium heat. Add onion, red bell pepper, and garlic. Cook, stirring frequently, for 10 minutes or until vegetables are soft. Add corned beef, mashed potatoes, and thyme and mix well. Season to taste with salt and pepper. (This can be done 1 day in advance and refrigerated, tightly covered. Add 15 minutes to the initial covered baking if chilled.)

2. Spread *hash* in the prepared baking pan and cover with aluminum foil. Bake for 20 minutes or until hot. Remove pan from oven, remove the foil, and create 6 to 8 indentations in top of hash, evenly spread apart. Break 1 egg into each indentation and sprinkle eggs with salt and pepper. Return the pan to the oven, uncovered, and bake for an additional 10 minutes or until egg whites are set. Serve immediately.

Ellen on Edibles

Hash is a general term for food that is finely chopped. The English word first appeared in the mid-seventeenth century; it comes from the French word *hacher*, which means "to chop." Because hash was frequently made with leftovers, inexpensive restaurants became known as "hash houses."

Herbed Potato, Sausage, and Red Pepper Bake

Serves: 6 to 8
Prep time: 15 minutes
Cook time: 50 minutes

12 oz. spicy or mild bulk pork sausage

1 medium onion, peeled and diced

1 red bell pepper, seeds and ribs removed, finely chopped

4 cups frozen diced potatoes, thawed

3 large eggs

¾ cup light cream

1 TB. chopped fresh sage or 1 tsp. dried, rubbed

1 TB. fresh thyme or ½ tsp. dried

Salt and freshly ground black pepper to taste

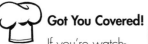 **Got You Covered!**

If you're watching fat grams, you can make any recipe calling for pork sausage with leaner and lighter chicken or turkey sausage. But remove the casings before you brown the sausage.

1. Preheat the oven to 350°F. Grease a 9×13-inch baking pan. Place a large skillet over medium-high heat. Add sausage, breaking up lumps with a fork, and cook, stirring occasionally, for 3 minutes or until sausage is browned. Add onion, red bell pepper, and potatoes to the skillet and cook, stirring occasionally, for 5 minutes or until potatoes soften. Remove the pan from heat, set aside, and let cool.

2. Combine eggs, cream, sage, thyme, salt, and pepper in a mixing bowl. Whisk well. Stir cooled vegetables into egg mixture, and scrape mixture into prepared pan.

3. Cover the pan with aluminum foil and bake for 30 minutes. Remove the foil and bake an additional 20 to 25 minutes or until potatoes are tender and a toothpick inserted into the center comes out clean. Cool 5 minutes; serve immediately.

Sausage, Cheese, and Potato Casserole

1 lb. mild or spicy bulk pork sausage

2 shallots, peeled and minced

3 TB. all-purpose flour

1½ cups half-and-half

1 cup (4 oz.) grated sharp cheddar cheese

1 (1-lb.) pkg. frozen hash-brown potatoes, thawed

Salt and freshly ground black pepper to taste

Serves: 6 to 8	
Prep time: 10 minutes	
Cook time: 50 minutes	

1. Preheat the oven to 350°F. Grease a 9×13-inch baking pan. Place a large skillet over medium-high heat. Add sausage and shallots, breaking up lumps with a fork, and cook, stirring occasionally, for 5 minutes or until sausage is browned and no longer pink.

2. Remove sausage from the pan with a slotted spoon and discard all but 2 tablespoons sausage fat. Reduce heat to low and return the skillet to the stove. Stir in flour and cook, stirring constantly, for 2 minutes. Slowly whisk in half-and-half and bring to a boil, whisking constantly until sauce is smooth and no lumps remain. Stir in cheddar cheese until melted. Return sausage mixture to the pan, along with potatoes, and season to taste with salt and pepper.

3. Scrape mixture into the prepared pan and cover with aluminum foil. Bake for 30 minutes. Remove the pan from the oven and stir. Return the covered pan to the oven for an additional 20 minutes or until potatoes are tender.

Sensational Strata: Easy Breakfast and Brunch Bread Puddings

In This Chapter

◆ One-dish breakfast and brunch bread puddings

◆ Strata with cheese—vegetarian, or not

◆ Sweet, cheeseless, French toast–like strata for a crowd

This generic family of savory or semi-savory bread puddings couldn't be easier to make. If you've got a loaf of any type of bread, a dozen eggs, and a quart of milk on hand, you're almost there.

As you'll see in the recipes in this chapter, bread soaked and cooked in custard is the only common denominator of strata. These homey casseroles can include breakfast meats such as bacon or sausage or a cornucopia of vegetables, or they can become sophisticated and elegant when seafood is folded in.

Although most savory strata include some sort of cheese, you can also produce sweet strata similar to a French toast pudding by omitting the cheese.

Strata Savvy

Strata can be made up to a day before they're baked and served. But if you have less time, don't fret. Although strata can spend overnight in the refrigerator, they really only need about 10 minutes to absorb the custard. That's why these recipes begin with soaking the bread, then preparing the other ingredients. Most of the additions need only a few minutes to cook, so in general, a strata is oven-ready in 15 minutes.

If the strata must go directly into the oven, slice the bread into thinner slices than the ½-inch slices specified in most of these recipes, and weight them down into the custard by placing a sheet of plastic wrap over the top of the pan and placing some canned goods or other weights on top of the plastic. Using this method, the strata will be ready to bake in less than 5 minutes.

Strata are a great way to use up stale bread or breakfast pastries. Do keep in mind that hard bread takes longer to absorb the egg custard than soft bread. If your baguette is a rock-hard lethal weapon, you're better off grinding it up for breadcrumbs.

Proper Proportions

Along with eggs and bread, milk is the other foundation ingredient of strata. You'll notice that all these recipes call for whole milk. You can go higher on the fat scale and use half-and-half, but it's not really necessary.

However, do not substitute 2 percent milk or skim milk for the whole milk. Milk with a lower fat content will produce a strata that tastes watery rather than rich. If skim or 2 percent milk is all you have in the house, add 1 tablespoon melted butter to the custard mixture for each 1 cup milk.

Serving Strata

In addition to providing a complete breakfast or brunch in one dish, strata can do double duty as a side dish to accompany any simple grilled or broiled item. If you're serving a strata from this chapter as a side dish, it will easily make 10 to 12 servings.

If the strata is your entrée, all you need is some sort of crisp salad or fruit salad to add additional color and texture to the plate. If you're serving the strata early in the day, use fruit salad; a green salad is always appropriate at brunch.

Sweet Sausage and Fennel Strata

8 large eggs

3½ cups whole milk

Salt and freshly ground black pepper to taste

1 cup grated mozzarella cheese

½ cup grated Parmesan cheese

¼ cup chopped fresh parsley

1 tsp. Italian seasoning

¾ lb. loaf French or Italian bread, cut into ½-inch slices

1½ lb. bulk sweet Italian sausage

1 (¾-lb.) fresh fennel bulb, leaves and stalks trimmed and thinly sliced

Serves: 6 to 8
Prep time: 15 minutes
Cook time: 45 minutes

1. Preheat the oven to 350°F. Grease a 10×14-inch baking pan. Combine eggs, whole milk, salt, and pepper in a mixing bowl and whisk well. Stir in mozzarella cheese, Parmesan cheese, parsley, and Italian seasoning. Arrange bread slices in the prepared baking pan and pour egg mixture over them, pressing down so bread will absorb liquid.

2. Heat a large skillet over medium-high heat. Add sausage and cook, breaking up large lumps, for 3 to 5 minutes or until sausage is browned. Remove sausage from the skillet with a slotted spoon and pour off all but 2 tablespoons sausage grease from the pan. Reduce heat to medium, add sliced fennel, and cook, stirring frequently, for 5 to 7 minutes or until fennel is crisp-tender. Stir sausage and fennel into bread mixture.

3. Cover the pan with aluminum foil and bake in the center of the oven for 30 minutes. Remove the foil and bake for an additional 15 to 20 minutes or until a toothpick inserted in the center comes out clean and the top is lightly browned. Allow to rest for 5 minutes and serve.

Half Baked

If you can't find bulk Italian sausage, buy the links. But be sure to squeeze the uncooked meat out of the casings and discard the casings. If the sausages are merely sliced and cooked, the thin pieces of casing will get into the strata, and they taste like rubber bands.

Three-Cheese Strata

Serves: 6 to 8
Prep time: 15 minutes
Cook time: 45 minutes

8 large eggs

3½ cups whole milk

Salt and freshly ground black pepper to taste

1 cup grated mozzarella cheese

1 cup grated sharp cheddar cheese

½ cup grated Parmesan cheese

¾ lb. loaf French or Italian bread, cut into ½-inch slices

 **Got You Covered!**

Grating cheese is a snap in a food processor fitted with a steel blade. If you're doing it by hand with a box grater, spray the grater with vegetable oil spray, and the cheese will grate far more easily.

1. Preheat the oven to 350°F. Grease a 10×14-inch baking pan. Combine eggs, whole milk, salt, and pepper in a mixing bowl and whisk well. Stir in mozzarella cheese, cheddar cheese, and Parmesan cheese. Arrange bread slices in the prepared baking pan and pour egg mixture over them, pressing down so bread will absorb liquid. Allow mixture to sit for 10 minutes.

2. Cover the pan with aluminum foil and bake in the center of the oven for 30 minutes. Remove the foil and bake for an additional 15 to 20 minutes or until a toothpick inserted in the center comes out clean and the top is lightly browned. Allow to rest for 5 minutes and serve.

Bacon, Corn, and Jalapeño Jack Strata

8 large eggs

3½ cups whole milk

Salt and freshly ground black pepper to taste

1½ cups grated jalapeño Jack cheese

¾ lb. loaf French or Italian bread, cut into ½-inch slices

1 lb. bacon, cut into 1-inch pieces

1 (10-oz.) pkg. frozen corn, thawed and drained

½ cup diced pimiento

Serves: 6 to 8	
Prep time: 15 minutes	
Cook time: 45 minutes	

1. Preheat the oven to 350°F. Grease a 10×14-inch baking pan. Combine eggs, whole milk, salt, and pepper in a mixing bowl and whisk well. Stir in jalapeño Jack cheese. Arrange bread slices in the prepared baking pan and pour egg mixture over them, pressing down so bread will absorb liquid.

2. Place a skillet over medium-high heat and add bacon pieces. Cook, stirring occasionally, until bacon is crisp. Remove bacon from the pan with slotted spoon and add bacon to bread mixture. Stir corn and pimiento into mixture.

3. Cover the pan with aluminum foil and bake in the center of the oven for 30 minutes. Remove the foil and bake for an additional 15 to 20 minutes or until a toothpick inserted in the center comes out clean and the top is lightly browned. Allow to rest for 5 minutes and serve.

 Got You Covered!

For a spicier version of this dish, substitute Mexican chorizo or Portuguese linguiça sausage for the bacon. Either one of those will really wake up your taste buds first thing in the morning!

Bacon, Cheddar, and Leek Strata

Serves: 6 to 8
Prep time: 20 minutes
Cook time: 45 minutes

8 large eggs

3½ cups whole milk

Salt and freshly ground black pepper to taste

2 TB. chopped fresh sage or 2 tsp. dried, rubbed

1½ cups grated sharp cheddar cheese, preferably orange

¾ lb. loaf French or Italian bread, cut into ½-inch slices

1 lb. bacon, cut into 1-inch pieces

3 large leeks, trimmed, thinly sliced, and well rinsed

 Half Baked

Leeks are notorious for the amount of sand and dirt naturally embedded in their layers during the growth process. Unlike scallions, which need a minor rinse after you discard the tops, leeks need a real cleaning. Be sure you cut through the tops and hold them upside down under cold running water to remove all the grit.

1. Preheat the oven to 350°F. Grease a 10×14-inch baking pan. Combine eggs, whole milk, salt, pepper, and sage in a mixing bowl and whisk well. Stir in cheddar cheese. Arrange bread slices in the prepared baking pan and pour egg mixture over them, pressing down so bread will absorb liquid.

2. Place a skillet over medium-high heat and add bacon pieces. Cook, stirring occasionally, until bacon is crisp. Remove bacon from the skillet with a slotted spoon and add to bread mixture.

3. Discard all but 2 tablespoons bacon fat from the skillet. Reduce heat to medium and add leeks to the skillet. Cook, stirring frequently, for 3 to 5 minutes or until leeks are soft. Stir leeks into bread mixture.

4. Cover the pan with aluminum foil and bake in the center of the oven for 30 minutes. Remove the foil and bake for an additional 15 to 20 minutes or until a toothpick inserted in the center comes out clean and the top is lightly browned. Allow to rest for 5 minutes and serve.

Bacon, Smoked Cheddar, and Sun-Dried Tomato Strata

8 large eggs

3½ cups whole milk

Salt and freshly ground black pepper to taste

1 tsp. *herbes de Provence*

1½ cups grated smoked cheddar cheese

¾ lb. loaf French or Italian bread, cut into ½-inch slices

1 lb. bacon, cut into 1-inch pieces

½ cup sun-dried tomatoes packed in oil, drained and finely chopped

Serves: 6 to 8	
Prep time: 15 minutes	
Cook time: 45 minutes	

1. Preheat the oven to 350°F. Grease a 10×14-inch baking pan. Combine eggs, whole milk, salt, pepper, and herbes de Provence in a mixing bowl and whisk well. Stir in cheddar cheese. Arrange bread slices in the prepared baking pan and pour egg mixture over them, pressing down so bread will absorb liquid.

2. Place the skillet over medium-high heat and add bacon pieces. Cook, stirring occasionally, until bacon is crisp. Remove bacon from the pan with a slotted spoon and add bacon to bread mixture along with sun-dried tomatoes.

3. Cover the pan with aluminum foil and bake in the center of the oven for 30 minutes. Remove the foil and bake for an additional 15 to 20 minutes or until a toothpick inserted in the center comes out clean and the top is lightly browned. Allow to rest for 5 minutes and serve.

Ellen on Edibles

Herbes de Provence, found in the spice section of many supermarkets and gourmet stores, is a dried blend of many herbs associated with the sunny cuisine of that part of France, including basil, thyme, fennel, rosemary, sage, and marjoram.

Spinach and Goat's Milk Cheese Strata

Serves: 6 to 8
Prep time: 15 minutes
Cook time: 45 minutes

8 large eggs

3½ cups whole milk

Salt and freshly ground black pepper to taste

2 tsp. fresh thyme or ½ tsp. dried

Pinch grated nutmeg

1½ cups mild *goat's milk cheese*, crumbled

¾ lb. loaf French or Italian bread, cut into ½-inch slices

2 TB. (¼ stick) butter

2 shallots, peeled and minced

1 garlic clove, peeled and minced

1 (10-oz.) pkg. frozen chopped spinach, thawed

 Ellen on Edibles

Goat's milk cheese, often referred to by its French name, *chevre*, is a pure white cheese with a delightful tart flavor that sets it apart from other cheeses. Goat's milk cheese comes in a variety of shapes, including cylinders, cones, and pyramids, and they are sometimes coated with edible ash, herbs, or pepper.

1. Preheat the oven to 350°F. Grease a 10×14-inch baking pan. Combine eggs, whole milk, salt, pepper, thyme, and nutmeg in a mixing bowl and whisk well. Stir in goat's milk cheese. Arrange bread slices in the prepared baking pan and pour egg mixture over them, pressing down so bread will absorb liquid.

2. Heat butter in a small skillet over medium heat. Add shallots and garlic and cook, stirring frequently, for 3 to 5 minutes or until shallots are translucent. While mixture is sautéing, place spinach in a colander and press with the back of a spoon to extract as much moisture as possible. Stir spinach and sautéed shallots into bread mixture.

3. Cover the pan with aluminum foil and bake in the center of the oven for 30 minutes. Remove the foil and bake for an additional 15 to 20 minutes or until a toothpick inserted in the center comes out clean and the top is lightly browned. Allow to rest for 5 minutes and serve.

Wild Mushroom and Gruyère Strata

6 dried shiitake mushrooms

8 large eggs

3½ cups whole milk

Salt and freshly ground black pepper to taste

2 tsp. fresh thyme, or ½ tsp. dried

1½ cups grated Gruyère cheese

¾ lb. loaf French or Italian bread, cut into ½-inch slices

3 TB. butter

2 TB. olive oil

¾ lb. fresh shiitake mushrooms, stems removed, wiped with a damp paper towel, and sliced

Serves: 6 to 8	
Prep time: 20 minutes	
Cook time: 45 minutes	

 Bake Lore

Although fresh shiitake mushrooms are a relative newcomer to the American produce section, they are the granddaddy of all culti-vated mushrooms. The Japanese have been cultivating them for more than 2,000 years. The ancient Greeks and Romans did not culti-vate mushrooms, con-trary to popular belief; they merely encouraged wild ones to grow. It was not until the eigh-teenth century, when Olivier de Serres was agronomist to French King Louis XIV, that mushroom cultivation began in Europe.

1. Preheat the oven to 350°F. Grease a 10×14-inch baking pan. Place dried shiitake mushrooms in a small bowl and cover them with very hot tap water. Press mushrooms down into water and set aside for 10 minutes.

2. Combine eggs, whole milk, salt, pepper, and thyme in a mix-ing bowl and whisk well. Stir in Gruyère cheese. Arrange bread slices in the prepared baking pan and pour egg mixture over them, pressing down so bread will absorb liquid.

3. Heat butter and oil in a large skillet over medium-high heat until butter is melted. Add fresh shiitake mushrooms and cook, stirring frequently, for 5 minutes or until mushrooms are browned. Drain dried mushrooms, discard stems, and thinly slice mushrooms. Stir all mushrooms into bread mixture.

4. Cover the pan with aluminum foil and bake in the center of the oven for 30 minutes. Remove the foil and bake for an additional 15 to 20 minutes or until a toothpick inserted in the center comes out clean and the top is lightly browned. Allow to rest for 5 minutes and serve.

Mango, Brie, and Green Chili Brioche Strata

Serves: 6 to 8
Prep time: 15 minutes
Cook time: 45 minutes

8 large eggs

3½ cups whole milk

Salt to taste

2 cups finely diced brie cheese

¾ lb. loaf *brioche*, cut into ¾-inch cubes (if brioche is unavailable, use ¾ lb. loaf French or Italian bread and add 4 TB. melted butter to custard mixture)

1 (4-oz.) can diced mild green chilies, drained

2 ripe mangoes, peeled and cut into ½-inch pieces

1. Preheat the oven to 350°F. Grease a 10×14-inch baking pan. Combine eggs, whole milk, and salt in a mixing bowl and whisk well. Stir in cheese. Arrange bread cubes in the prepared baking pan and pour egg mixture over them, pressing down so bread will absorb liquid. Stir green chilies and mangoes into bread mixture and allow mixture to sit for 10 minutes.

2. Cover the pan with aluminum foil and bake in the center of the oven for 30 minutes. Remove the foil and bake for an additional 15 to 20 minutes or until a toothpick inserted in the center comes out clean and the top is lightly browned. Allow to rest for 5 minutes and serve.

 Ellen on Edibles _____

Brioche (pronounced *BREE-ohsh*) is a French yeast bread that is rich with both butter and eggs. An increasing number of American bakeries are beginning to carry this crown-shaped loaf. However, if you can't find it, challah, a Jewish-style egg bread, is a good substitution. Add a few tablespoons melted butter to the custard mixture to give it additional richness.

Crab and Cilantro Pesto Strata

8 large eggs

3½ cups whole milk

Salt and freshly ground black pepper to taste

¾ lb. loaf French or Italian bread, cut into ½-inch slices

1 cup grated Parmesan cheese

1 cup fresh cilantro leaves, rinsed and patted dry

3 garlic cloves, peeled

½ cup pine nuts

½ cup olive oil

¾ lb. fresh crabmeat, picked over to remove shell fragments

Serves: 6 to 8
Prep time: 15 minutes
Cook time: 45 minutes

1. Preheat the oven to 350°F. Grease a 10×14-inch baking pan. Combine eggs, whole milk, salt, and pepper in a mixing bowl and whisk well. Arrange bread slices in the prepared baking pan and pour egg mixture over them, pressing down so bread will absorb liquid.

2. Combine Parmesan cheese, cilantro, garlic, pine nuts, and olive oil in a food processor fitted with a steel blade. Pureé until smooth, scraping down the sides of the work bowl as necessary. Stir cilantro pesto and crabmeat into bread mixture.

3. Cover the pan with aluminum foil and bake in the center of the oven for 30 minutes. Remove the foil and bake for an additional 15 to 20 minutes or until a toothpick inserted in the center comes out clean and the top is lightly browned. Allow to rest for 5 minutes and serve.

Got You Covered!

Already picked-over crabmeat from the seafood department is a tremendous time-saver, but it's far from perfect. The best way to ensure that no shell fragments find their way into a dish is to spread out the crab on a dark-colored plate. You'll see many fragments against the dark background so you can pick them out easily. Then rub the morsels between your fingers, being careful not to break up large lumps. Unless you have a shellfish allergy, please don't substitute imitation crabmeat, actually made from Pollack, for real crabmeat.

Dilled Shrimp, Corn, and Scallion Strata

Serves: 6 to 8
Prep time: 15 minutes
Cook time: 45 minutes

8 large eggs

3½ cups whole milk

Salt and freshly ground black pepper to taste

1 cup grated mozzarella cheese

¾ lb. loaf French or Italian bread, cut into ½-inch slices

3 TB. butter

6 scallions, trimmed with all but 2 inches of green tops discarded, thinly sliced

½ lb. cooked peeled and *deveined* shrimp, cut into ½-inch pieces if large

1 (10-oz.) pkg. frozen corn kernels, thawed

¼ cup chopped fresh dill or 2 TB. dried

Ellen on Edibles

Devein means to remove the black vein, actually the intestinal tract, from shrimp. Do this with the tip of a sharp paring knife or with a specialized tool called a *deveiner.*

1. Preheat the oven to 350°F. Grease a 10×14-inch baking pan. Combine eggs, whole milk, salt, and pepper in a mixing bowl and whisk well. Stir in mozzarella cheese. Arrange bread slices in the prepared baking pan and pour egg mixture over them, pressing down so bread will absorb liquid.

2. Melt butter in a small skillet over medium heat. Add scallions, and cook, stirring frequently, for 3 minutes or until scallions are translucent. Stir scallions, shrimp, corn, and dill into bread mixture.

3. Cover the pan with aluminum foil and bake in the center of the oven for 30 minutes. Remove the foil and bake for an additional 15 to 20 minutes or until a toothpick inserted in the center comes out clean and the top is lightly browned. Allow to rest for 5 minutes and serve.

Ham and Vegetable Cornbread Strata

8 large eggs

3½ cups whole milk

Salt and freshly ground black pepper to taste

2 tsp. fresh thyme or ½ tsp. dried

1½ cups grated mild cheddar cheese

6 cups finely diced cornbread

¾ lb. smoked ham, cut into ½-inch dice

3 TB. butter

1 large onion, peeled and diced

1 red bell pepper, seeds and ribs removed, and finely chopped

2 celery stalks, trimmed and thinly sliced

Serves: *6 to 8*
Prep time: 15 minutes
Cook time: 45 minutes

1. Preheat the oven to 350°F. Grease a 10×14-inch baking pan. Combine eggs, whole milk, salt, pepper, and thyme in a mixing bowl and whisk well. Stir in cheddar cheese. Arrange cornbread pieces in the prepared baking pan and pour egg mixture over them, pressing down so bread will absorb liquid. Stir in ham.

2. Melt butter in a medium skillet over medium heat. Add onion, red bell pepper, and celery. Cook, stirring often, for 3 to 5 minutes or until onions are translucent. Stir vegetables into bread mixture.

3. Cover the pan with aluminum foil and bake in the center of the oven for 30 minutes. Remove the foil and bake for an additional 15 to 20 minutes or until a toothpick inserted in the center comes out clean and the top is lightly browned. Allow to rest for 5 minutes and serve.

 Half Baked

When selecting cornbread for this or any other savory recipe, buy or make one that does not contain sugar or only a modest amount of sugar. Some cornbread mixes produce a product that is more a cake than a bread. That will be too sweet for this savory strata recipe. If the cornbread is very moist, reduce the amount of milk by ¼ cup.

Sausage, Apple, and Sage Raisin Bread Strata

Serves: 6 to 8
Prep time: 15 minutes
Cook time: 45 minutes

8 large eggs

3½ cups whole milk

Salt and freshly ground black pepper to taste

1 cup grated mozzarella cheese

¾ lb. loaf raisin bread, cut into ½-inch cubes (if raisin bread is unavailable, use ¾ lb. loaf French or Italian bread and add ½ cup raisins and an additional ½ tsp. cinnamon to custard mixture)

1 (12-oz.) roll bulk breakfast sausage

2 TB. (¼ stick) butter

1 small onion, peeled and diced

1 large McIntosh or Golden Delicious apple, peeled, cored, quartered, and thinly sliced

3 TB. granulated sugar

¼ cup chopped fresh sage or 1 TB. dried, rubbed

½ tsp. ground cinnamon

 Bake Lore

Although there isn't really a Jolly Green Giant, there certainly was a Johnny Appleseed. Named John Chapman, he was born in Massachusetts in 1774. Unlike the artistic depictions of his propagating apples by tossing seeds out of his backpack, he actually started nurseries for apple tree seedlings in the Allegheny Valley in 1800. By the time of his death in 1845, Chapman had pushed as far west as Indiana, establishing groves of apple trees as he went.

1. Preheat the oven to 350°F. Grease a 10×14-inch baking pan. Combine eggs, whole milk, salt, and pepper in a mixing bowl and whisk well. Stir in mozzarella cheese. Arrange bread cubes in the prepared baking pan and pour egg mixture over them, pressing down so bread will absorb liquid.

2. Place a large skillet over medium-high heat. Add sausage, breaking up lumps with a fork. Cook sausage, stirring frequently, for 5 minutes or until browned and no longer pink. Remove sausage from the skillet with a slotted spoon and add to bread mixture. Discard sausage grease.

3. Return the skillet to the stove and reduce the heat to medium. Add butter and onion. Cook, stirring frequently, for 3 minutes or until onion is translucent. Add apple, sugar, sage, and cinnamon to the skillet. Cook, stirring frequently, for 3 minutes or until apple begins to soften. Stir apple mixture into bread mixture.

4. Cover the pan with aluminum foil and bake in the center of the oven for 30 minutes. Remove the foil and bake for an additional 15 to 20 minutes or until a toothpick inserted in the center comes out clean and the top is lightly browned. Allow to rest for 5 minutes and serve.

Blueberry French Toast Strata

8 large eggs

3½ cups whole milk

Salt to taste

⅓ cup granulated sugar

1 TB. grated lemon zest

1 tsp. pure vanilla extract

¾ lb. loaf challah, Portuguese sweet bread, or white bread, cut into ½-inch slices

1 pt. fresh or 2 cups dry-packed frozen blueberries, thawed

Serves: 6 to 8	
Prep time: 15 minutes	
Cook time: 45 minutes	

1. Preheat the oven to 350°F. Grease a 10×14-inch baking pan. Combine eggs, whole milk, salt, granulated sugar, lemon zest, and vanilla extract in a mixing bowl and whisk well. Arrange bread slices in the prepared baking pan and pour egg mixture over them, pressing down so bread will absorb liquid. Allow mixture to sit for 10 minutes. Stir blueberries into bread mixture.

2. Cover the pan with aluminum foil and bake in the center of the oven for 30 minutes. Remove the foil and bake for an additional 15 to 20 minutes or until a toothpick inserted in the center comes out clean and the top is lightly browned. Allow to rest for 5 minutes and serve.

Maple French Toast Strata

Serves: 6 to 8
Prep time: 15 minutes
Cook time: 45 minutes

8 large eggs

3½ cups whole milk

½ cup pure maple syrup

1 tsp. ground cinnamon

Salt to taste

¾ lb. loaf *challah*, Portuguese sweet bread, or white bread, cut into ½-inch slices

Ellen on Edibles

Challah is an egg-rich ceremonial Jewish bread served on the Sabbath and holidays. It has a light, airy texture and is traditionally braided into an oval loaf.

1. Preheat the oven to 350°F. Grease a 10×14-inch baking pan. Combine eggs, whole milk, maple syrup, cinnamon, and salt in a mixing bowl and whisk well. Arrange bread slices in the prepared baking pan and pour egg mixture over them, pressing down so bread will absorb liquid. Allow mixture to sit for 10 minutes.

2. Cover the pan with aluminum foil and bake in the center of the oven for 30 minutes. Remove the foil and bake for an additional 15 to 20 minutes or until a toothpick inserted in the center comes out clean and the top is lightly browned. Allow to rest for 5 minutes and serve.

Part 3

From the Seas

One of the greatest changes in American supermarkets in recent years is the expansion of the fresh fish department. The growing demand by cooks to prepare healthful and nutritious fresh fish has been met by advances in modern transportation that allow fish to reach inland markets from all coasts long before it's ready for Social Security.

The recipes in Part 3 are divided by the type of fish being prepared. Chapter 4 gives canned tuna—a pantry staple—some fresh treatments. Chapter 5 is devoted to fillets and steaks from fish that swim in the lakes and oceans. Chapter 6 showcases ever-popular shrimp, along with other crustaceans and mollusks.

Fresh fish is far faster to cook than most meats, so the recipes in this chapter can be served the night they're prepared, even if the cook doesn't start preparation until after getting home from work.

Chapter 4

Fish from the Pantry: One-Dish Meals with Canned Tuna

In This Chapter

- ◆ Updated versions of classic creamy pasta and tuna combinations
- ◆ Quick and healthful meals full of primarily pantry ingredients
- ◆ Tuna casseroles with international flair

Shelf-stable foods such as tuna and pasta are dinner insurance. With those ingredients tucked into your pantry, a meal is but minutes away.

Many of us have fond memories of Tuna Noodle Casserole, and if it remains part of your meal rotation, you already know how to make it. But there are many ways of preparing it beyond adding the can of condensed soup to create a one-dish meal, even a one-dish meal using convenience products. This chapter will expand your horizons.

Some recipes in this and other chapters are referred to as "overnight bakes." These dishes use small pastas that begin to soften during the specified refrigerated time, at least 8 hours. That means they will cook al dente during the final baking and require no precooking.

Talking Tuna

You can find a dizzying array of cans and pouches of tuna on your supermarket shelves. They are labeled by myriad brands, both national and imported, but they essentially fall into four categories: solid white tuna packed in water, solid white tuna packed in oil, and the same packing options for light tuna. Water-packed tuna is a relative newcomer to the market, following decades of oil-packed tuna. Although the water does trim the fat from the fish, it also trims much of the flavor because it tends to be less moist.

There's no question that water-packed solid white tuna yields the most impressive chunks—and has concomitantly the highest price. Light tuna is darker in color and tends to fall apart after it's drained. It's less expensive, and for making these casseroles, there's no difference in the finished flavor. It's a matter of aesthetics and price.

Tuna packed in pure olive oil rather than vegetable oil, usually imported from Italy, adds a more substantial flavor to dishes, especially if you utilize the oil for cooking the vegetables in a recipe.

Canning the Can

One of the greatest advances in food processing since the advent of commercial canning was the creation of 3-ounce, shelf-stable, single-serving plastic pouches of tuna. The fish has more flavor, and you have the convenience of tearing open a pouch instead of potentially dripping water or oil around as you wrestle with the can opener.

Salmon and Other Substitutes

You can substitute bright pink salmon, loaded with healthful omega-3 fatty acids even in its canned form, for tuna in any of these recipes. Salmon is packed in 7½-ounce cans rather than the traditional 6-ounce cans of tuna because canned salmon contains both skin and bones. When these are discarded, the edible amount of fish in the can is identical to a can of tuna.

Due to a high mercury content, most health authorities agree that you should limit the consumption of canned tuna to no more than a few times a week. If you have a favorite tuna recipe, it will be just as flavorful if you make it with canned salmon.

Tuna Pasta Alfredo Bake with Mushrooms and Green Beans

1 lb. rigatoni or penne pasta

3 TB. butter

1 TB. olive oil

½ lb. white mushrooms, trimmed, wiped with a damp paper towel, and sliced

1 garlic clove, peeled and minced

1 (10-oz.) container Alfredo or four-cheese pasta sauce from the supermarket's refrigerated aisle

½ cup grated mozzarella cheese

¼ cup grated Parmesan cheese

1 TB. Italian seasoning

¾ cup milk

2 (6-oz.) cans tuna, drained and broken into chunks or 4 (3-oz.) pouches, broken into chunks

1 (10-oz.) pkg. frozen cut green beans, thawed

Salt and freshly ground black pepper to taste

½ cup Italian breadcrumbs

Serves: 6 to 8	
Prep time: 15 minutes	
Cook time: 25 minutes	

1. Preheat the oven to 375°F. Grease a 10×14-inch baking pan. Set aside.

2. Bring a large pot of salted water to a boil over high heat. Add rigatoni and cook according to the package directions until al dente. Drain and return to the pot.

3. While rigatoni is cooking, heat butter and oil in a large skillet over medium-high heat until butter is melted. Add mushrooms and garlic and cook, stirring frequently, for 3 to 5 minutes or until mushrooms are cooked and liquid has evaporated. Scrape mushrooms into rigatoni and add Alfredo sauce, mozzarella cheese, Parmesan cheese, Italian seasoning, milk, tuna, and green beans. Season to taste with salt and pepper.

4. Scrape mixture into the prepared baking pan, level top with a rubber spatula, and sprinkle with Italian breadcrumbs. Cover the pan with aluminum foil and bake for 10 minutes. Remove the foil and bake for an additional 15 minutes or until hot and bubbly. Serve immediately.

Ellen on Edibles

Italian breadcrumbs are toasted breadcrumbs that are then seasoned with parsley, other herbs, garlic, and Parmesan cheese. If you only have plain breadcrumbs, to replicate the flavor, add 1 teaspoon Italian seasoning, ½ teaspoon garlic powder, and 3 tablespoons Parmesan cheese to each 1 cup plain breadcrumbs.

Updated Tuna Noodle Casserole with Potato-Chip Topping

Serves: 6 to 8
Prep time: 20 minutes
Cook time: 30 minutes

6 oz. medium egg noodles

5 TB. butter

4 scallions, trimmed with all but 2 inches of green tops discarded, chopped

½ cup chopped celery

2 garlic cloves, peeled and minced

½ lb. white mushrooms, trimmed, wiped with a damp paper towel, and sliced

¼ cup all-purpose flour

2 cups milk

1 TB. chopped fresh rosemary or 1 tsp. dried

1 TB. fresh thyme or 1 tsp. dried

Salt and freshly ground black pepper to taste

2 (6-oz.) cans tuna, drained and broken into chunks, or 4 (3-oz.) pouches, broken into chunks

1 (5-oz.) bag potato chips, crushed

Got You Covered!

If you can't relate to a Tuna Noodle Casserole that's made without a can of cream of something soup, here's an adaptation: cut back to 2 tablespoons butter, omit flour, and change the amount of milk to ½ cup. Then add 1 (10.75-ounce) can condensed cream of mushroom or cream of celery soup. But at least please try this version, too!

1. Preheat the oven to 375°F. Grease a 10×14-inch baking pan. Bring a large pot of salted water to a boil and cook egg noodles according to the package directions. Drain and return to the pot.

2. Melt 2 tablespoons butter in a large skillet over medium-high heat. Add scallions, celery, garlic, and mushrooms. Cook, stirring frequently, for 5 minutes or until celery begins to soften. Add vegetables to noodles and return the skillet to the stove.

3. Melt remaining 3 tablespoons butter in the same skillet over low heat. Stir in flour and cook, stirring constantly, for 2 minutes. Slowly whisk in milk and bring to a boil over medium heat, whisking constantly. Simmer 1 minute, stir in rosemary and thyme, and season sauce to taste with salt and pepper. Pour sauce over noodles and gently fold in tuna.

4. Scrape mixture into the prepared baking pan, level top with a rubber spatula, and sprinkle with potato chips. (You can do this a day in advance and refrigerate, tightly covered. Add 10 minutes to initial covered baking time.)

5. Cover the pan with aluminum foil and bake for 10 minutes. Remove the foil and bake for an additional 20 minutes or until hot and bubbly. Serve immediately.

Tuna Linguine Skillet with Oregano Tomato Sauce and Kalamata Olives

1 lb. linguine or other thin pasta

2 TB. olive oil

1 small onion, peeled and diced

3 garlic cloves, peeled and minced

1 celery stalk, trimmed and thinly sliced

1 (28-oz.) can crushed tomatoes in tomato purée

½ cup dry white wine

¾ cup pitted kalamata olives, chopped

¼ cup small capers, drained and rinsed

¼ cup chopped fresh parsley

3 TB. chopped fresh oregano or 1 TB. dried

1 bay leaf

Salt and freshly ground black pepper to taste

2 (6-oz.) cans tuna, drained and broken into chunks, or 4 (3-oz.) pouches, broken into chunks

½ cup grated Parmesan cheese

Serves: 6 to 8
Prep time: 15 minutes
Cook time: 21 minutes

1. Bring a large pot of salted water to a boil. Add linguini and cook until al dente. Drain and set aside.

2. Heat oil in a skillet over medium-high heat. Add onion, garlic, and celery. Cook, stirring frequently, for 3 minutes or until onion is translucent. Add tomatoes, wine, olives, capers, parsley, oregano, and bay leaf. Bring to a boil, reduce heat to medium, and simmer uncovered for 15 minutes. Season to taste with salt and pepper and stir in cooked linguini and tuna. Cover and cook for 3 minutes or until pasta is hot.

3. Remove and discard bay leaf. Serve immediately, sprinkling individual servings with Parmesan cheese.

 Half Baked

The key word for the olives in this recipe is *pitted*. It's easy to find imported Greek kalamata olives already pitted, but it's more important to find a pitted olive than one hailing from Kalamata. Some markets have pitted French olives, and there is always the ubiquitous can. Trust me. You don't want to spend time pitting tiny olives.

Tex-Mex Tuna, Monterey Jack, and Tortilla Casserole

Serves: 6 to 8
Prep time: 10 minutes
Cook time: 30 minutes

2 TB. (¼ stick) butter

1 medium onion, peeled and diced

2 garlic cloves, peeled and minced

1½ tsp. dried oregano, preferably Mexican

1 (4-oz.) can diced mild green chilies, drained

6 (6-in.) corn tortillas, cut into ½-inch strips

1 cup grated Monterey Jack cheese

2 (6-oz.) cans tuna, drained and broken into chunks, or 4 (3-oz.) pouches, broken into chunks

3 large eggs

1½ cups whole milk

¼ cup chopped fresh cilantro

Salt and freshly ground black pepper to taste

Got You Covered!

Heat releases the flavor and aroma of dried herbs and spices. For blends such as curry powder or chili powder, it also removes any "raw" taste. Add these dried ingredients at the beginning of the cooking process. Add fresh herbs more toward the end.

1. Preheat the oven to 350°F. Grease a 9×13-inch baking pan.

2. Melt butter in a small skillet over medium-high heat. Add onion, garlic, and oregano. Cook, stirring frequently, for 3 minutes or until onions are translucent. Stir green chilies into onion mixture and set aside.

3. Place ½ tortilla strips in the prepared baking pan and top with ½ Monterey Jack cheese, ½ tuna, and ½ onion mixture. Repeat with second layer.

4. Whisk eggs with milk and cilantro and season to taste with salt and pepper. Pour egg mixture into the pan and cover with aluminum foil. Bake for 15 minutes, remove the foil, and bake for an additional 15 minutes or until top is browned and a toothpick inserted in the center comes out clean.

Skillet Tuna and Pasta with Provençale Vegetables

1 (1-lb.) eggplant, peeled and cut into ½-inch cubes

Salt

1 lb. small pasta shells

⅓ cup olive oil

2 celery stalks, trimmed and diced

1 medium onion, peeled and diced

4 garlic cloves, peeled and minced

1 (4-oz.) jar sliced pimientos, drained and rinsed

¼ cup red wine vinegar

1 TB. granulated sugar

1 (14.5-oz.) can diced Italian plum tomatoes, undrained

½ cup water

2 TB. tomato paste

½ cup sliced green or black olives

2 (6-oz.) cans tuna, drained and broken into chunks, or 4 (3-oz.) pouches, broken into chunks

Freshly ground black pepper

Serves: 6 to 8
Prep time: 30 minutes
Cook time: 25 minutes

1. Place eggplant in a colander and sprinkle liberally with salt. Place a plate on top of eggplant and weight the plate with cans. Place the colander in the sink or on a plate and allow eggplant to drain for 30 minutes. Rinse eggplant cubes and squeeze dry with your hands. Wring out remaining water with a cloth tea towel and set aside. Bring a large pot of salted water to a boil and cook pasta shells until *al dente*. Drain and set aside.

2. While eggplant is sitting, heat ½ olive oil in a skillet over medium-high heat. Add celery, onion, and garlic. Cook, stirring frequently, for 3 to 5 minutes or until onion is translucent and celery begins to soften. Remove vegetables from the skillet with a slotted spoon.

3. Pour remaining olive oil into the skillet and heat over medium-high heat. Add eggplant cubes and cook, stirring frequently, for 5 minutes or until lightly browned. Return celery mixture to the skillet and add pimientos, vinegar, sugar, tomatoes, water, tomato paste, and olives.

4. Bring to a boil, reduce heat to low, and simmer, covered, stirring occasionally, for about 15 minutes or until vegetables are cooked but still retain their texture. Add tuna and cooked shells and cook an additional 2 minutes, covered. Season to taste with salt and pepper and serve immediately.

Ellen on Edibles

Al dente is Italian for "against the teeth" and refers to pasta (or another ingredient such as rice) that is neither soft nor hard, but just slightly firm when you bite it. For these recipes, it is very important to not overcook pasta, because it is subjected to additional cooking in the finished dish.

Overnight Tuna, Spinach, and Macaroni Bake

Serves: 6 to 8
Prep time: 15 minutes, plus 8 hours chilling
Cook time: 50 minutes

3 TB. butter

2 shallots, peeled and minced

1 garlic clove, peeled and minced

¼ cup all-purpose flour

2 cups milk

1½ cups grated Gruyère cheese

¼ cup chopped fresh parsley

2 tsp. herbes de Provence

Salt and freshly ground black pepper to taste

1 (10-oz.) pkg. frozen leaf spinach, thawed and squeezed dry

2 cups macaroni

2 (6-oz.) cans tuna, drained and broken into chunks, or 4 (3-oz.) pouches, broken into chunks

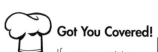

Got You Covered!

If you want to make an "overnight bake" on the same day, precook the pasta for a few minutes less than package directions, and decrease the milk to 1½ cups.

1. Grease a 2-quart casserole dish with a cover. Melt butter in a saucepan over medium heat. Add shallots and garlic and cook, stirring frequently, for 3 minutes or until shallots are translucent. Reduce heat to low, stir in flour, and cook, stirring constantly, for 2 minutes. Raise heat to medium, whisk in milk, and bring to a boil, whisking constantly. Stir in Gruyère cheese, parsley, herbes de Provence, salt, and pepper. Simmer for 2 minutes or until cheese is melted, stirring occasionally. Stir in spinach, macaroni, and tuna. Scrape mixture into the prepared casserole dish, cover, and refrigerate for at least 8 hours or overnight.

2. Preheat the oven to 350°F. Bake casserole, covered, for 50 minutes to 1 hour or until macaroni is tender. Serve immediately.

Tuna and Herbed Rice Stuffed Red Bell Peppers

1 cup long-grain rice

2 cups tomato juice

¼ cup chopped fresh parsley

1 TB. fresh thyme or 1 tsp. dried

1 TB. fresh chopped tarragon or 1 tsp. dried

Salt and freshly ground black pepper to taste

½ cup grated Swiss cheese

2 TB. (¼ stick) butter

1 small onion, peeled and diced

2 garlic cloves, peeled and minced

¼ lb. white mushrooms, trimmed, wiped with a damp paper towel, and chopped

1 (10-oz.) pkg. frozen mixed vegetables, thawed

2 (6-oz.) cans tuna, drained and broken into chunks, or 4 (3-oz.) pouches, broken into chunks

6 to 8 red bell peppers

Serves: 6 to 8	
Prep time: 20 minutes	
Cook time: 40 minutes	

1. Preheat the oven to 350°F. Combine rice, tomato juice, parsley, thyme, and tarragon in a saucepan. Season to taste with salt and pepper and bring to a boil over high heat. Reduce heat to low and simmer rice for 15 to 20 minutes or until tender and liquid is evaporated. Stir in Swiss cheese and set aside.

2. While rice is cooking, melt butter in a medium skillet over medium-high heat. Add onion, garlic, and mushrooms. Cook, stirring frequently, for 3 to 5 minutes or until onion is translucent and mushrooms are soft. Stir vegetable mixture, frozen mixed vegetables, and tuna into rice.

3. Cut top ½ inch off red bell peppers and discard caps. Scoop out seeds and ribs and discard. Cut a small slice off bottoms of peppers so they sit securely. Spoon tuna mixture into peppers and place them in a baking pan large enough to hold them all upright in a single layer.

4. Cover the pan with aluminum foil and bake for 40 to 50 minutes or until peppers are soft. Serve immediately.

Got You Covered!

For a spicier dish, substitute Bloody Mary mix for the tomato juice, or add a few dashes of hot red pepper sauce to the tomato juice when cooking the rice.

Tuna and Vegetable Fusilli Bake with Creamy Pesto Sauce

Serves: 6 to 8
Prep time: 10 minutes
Cook time: 30 minutes

1 lb. fusilli

1 (10-oz.) container Alfredo sauce from the supermarket's refrigerated aisle

½ cup milk

¼ cup pesto sauce from the supermarket's refrigerated aisle

1 (10-oz.) pkg. frozen mixed vegetables, thawed

2 (6-oz.) cans tuna, drained and broken into chunks, or 4 (3-oz.) pouches, broken into chunks

Salt and freshly ground black pepper to taste

½ cup Italian breadcrumbs

¼ cup grated Parmesan cheese

1 TB. Italian seasoning

3 TB. olive oil

Bake Lore

Alfredo sauce, a rich cream sauce with grated Parmesan cheese, is credited to a Roman restaurateur, Alfredo di Lello, who created the sauce for his patrons in the early 1920s.

1. Preheat the oven to 375°F. Grease a 9×13-inch baking pan. Bring a large pot of salted water to a boil. Cook fusilli according to the package directions until al dente. Drain and return pasta to the pot.

2. Add Alfredo sauce, milk, and pesto sauce and stir well. Fold in mixed vegetables and tuna and season to taste with salt and pepper. Scrape mixture into the prepared pan and level top with a rubber spatula. Combine breadcrumbs, Parmesan cheese, Italian seasoning, and olive oil in a small bowl. Drizzle breadcrumb mixture over tuna mixture.

3. Cover the pan with aluminum foil and bake for 15 minutes. Remove the foil and bake for an additional 15 minutes or until bubbly. Serve immediately.

Tuna Skillet au Gratin

1½ lb. frozen diced potatoes with onion and peppers (O'Brien potatoes), not thawed

1½ cups milk

Salt and freshly ground black pepper to taste

1 (10-oz.) pkg. frozen peas and carrots, thawed

2 (6-oz.) cans tuna, drained and broken into chunks, or 4 (3-oz.) pouches, broken into chunks

1½ cups grated mild or sharp cheddar cheese

Serves: 6 to 8	
Prep time: 5 minutes	
Cook time: 15 minutes	

1. Place potatoes and milk in a large skillet and heat over medium-high heat, stirring frequently to break up lumps of potatoes. Reduce heat to low, cover, and cook for 10 to 15 minutes or until potatoes are tender. Season to taste with salt and pepper.

2. Stir in peas and carrots, tuna, and cheddar cheese. Cook over low heat for 5 minutes or until cheese is melted and the dish is hot. Serve immediately.

Got You Covered!

Changing the cheese and vegetable in this dish creates an entirely new flavor, so feel free to experiment. Using jalapeño Jack cheese will make it spicy; using Swiss or Gruyère will give it a more savory appeal. You can substitute a package of chopped broccoli or sliced green beans for the peas and carrots, too.

Lemon Dill Tuna Bake

Serves: 6 to 8
Prep time: 15 minutes
Cook time: 45 minutes

1 lb. small shells or gemelli pasta

3 TB. butter

1 TB. vegetable oil

1 shallot, peeled and minced

½ lb. fresh shiitake mushrooms, stems removed, wiped with a damp paper towel, and sliced

2 TB. all-purpose flour

1 (14.5-oz.) can chicken stock or vegetable stock

⅓ cup half-and-half

1 TB. grated lemon zest

¼ cup chopped fresh dill or 2 TB. dried

1 (10-oz.) pkg. frozen peas, thawed

2 (6-oz.) cans tuna, drained and broken into chunks, or 4 (3-oz.) pouches, broken into chunks

Salt and freshly ground black pepper to taste

1. Preheat the oven to 350°F. Grease a 9×13-inch baking pan. Bring a large pot of salted water to a boil. Cook shells according to the package directions, drain, and set aside.

2. Melt 1 tablespoon butter and oil in a medium skillet over medium-high heat. Add shallot and mushrooms. Cook, stirring frequently, for 3 to 5 minutes or until mushrooms are soft. Remove from the skillet with a slotted spoon.

3. Reduce the heat to low and add remaining 2 tablespoons butter to the pan. Stir in flour and cook, stirring constantly, for 2 minutes. Whisk in chicken stock and half-and-half, and bring to a boil over medium heat, stirring occasionally. Simmer for 2 minutes; then stir in shells, mushrooms, lemon zest, dill, peas, and tuna. Season to taste with salt and pepper and scrape mixture into the prepared pan; level top with a rubber spatula.

4. Cover the pan with aluminum foil and bake for 25 minutes. Remove the foil and bake for an additional 20 to 25 minutes or until bubbly.

Half Baked

Never substitute lemon juice for lemon zest in a recipe. Lemon zest adds aroma and some delicate flavor without the acidity of the juice. Using lemon pepper in place of freshly ground pepper will enhance a dish in the same way.

Fishy Business: Recipes Using Fin Fish Steaks and Fillets

In This Chapter

- ◆ Hearty one-dish fish stews you can prepare in advance
- ◆ Fast and easy Asian fish bakes
- ◆ Healthful fish meals drawn from Mediterranean cuisines

It's a chicken and egg situation. Are Americans eating more fish because it's more widely available? Or is the fish department growing because people are eating more fish?

Regardless of the reason, more countries border on an ocean or major lake than are land-locked. So the majority of the world's cuisines include great fish dishes. The recipes in this chapter are all for fin fish; see Chapter 6 for dishes that contain shellfish.

Choosing the Choicest

It's worth the effort to search your neighborhood for the best fish source you can find. Look for a market that offers the most varied selection, that keeps its fish on chipped ice to maintain moisture, and that has a level of personal service that allows you to special order specific varieties or cuts of fish.

When making your fish selection, keep a few simple guidelines in mind. Above all, do not buy any fish that actually smells fishy, indicating that it is no longer fresh or hasn't been cut or stored properly. Fresh fish has the mild, clean scent of the sea—nothing more. If possible, select a whole fish and then have it cut to your specifications, such as fillets or steaks, because there are more signs to judge the freshness of a whole fish than any of the parts comprising it.

Look for bright shiny colors in the fish scales, because as a fish sits, its skin becomes more pale and dull looking. Then peer into the eyes; they should be black and beady. If they're milky or sunken, the fish has been dead too long. And the last test, if the fish isn't behind glass, is to gently poke its flesh. If the indentation remains, the fish is old.

Also, fish fillets or steaks should look bright, lustrous, and moist, with no signs of discoloration or drying.

Fish Families

Although these recipes are written for specific fish, it's more important to use the freshest fish in the market than the particular species. All fish fall into three basic families, and you can easily substitute one species for another. Use the following table to make life at the fish counter easier.

A Guide to Fish

Description	Species	Characteristics
Firm, lean fish	Black sea bass, cod family, flat fish (flounder, sole, halibut), grouper, lingcod, ocean perch, perch, pike, porgy, red snapper, smelt, striped bass, turbot, salmon, trout, drum family, tilefish	Low fat, mild to delicate flavor, firm flesh, flakes when cooked
Meaty fish	Catfish, carp, eel, monkfish (anglerfish), orange roughy, pike, salmon, shark, sturgeon, swordfish, some tuna varieties, mahi-mahi (dolphinfish), whitefish, pompano, yellowtail	Low to high fat, diverse flavors and textures, usually thick steaks or filets
Fatty or strong-flavored fish	Bluefish, mackerel, some tuna varieties	High fat, pronounced flavor

Preparation Pointers

Rinse all fish under cold running water before cutting or cooking. With fillets, run your fingers in every direction along the top of the fillet before cooking, and feel for any pesky little bones.

You can remove bones easily in two ways. Larger bones will come out if they're stroked with a vegetable peeler, and you can pull out smaller bones with tweezers. This is not a long process, but it's a gesture that will be greatly appreciated by all who eat the fish.

Overcooking is a common plight for fish dishes. That's why we add the fish as the last ingredient in these recipes. To test for doneness, flake the fish with a fork; cooked fish will flake easily, and the color will be opaque rather than translucent. While cooking, fish flakes become milky and opaque from the outside in.

Aquatic Attributes

Fish is high in protein and low to moderate in fat, cholesterol, and sodium. A 3-ounce portion of fish has between 47 and 170 calories, depending on the species. Fish is an excellent source of B vitamins, iodine, phosphorus, potassium, iron, and calcium.

The most important nutrient in fish may be the omega-3 fatty acids. These are the primary polyunsaturated fatty acids found in the fat and oils of fish. They have been found to lower the levels of low-density lipoproteins (LDL), the "bad" cholesterol, and raise the levels of high-density lipoproteins (HDL), the "good" cholesterol. Fatty fish that live in cold water, such as mackerel and salmon, seem to have the most omega-3 fatty acids, although all fish have some.

Expanding Options

In addition to substituting any number of fish species for the ones listed in these recipes, if you like a concept but you're more in the mood for poultry, you're in luck. You can make any of these recipes with boneless, skinless chicken breasts.

One difference to keep in mind, however, is the cooking time. For fish cut into cubes, rather than allowing the fish to poach for 5 minutes, keep the liquid at a simmer. For whole pieces, pound the chicken breasts to an even, ½-inch thickness. Then the chicken will cook in the same time as the fish fillets.

Chinese-Style Sea Bass with Mixed Vegetables and Jasmine Rice

Serves: 6 to 8
Prep time: 15 minutes
Cook time: 15 minutes

1½ cups jasmine rice

3 TB. Asian sesame oil

6 scallions, trimmed and cut into 1-inch pieces

5 garlic cloves, peeled and minced

3 TB. grated fresh ginger

1 small jalapeño pepper, seeds and ribs removed, and finely chopped

1 lb. fresh asparagus, woody stems removed, and sliced on the diagonal into 1-inch pieces

1 large red bell pepper, seeds and ribs removed, thinly sliced

1 medium red onion, peeled and thinly sliced

1½ lb. sea bass fillets, rinsed and cut into 6 to 8 serving-size pieces

¼ cup soy sauce

¼ cup plum wine or sweet sherry

¾ cup fish stock or chicken stock

1 TB. cornstarch mixed with 2 TB. cold water

¼ cup black sesame seeds or toasted white sesame seeds

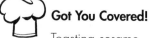 **Got You Covered!**

Toasting sesame seeds is a quick process. Place them in a small dry skillet over medium-high heat and shake the pan as they begin to brown. The entire process takes less than 1 minute.

1. Cook rice according to package directions and set aside.

2. Heat sesame oil in a large skillet over medium-high heat. Add scallions, garlic, ginger, and jalapeño pepper. Cook, stirring constantly, for 30 seconds. Add asparagus, red bell pepper, and red onion to the skillet. Cook, stirring frequently, for 2 minutes.

3. Add sea bass to the skillet, along with soy sauce, plum wine, and fish stock. Bring to a boil, cover, reduce heat to low, and simmer 5 minutes. Gently turn sea bass with a slotted spatula and cook, covered, for an additional 3 minutes or until fish is opaque.

4. Remove sea bass and vegetables from the skillet with a slotted spatula and keep hot. Add cornstarch mixture to the skillet and simmer for 1 minute or until lightly thickened. Stir rice into sauce and heat through. Place rice on a serving platter or plates and spoon fish and vegetables over it. Sprinkle with sesame seeds and serve.

Baked Cod with Tomatoes, Fennel, and Arborio Rice

¼ cup olive oil

1 large onion, peeled and thinly sliced

3 garlic cloves, peeled and minced

2 fennel bulbs, trimmed, cored, and thinly sliced

1½ cups Arborio rice

1 (28-oz.) can diced tomatoes, undrained

2 cups fish stock, bottled clam juice, or tomato juice

1 cup dry white wine

½ cup orange juice

¼ cup *Pernod*

1 TB. grated orange zest

2 bay leaves

Salt and freshly ground black pepper to taste

1½ to 2 lb. thick cod fillets, rinsed and cut into serving-size pieces

Serves: 6 to 8
Prep time: 20 minutes
Cook time: 30 minutes

1. Preheat the oven to 425°F. Heat olive oil in a large saucepan over medium heat. Add onion and garlic and cook, stirring frequently, for 3 minutes or until onion is translucent. Add fennel and rice and cook for 2 minutes, stirring frequently. Add tomatoes, fish stock, wine, orange juice, Pernod, orange zest, and bay leaves to the saucepan. Bring to a boil, reduce the heat, and simmer, uncovered, stirring occasionally, for 10 minutes. Season to taste with salt and pepper. (You can do this a day in advance and refrigerate, tightly covered. Add 15 minutes to initial oven baking time.)

2. Transfer vegetable mixture to a 10×14-inch baking pan. Cover the pan with aluminum foil and bake for 20 minutes. Remove the pan from the oven and stir well. Sprinkle cod with salt and pepper and place it on top of vegetables. Bake uncovered for about 10 to 15 minutes or until cod is opaque. Remove and discard bay leaves and serve immediately.

 Ellen on Edibles

Pernod is a light green, licorice-flavored liqueur popular in France. It's usually mixed with water, at which time it turns milky white. Ouzo, a Greek concoction, is similar in flavor.

Mahi-Mahi with Asian Vegetables and Rice in Macadamia Cream Sauce

Serves: 6 to 8	
Prep time: 15 minutes	
Cook time: 25 minutes	

1½ cups jasmine rice

2 TB. Asian sesame oil

3 scallions, trimmed with all but 2 inches of green tops discarded, chopped

2 garlic cloves, peeled and minced

2 TB. grated fresh ginger

⅓ lb. fresh shiitake mushrooms, stems removed, wiped with a damp paper towel, and sliced

½ lb. snow peas, rinsed and stemmed

¾ lb. baby bok choy, trimmed, rinsed and patted dry on paper towels, and sliced in half (or quartered if larger than 3 inches in diameter)

1½ lb. mahi-mahi fillet, rinsed and cut into 1-inch slices

1 cup chopped salted macadamia nuts

1 (14-oz.) can light coconut milk

2 TB. *nam pla* (Thai fish sauce), available in the Asian section of most supermarkets and at Asian grocery stores

Salt and freshly ground black pepper to taste

¼ cup chopped fresh cilantro

Ellen on Edibles

Nam pla, a salty sauce with an extremely pungent odor, is made from fermented fish and used as a dipping sauce/condiment and seasoning ingredient throughout Southeast Asia. Nam pla is the Thai term; it's known as *nuoc nam* in Vietnam and *shottsuru* in Japan.

1. Preheat the oven to 350°F. Grease a 9×13-inch baking pan. Cook rice according to the package directions and set aside.

2. Heat sesame oil in a medium skillet over medium-high heat. Add scallions, garlic, and ginger. Cook, stirring constantly, for 30 seconds. Add shiitake mushrooms and cook, stirring frequently, for 3 minutes or until mushrooms are soft. Add snow peas and bok choy to the skillet and cook for 30 seconds.

3. Place mahi-mahi in the prepared baking pan and scatter vegetables and macadamia nuts on top. Combine coconut milk, nam pla, salt, and pepper and pour over mahi-mahi. Cover the pan with aluminum foil and bake for 10 minutes. Remove the foil, stir in rice, and bake for an additional 10 minutes. Sprinkle with cilantro and serve immediately.

Provençale Swordfish with Potatoes and Olives

¼ cup olive oil

1 large onion, peeled and thinly sliced

3 garlic cloves, peeled and minced

1 (14.5-oz.) can diced tomatoes, undrained

2 TB. chopped fresh parsley

1 TB. herbes de Provence

1 bay leaf

3 large baking potatoes, peeled and thinly sliced

1 (10-oz.) pkg. frozen artichoke hearts, thawed and halved

⅓ cup pitted oil-cured black olives, halved

¼ cup small capers, rinsed

Salt and freshly ground black pepper to taste

1½ to 2 lb. swordfish steaks, 1-inch thick, rinsed and cut into 6 to 8 serving-size pieces

Serves: 6 to 8
Prep time: 15 minutes
Cook time: 25 minutes

1. Preheat the oven to 350°F. Grease a 10×14-inch baking pan. Heat olive oil in a large skillet over medium-high heat. Add onion and garlic and cook, stirring frequently, for 3 minutes or until onion is translucent. Add tomatoes, parsley, herbes de Provence, bay leaf, potatoes, artichoke hearts, olives, and capers to the skillet. Bring to a boil and simmer, uncovered, for 7 to 10 minutes or until potatoes begin to soften. Remove and discard bay leaf and season to taste with salt and pepper.

2. Spread half of mixture into the prepared pan and top with swordfish steaks. Top swordfish with remaining vegetable mixture. Cover the pan with aluminum foil and bake for 25 minutes or until potatoes are tender and swordfish is opaque. Serve immediately.

Bake Lore

Provençale is the term given to dishes that are derived from the sunny cuisine of southern France, Provence. Certain ingredients, such as tomatoes and olives, characterize this style of cooking, and it's extremely healthful and olive oil based, rather than butter based.

Thai-Style Skillet Cod with Pineapple, Asian Vegetables, and Jasmine Rice

Serves: 6 to 8
Prep time: 20 minutes
Cook time: 15 minutes

1½ cups jasmine rice

1½ to 2 lb. cod fillet, rinsed

4 shallots, peeled and halved

5 garlic cloves, peeled

1 (1-in.) piece fresh ginger, peeled and sliced

1 stalk lemongrass, trimmed and sliced

1 small serrano or Thai chili, seeds and ribs removed

1 (14-oz.) can light coconut milk

¼ cup whole milk

¼ cup nam pla (Thai fish sauce)

3 TB. lemon juice

½ ripe pineapple, cored and cut into ½-inch dice

½ lb. snow peas, rinsed and stemmed

1½ cups sliced bok choy

1 cup fresh bean sprouts, rinsed

¼ cup chopped fresh cilantro

1. Bring a large pot of salted water to a boil. Add rice, reduce heat to low, and simmer, covered, for 10 minutes. Drain and set aside.

2. Cut off ¼-pound piece of cod; cut remaining cod into 6 to 8 serving-size pieces. Place ¼-pound piece in a microwave-safe dish. Sprinkle with 2 tablespoons water and cover the dish tightly with plastic wrap. Microwave on high (100 percent) power for 1 minute. Allow to sit for 1 minute. Carefully remove and discard the plastic wrap and place fish in a food processor fitted with a steel blade or in a blender.

3. Add shallots, garlic, ginger, lemongrass, serrano chili, ½ cup coconut milk, milk, nam pla, and lemon juice to food processor and purée until smooth, scraping the sides of bowl as necessary.

4. Scrape to a large skillet and add remaining 1½ cups coconut milk. Bring to a boil over medium heat. Add pineapple and rice and simmer, covered, for 5 minutes.

5. Place pieces of cod, snow peas, and bok choy on top of rice. Cover the skillet and simmer for 5 minutes. Carefully turn fish, add bean sprouts and cilantro, and stir gently. Cover and cook for an additional 3 to 5 minutes or until cod is opaque. Serve immediately.

 **Got You Covered!**

Unlike the difference between skim milk and whole milk, there's virtually no difference in taste and texture between light coconut milk and regular coconut milk. What is different is the amount of fat, most of it saturated. Use light coconut milk whenever possible to keep foods healthful.

Monkfish Stew with Summer Squash and New Potatoes in Rosemary White Wine Sauce

3 TB. olive oil

3 shallots, peeled and minced

2 garlic cloves, peeled and minced

½ lb. white mushrooms, trimmed, wiped with a damp paper towel, and sliced

¼ cup chopped fresh parsley

3 TB. chopped fresh rosemary or 1 TB. dried

1 bay leaf

1 cup dry white wine

2 cups fish stock or bottled clam juice

1 lb. small new potatoes, scrubbed and cut into quarters

2 yellow summer squash, trimmed, halved lengthwise, and cut into ½-inch slices

1½ lb. *monkfish* fillets, rinsed

Salt and freshly ground black pepper to taste

2 tsp. cornstarch, mixed with 2 TB. cold water

Serves: 6 to 8
Prep time: 15 minutes
Cook time: 25 minutes

1. Heat olive oil in a Dutch oven over medium-high heat. Add shallots and garlic and cook, stirring frequently, for 2 minutes. Add mushrooms and cook, stirring frequently, for 3 minutes or until mushrooms are soft and shallots are translucent. Add parsley, rosemary, bay leaf, white wine, fish stock, and potatoes to the Dutch oven. Bring to a boil over high heat; then reduce heat to low, cover, and simmer for 15 minutes. Add squash and simmer for 5 minutes. (You can do this a day in advance and refrigerate, tightly covered. Before continuing, reheat to a simmer.)

2. Remove all membranes from monkfish by holding the thin end of each fillet and scraping away membranes with a knife. Slice each fillet into ½-inch slices across the grain. Add monkfish to simmering stew, return to a boil, and cover. Simmer for 3 to 5 minutes or until monkfish is opaque. Season to taste with salt and pepper and remove and discard bay leaf. Stir in cornstarch mixture, bring to a simmer, and cook for 1 minute or until lightly thickened. Serve immediately.

 Ellen on Edibles

Monkfish is called "poor man's lobster" by many people because its sweet, mild flavor is similar. Its official name is angler fish because it attracts its prey by releasing a long filament that grows from its head. Smaller fish think it's a worm, or angler, and swim closer, only to be gobbled up by the angler's huge mouth. It's called *lotte* in French.

Portuguese Seafood Stew

Serves: 6 to 8
Prep time: 10 minutes
Cook time: 20 minutes

¼ lb. bacon, cut into 1-inch pieces

1 medium onion, peeled and diced

1 carrot, trimmed, peeled, and thinly sliced

1 celery stalk, trimmed and thinly sliced

3 garlic cloves, peeled and minced

½ lb. mild linguiça sausage, diced

1 (14.5-oz.) can diced tomatoes, undrained

2 oranges, zest grated and juiced

½ cup dry red wine

3 cups fish stock or bottled clam juice

3 TB. chopped fresh basil or 1 tsp. dried

2 TB. chopped fresh parsley

2 tsp. fresh thyme or ½ tsp. dried

1 bay leaf

3 large boiling potatoes, scrubbed and cut into ½-inch dice

Salt and freshly ground black pepper to taste

1 lb. thick cod fillet, rinsed and cut into 1-inch cubes

½ lb. swordfish fillet, rinsed, skin discarded, and cut into 1-inch cubes

1. Cook bacon in a Dutch oven or large saucepan over medium heat until crisp. Remove bacon with a slotted spoon and discard all but 2 tablespoons fat from the Dutch oven.

2. Add onion, carrot, celery, and garlic. Cook, stirring frequently, for 3 minutes or until onion is translucent. Add linguiça and cook for 3 minutes. Add tomatoes, orange zest, orange juice, red wine, fish stock, basil, parsley, thyme, bay leaf, and potatoes. Bring to a boil and cook over medium-high heat, stirring occasionally, until liquid has reduced in volume by ⅓. Season to taste with salt and pepper. (You can do this a day in advance and refrigerate, tightly covered. Before continuing, reheat over medium heat to a simmer.)

3. Add cod and swordfish and return to a boil. Turn off the heat, cover the Dutch oven, and allow to sit for 5 minutes. Serve immediately.

Got You Covered!

One of the pitfalls of many fish dishes is overcooking the fish. When broiling or grilling, the fish should cook for a total of 10 minutes for each inch of thickness. For stews and casseroles such as this one, the way to ensure the small cubes will not be overcooked is to cover the pan and allow the fish to gently poach in simmering liquid.

Overnight Salmon, Asparagus, and Pasta Bake

Serves: 6 to 8	
Prep time: 10 minutes, plus 8 hours chilling	
Cook time: 50 minutes	

4 TB. (½ stick) butter

¼ cup all-purpose flour

1 cup fish stock or chicken stock

1 cup milk

1 cup grated Gruyère cheese

1 TB. fresh thyme or 1 tsp. dried

Salt and freshly ground black pepper to taste

2½ cups small pasta shells

1½ lb. fresh asparagus, woody stems removed, and cut into 1-inch pieces

1½ lb. fresh salmon fillet, rinsed and cut into 1-inch cubes

1. Grease a 9×13-inch baking pan. Melt butter in a small saucepan over low heat. Stir in flour and cook, stirring constantly, for 2 minutes. Whisk in fish stock and milk, increase heat to medium-high, and bring to a boil. Reduce heat to low and simmer sauce for 2 minutes. Stir in Gruyère cheese and thyme and season to taste with salt and pepper.

2. Pour sauce into the prepared pan and stir in pasta shells. Cover the pan tightly and refrigerate for at least 8 hours or overnight.

3. Preheat the oven to 350°F. Remove the pan from the refrigerator and stir in asparagus and salmon. Cover the pan with aluminum foil and bake for 50 minutes or until pasta is tender. Serve immediately.

Half Baked

When cooking in advance, it's important to never refrigerate raw food with cooked food. That's why in this recipe the salmon is refrigerated separately from the sauce and pasta. When raw, fish, poultry, and meat can contain naturally occurring bacteria, such as salmonella, that bacteria is killed during the cooking process. However, it can create a microbiological field day if it's combined with cooked food.

Sole Almandine with Vegetable and Rice Stuffing

Serves: 6 to 8	
Prep time: 25 minutes	
Cook time: 20 minutes	

4 TB. (½ stick) butter

6 scallions, trimmed and thinly sliced

2 garlic cloves, peeled and minced

¼ lb. fresh shiitake mushrooms, stems removed, wiped with a damp paper towel, and thinly sliced

2 cups cooked white rice

¼ cup all-purpose flour

2 cups milk

1 TB. herbes de Provence

3 TB. chopped fresh parsley

Salt and freshly ground black pepper to taste

6 to 8 thin sole fillets, rinsed

½ cup *crème fraîche*

⅓ cup dry sherry

1 cup sliced, toasted almonds

Ellen on Edibles

Crème fraîche is a thickened cream with a tangy taste and a rich texture. It's better for soups and sauces than sour cream because it can be boiled without curdling. Make it at home by stirring 2 tablespoons buttermilk into 1 cup heavy cream. Allow to stand at room temperature for 12 hours or until thick. Then refrigerate for up to 10 days.

1. Melt 2 tablespoons butter in a skillet over medium heat. Add scallions and garlic and cook, stirring frequently, for 2 minutes. Add mushrooms, increase heat to medium-high, and cook, stirring frequently, for 3 to 5 minutes or until mushrooms are soft. Add rice and keep warm.

2. Melt remaining 2 tablespoons butter in a saucepan over low heat. Add flour and cook, stirring constantly, for 2 minutes. Whisk in milk and bring to a boil over medium heat, whisking constantly. Reduce heat to low and simmer sauce for 2 minutes. Stir in herbes de Provence and parsley and season to taste with salt and pepper. Add ⅔ cup sauce to rice mixture, stir well, and season again with salt and pepper if necessary. Reserve remaining sauce.

3. Increase the oven heat to 400°F. Grease a 10×14-inch baking pan. Place 1 sole fillet on a plate and place ¼ cup rice stuffing in the center. Fold fillet to enclose stuffing and place in prepared baking pan, seam side down. Repeat with remaining fillets and stuffing.

4. Combine sauce, crème fraîche, and sherry. Pour sauce over sole fillets and cover the pan with aluminum foil. Bake for 10 minutes, remove foil, and bake for an additional 10 minutes or until sole is opaque. Serve immediately, sprinkled with toasted almonds.

Skillet-Braised Halibut in White Wine with Pearl Onions, Oranges, and Couscous

2 TB. olive oil

3 scallions, trimmed with all but 2 inches of green tops discarded, thinly sliced

1 celery stalk, trimmed and sliced

3 garlic cloves, peeled and minced

1 (16-oz.) pkg. frozen pearl onions, thawed

1 (14.5-oz.) can diced tomatoes, undrained

¼ cup chopped fresh parsley

1½ cups fish stock or chicken stock

½ cup dry white wine

1 cup orange juice

1 bay leaf

Salt and freshly ground black pepper to taste

1½ to 2 lb. halibut fillets, cut into 6 to 8 pieces, rinsed

2 navel oranges, rind and white pith removed, and cut into ½-inch cubes

¾ lb. sugar snap peas, rinsed and stemmed

2 cups *couscous*

Serves: 6 to 8	
Prep time: 15 minutes	
Cook time: 20 minutes	

1. Heat olive oil in a large skillet over medium heat. Add scallions, celery, and garlic and cook, stirring frequently, for 3 minutes. Add pearl onions, tomatoes, parsley, fish stock, white wine, orange juice, and bay leaf to the skillet. Season to taste with salt and pepper. Bring to a boil and simmer, uncovered, for 3 minutes.

2. Add halibut fillets and orange pieces to the skillet. Cover, bring to a boil, reduce heat to low, and cook for 5 minutes. Turn halibut gently with a slotted spatula, add sugar snap peas, and cook for an additional 5 minutes. Remove halibut from the skillet with a slotted spatula and keep it hot, covered with aluminum foil.

3. Stir couscous into cooking liquid, cover, and remove from heat. Allow to sit 5 minutes. Distribute halibut on serving plates, fluff couscous with a fork, and spoon some next to each portion of halibut. Serve immediately.

 Ellen on Edibles

Couscous (pronounced *KOOS-koos*) is a granular pasta made from semolina and is a staple of North African cuisine. Because the grains are about the size of coarse sand, it cooks in minutes in simmering liquid and absorbs the flavor of its cooking liquid.

Grouper with Yellow Rice, Peas, and Pimientos

Serves: 6 to 8
Prep time: 21 minutes
Cook time: 15 minutes

½ cup olive oil

1 large onion, peeled and chopped

1 large green bell pepper, seeds and ribs removed, chopped

5 garlic cloves, peeled and minced

1 (14.5-oz.) can diced tomatoes, undrained

1 cup sliced pimientos, drained and rinsed

¾ cup dry sherry

2 bay leaves

2 tsp. ground cumin

2 tsp. dried oregano

3 (5-oz.) pkg. yellow rice

3 cups fish stock, bottled clam juice, or chicken stock

6 to 8 grouper fillets

Salt and freshly ground black pepper to taste

1 (10-oz.) pkg. frozen peas, thawed

1. Heat 2 tablespoons olive oil in a medium saucepan over medium-high heat. Add onion, green bell pepper, and garlic. Cook, stirring frequently, for 3 minutes or until onion is translucent. Stir in tomatoes with liquid, pimientos, sherry, bay leaves, cumin, and oregano. Bring to a boil, reduce heat to medium, and simmer, uncovered, for 3 minutes.

2. Preheat the oven to 325°F. Grease a 10×14-inch baking pan. Stir rice and fish stock into the saucepan. Bring to a boil, reduce heat to low, and simmer, covered, for 15 minutes or until rice is almost tender.

3. While rice is cooking, heat remaining olive oil in a large skillet over medium-high heat. Sprinkle grouper with salt and pepper, place in the skillet, and brown briefly on both sides, turning fillets gently with slotted spatula. Stir peas into rice and scrape mixture into the prepared baking pan.

4. Place grouper on top of rice mixture and cover the baking pan with aluminum foil. Bake for 15 minutes or until rice is tender and grouper is opaque.

 **Got You Covered!**

Although many recipes call for some sort of alcoholic beverage as an ingredient (as this one calls for sherry), you need not worry that you can't serve the dish to teetotalers or toddlers. The alcohol evaporates when the liquid boils.

Chapter 6

Creative Crustaceans and Marvelous Mollusks: Casseroles with Shellfish

In This Chapter

- ◆ Fast Asian- and Latin American–inspired shrimp meals
- ◆ Rice and pasta dishes
- ◆ Cover and bake scallops and oysters

Regardless of where Americans live, studies show that shrimp, from the warm waters of the Atlantic and Pacific coasts as well as the Gulf of Mexico, remains the most popular species of seafood consumed. Increasingly, high-quality shrimp is also being imported from Latin America and Asia, which has increased the supply and brought down the price.

In addition to being low in calories, shrimp takes to countless preparations. You'll find many ways to cook them in this chapter, with seasonings that span the globe. You'll also discover ways to cook other shellfish, such as scallops and oysters.

Craving Crustaceans

Shellfish come in two main categories. Crustaceans are one family; they include shrimp, prawns, crab, and lobster. While all shellfish have—you guessed it—shells, crustaceans have elongated bodies that are jointed, so they can swim and maneuver in the water.

There are hundreds of shrimp species, most of which can be divided into two broad classifications—warm-water shrimp and cold-water shrimp. As a general rule, the colder the water, the smaller the shrimp, and some authorities maintain that small shrimp have a more delicious flavor than large. Shrimp come in all manner of colors including reddish to light brown, pink, deep red, grayish-white, yellow, gray-green, and dark green; and all colors can have color mottling on their shells.

Raw shrimp should smell of the sea with no hint of ammonia. Cooked, shelled shrimp should look plump and succulent. Before storing fresh, uncooked shrimp, rinse them under cold, running water and drain thoroughly. Tightly cover and refrigerate for up to 2 days. Cooked shrimp can be refrigerated for up to 3 days. Freeze shrimp for up to 3 months.

Sizing Up the Situation

Shrimp are sorted by "count," which means their size and the number that comprises 1 pound, and the smaller the number of shrimp in a pound, the higher the price will be. The general size categories into which shrimp fall are as follows:

♦ *Colossal*, which count up as less than 10 per pound. These are sometimes referred to as U8s as well.

♦ *Jumbo* is the term for shrimp that count up at 11 to 15 per pound. These yield the highest proportion of meat to shell.

♦ An *extra large* label means 16 to 20 per pound. These are frequently called "cocktail shrimp," because they look impressive in a shrimp cocktail.

♦ *Large*, which represents 21 to 30 shrimp per pound, is the most common size for shrimp found in the supermarket, both cooked and raw. They deliver the best price value relationship, and should be used for the dishes in this chapter unless another size is specified.

♦ *Small* shrimp, 36 to 45 per pound, and *miniature* shrimp, more than 45 per pound, are usually sold as "salad shrimp." Unless they are cooked and peeled, stay away, because the labor involved in preparing them for cooking or eating is monumental.

Regardless of the color of the shell, raw shrimp are termed "green shrimp."

The Dilemma of Deveining

To devein a shrimp means to remove the gray-black vein (the intestinal tract) from the back of a shrimp. You can do this with the tip of a sharp knife or a special tool called a deveiner.

On small and medium shrimp, deveining is more for cosmetic purposes. However, because the intestinal vein of large shrimp contains grit, you should always remove it. For these recipes, devein the shrimp before cooking, and discard all peel, which is actually the shrimp's paperlike shell.

Frozen Assets

Most shrimp eaten by Americans have been previously frozen, and this category is growing as imports from Latin America and Asia increase. Frozen shrimp are found both raw and cooked. It's rare to find cooked shrimp that haven't been deveined, and most are also peeled to some extent. Salad shrimp are always totally peeled, and larger sizes usually have the peel remaining on the tail section.

Raw shrimp are another story, and how much preparation they require varies widely. Some raw shrimp require both peeling and deveining. Some raw shrimp have undergone both processes; however, you'll pay premium price for the processing.

Mad for Mollusks

The other category of shellfish are the mollusks, which protect their soft bodies with hard shells. Some mollusks, such as snails, have one-piece shells (and are called univalves), but most of the mollusk species we think of—such as clams, oysters, and scallops—are classified as bivalves because they have a two-part, hinged shell.

Removing bivalves from their shells is a labor-intensive process referred to as shucking. Increasingly, fish processors are doing this for us. Pints of shucked oysters, scallops by the pound, and minced fresh clams are becoming the rule rather than the exception, so look for a store that sells preshucked mollusks.

All bivalves come in various sizes depending on the harvest location. Oysters are identified by the place of origin and have names such as Blue Point (for the waters off New York's Long Island) and Olympia (which are native to the Pacific Northwest).

Clams and scallops are graded by size. Littleneck clams are the smallest, followed in size by cherrystone clams and quahogs. Sea scallops are about four times the size of bay scallops and can be cut into quarters for a recipe calling for the tiny bay scallops.

Bacon, Shrimp, Peas, and Yellow Rice in Tequila Chili Sauce

Serves: 6 to 8
Prep time: 20 minutes
Cook time: 15 minutes

2 (5-oz.) pkg. yellow rice

4 large dried *ancho chilies*, stemmed, seeded, and broken into small pieces

½ cup boiling water

2 TB. balsamic vinegar

4 garlic cloves

2 tsp. dried oregano, preferably Mexican

½ lb. bacon, cut into 1-inch pieces

1½ lb. large (21 to 30 per lb.) raw shrimp, peeled, deveined, rinsed, and patted dry with paper towels

1 (10-oz.) pkg. frozen peas, thawed

⅓ cup tequila

1 cup half-and-half

Salt and freshly ground black pepper to taste

Ellen on Edibles

Ancho (pro-nounced *AHN-choo*) **chilies** are the sweetest of the dried chili peppers. They are the mild green poblano chilies in their fresh form and they add a rich, almost fruity flavor to foods. They're about 3 to 4 inches long, and they always need to be soaked before using them.

1. Cook rice according to package directions and set aside. Place ancho chilies in a small bowl and pour boiling water over them. Soak for 15 minutes; then drain chilies and combine them in a blender with vinegar, garlic, and oregano. Purée until smooth. Scrape into a small bowl and set aside.

2. Place bacon in a large skillet over medium-high heat and cook until crisp; remove with a slotted spoon and set aside. Discard all but 2 tablespoons bacon fat. Add shrimp to the skillet and cook 2 to 3 minutes over medium-high heat or until pink. Remove shrimp from the skillet with a slotted spoon and keep warm.

3. Add peas, ancho chili paste, tequila, and half-and-half to the skillet and bring to a boil over medium-high heat. Reduce heat to low and simmer for 5 to 7 minutes or until reduced in volume by half.

4. Stir bacon and shrimp into the skillet and heat through. Season to taste with salt and pepper and serve immediately on top of rice.

Greek Oregano Shrimp with Tomatoes, Feta, and Orzo

2½ cups orzo

2 TB. olive oil

1 large onion, peeled and diced

3 garlic cloves, peeled and minced

1 (14.5-oz.) can diced tomatoes, undrained

½ cup chopped fresh basil or 2 TB. dried

½ cup chopped fresh dill or 2 TB. dried

Freshly ground black pepper to taste

1½ lb. large (21 to 30 per lb.) raw shrimp, peeled, deveined, rinsed, and patted dry with paper towels

½ lb. feta cheese, crumbled

¼ cup chopped fresh oregano or 1 TB. dried

Serves: 6 to 8
Prep time: 15 minutes
Cook time: 20 minutes

1. Preheat the oven to 450°F. Grease a 9×13-inch baking pan. Bring a large pot of salted water to a boil over high heat. Add orzo and boil for 7 minutes or until orzo is double in size but still slightly hard. (The amount of time depends on the brand of orzo.) Drain.

2. While orzo is boiling, heat olive oil in a medium skillet over medium-high heat. Add onion and garlic and cook, stirring frequently, for 3 minutes or until onion is translucent. Add tomatoes, basil, dill, and black pepper. Bring to a boil, reduce heat to low, and simmer for 3 minutes. Add orzo and stir well.

3. Scrape mixture into the prepared baking pan and arrange shrimp on top. Sprinkle feta and oregano over shrimp and cover pan with aluminum foil. Bake for 20 minutes or until shrimp are pink and cooked through and feta is melted. Serve immediately.

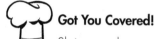 **Got You Covered!**

Shrimp and other seafood cook in far less time than it takes even tiny pasta like orzo to reach al dente. That's why the pasta in this and many other dishes is partially cooked before baking. That parboiling brings all the elements in the dish to the finish line at the right point.

Spicy Southwest Shrimp with Pinto Beans and Polenta Crust

Serves: 6 to 8
Prep time: 15 minutes
Cook time: 30 minutes

¼ lb. chorizo sausage, thinly sliced

2 medium onions, peeled and diced

5 garlic cloves, minced

3 jalapeño peppers, seeds and ribs removed, finely chopped

1 TB. ground cumin

2 medium tomatoes, cored, seeded, and diced

2 (15-oz.) cans pinto beans, drained and rinsed

1½ cups fish stock or bottled clam juice

Salt and freshly ground black pepper to taste

1½ lb. large (21 to 30 per lb.) raw shrimp, peeled, deveined, rinsed, and patted dry with paper towels

3 TB. chopped fresh cilantro

2 tsp. fresh thyme or ½ tsp. dried

1 (18-oz.) roll prepared polenta, sliced into 1-inch slices

½ cup grated Monterey Jack cheese

Got You Covered!

Polenta is basically an Italian cornmeal mush. If you can't find it prepared, whisk 1 cup yellow cornmeal into 2 cups water or stock, and season with salt and pepper. Bring to a boil over medium-high heat, whisking constantly. Reduce heat to low and cook, stirring constantly, for 5 to 7 minutes or until it begins to leave the sides of the pan. Scrape mixture into greased 9×13-inch baking pan and chill.

1. Preheat the oven to 400°F. Grease a 2-quart casserole. Place chorizo in a saucepan over medium-high heat. Cook, stirring occasionally, for 3 minutes. Add onions and garlic, reduce heat to medium, and cook, stirring constantly, for 2 minutes. Add jalapeño pepper and cumin and continue to cook for 1 minute. Add tomatoes, beans, and fish stock. Bring to a boil, reduce heat to low, and simmer for 10 minutes. Season to taste with salt and pepper. (You can do this 1 day in advance and refrigerate, tightly covered. Before continuing, reheat over low heat, stirring occasionally.)

2. Stir shrimp, cilantro, and thyme into bean mixture, scrape into a prepared baking pan, and arrange polenta slices on top. Cover the pan with aluminum foil and bake for 15 minutes. Remove the foil, sprinkle Monterey Jack cheese on top of polenta, and bake for an additional 15 minutes or until cheese is melted and shrimp are cooked. Serve immediately.

Chinese Shrimp and Noodles in Black Bean Sauce with Bok Choy

½ lb. Chinese noodles or linguine, cut into 2-inch sections

3 TB. Chinese *fermented black beans* (available in the Asian section of most supermarkets and at Asian grocery stores), coarsely chopped but not rinsed

⅓ cup dry sherry

6 scallions, trimmed and thinly sliced (including green tops)

2 TB. Asian sesame oil

4 garlic cloves, peeled and minced

3 TB. finely minced fresh ginger

½ lb. bok choy, rinsed and patted dry on paper towels, trimmed, and cut into ½-inch slices, including leaves

1 red bell pepper, seeds and ribs removed, thinly sliced

¼ cup soy sauce

2 TB. Chinese oyster sauce

1 TB. Asian chili sauce, or ½ tsp. hot red pepper sauce

1½ lb. large (21 to 30 per lb.) raw shrimp, peeled, deveined, rinsed, and patted dry with paper towels

Serves: 6 to 8
Prep time: 15 minutes
Cook time: 10 minutes

 Ellen on Edibles

Fermented black beans are small black soybeans with a pungent flavor that have been preserved in salt before being packed. They should be chopped and soaked in some sort of liquid to soften them and release their flavor prior to cooking. Because they are salted as a preservative, they last for up to 2 years if refrigerated once opened.

1. Cook noodles according to the package directions. Drain and set aside.

2. Stir black beans into sherry to plump for 10 minutes. Reserve 3 tablespoons scallions. Heat sesame oil in a large skillet over medium-high heat. Add remaining scallions, garlic, and ginger and cook, stirring constantly, for 2 minutes.

3. Add bok choy and red bell pepper to the skillet and cook, stirring constantly, for 2 minutes. Add sherry mixture, soy sauce, oyster sauce, chili sauce, shrimp, and noodles. Cover and cook over medium heat for 3 minutes or until shrimp are pink and cooked through. Sprinkle with remaining 3 tablespoons scallions and serve immediately.

Caribbean Curried Seafood Pilau with Black Beans and Rice

Serves: 6 to 8
Prep time: 15 minutes
Cook time: 30 minutes

2 TB. olive oil

2 medium onions, peeled and diced

4 garlic cloves, peeled and minced

1 jalapeño or Scotch bonnet pepper, seeds and ribs removed, finely chopped

2 TB. curry powder

1½ cups long-grain rice

2 tomatoes, cored, seeded, and diced

2 (14-oz.) cans light coconut milk

Salt and freshly ground black pepper to taste

1 (15-oz.) can black beans, drained and rinsed well

1 (10-oz.) package frozen peas, thawed

1 lb. large (21 to 30 per lb.) raw shrimp, peeled, deveined, rinsed, and patted dry with paper towels

½ lb. lump crabmeat, picked over to remove shell fragments

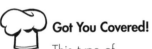 **Got You Covered!**

This type of recipe is open to many substitutions of seafood. In lieu of the crabmeat, you could increase the amount of shrimp or add bay scallops or some combination of fin fish cut into ½-inch cubes. The important factor is to come up with the right quantity of fish and have it the same size so it will cook evenly.

1. Heat oil in a saucepan over medium-high heat. Add onions, garlic, and jalapeño pepper. Cook for 3 minutes or until onion is translucent. Reduce heat to low, add curry powder and rice, and cook, stirring constantly, for 2 minutes. Add tomatoes and coconut milk and season to taste with salt and pepper. Bring to a boil over medium heat, stirring occasionally. Cover, reduce heat to low, and cook for 15 to 18 minutes or until rice is almost tender and liquid is almost all absorbed. (You can do this a day in advance and refrigerate, tightly covered. Before continuing, reheat rice mixture over low heat or in a microwave-safe dish, covered with plastic wrap, heating on high [100 percent] for 1 minute, then at 30-second intervals until hot.)

2. Stir black beans, peas, shrimp, and crabmeat into rice. Cook, covered, over low heat, stirring gently occasionally, for 3 to 5 minutes or until shrimp are pink and cooked through. Serve immediately.

Tex-Mex Shrimp and Pasta Bake

1 lb. thin spaghetti, broken into 2-inch lengths

2 TB. (¼ stick) butter

1 medium onion, peeled and diced

3 garlic cloves, peeled and minced

2 tsp. ground cumin

1 tsp. dried oregano, preferably Mexican

3 large eggs

1½ cups half-and-half

1 cup bottled tomato salsa

¼ cup chopped fresh cilantro

Salt and freshly ground black pepper to taste

1½ lb. cooked shrimp, peeled and deveined

1½ cups grated jalapeño Jack cheese

Serves: 6 to 8	
Prep time: 15 minutes	
Cook time: 30 minutes	

1. Preheat the oven to 350°F. Grease a 10×14-inch baking pan. Bring a large pot of salted water to a boil and cook spaghetti according to the package instructions until al dente. Drain and set aside.

2. Melt butter in a skillet over medium-high heat. Add onion and garlic and cook, stirring frequently, for 3 minutes or until onion is translucent. Stir in cumin and oregano, reduce heat to low, and cook for 1 minute. Remove from heat and let cool.

3. Whisk eggs with half-and half, salsa, and cilantro. Season to taste with salt and pepper and stir in onion mixture. Layer ½ pasta in the prepared pan and top with ½ shrimp and ½ jalapeño Jack cheese. Repeat with remaining pasta, shrimp, and cheese and pour egg mixture over the top.

4. Cover the pan with aluminum foil and bake for 15 minutes. Remove the foil and bake for an additional 15 to 20 minutes or until top is browned and a toothpick inserted in the center comes out clean. Allow to sit for 5 minutes and serve.

Got You Covered!

Cooking shrimp is easy. If frozen, thaw the shrimp in a bowl of cold water or in the refrigerator. Bring a large pot of salted water to a boil. Add the shrimp, cover the pan, and as soon as the water begins to simmer again, take the pan off the heat. Wait 5 minutes and the shrimp will be cooked.

Skillet Shrimp Creole in Spicy Tomato Sauce with Mixed Peppers and Rice

Serves: 6 to 8
Prep time: 15 minutes
Cook time: 25 minutes

 Bake Lore

In the eighteenth century, the Spaniards governing New Orleans named all residents of European heritage *Criollo*, which was transformed into *Creole* by the predominant French population. Creole cooking today reflects the amalgam of French, Spanish, and African cuisines that characterize food in Louisiana. In contrast to rural Cajun cooking, Creole food is more refined and uses more tomatoes and is less intensely spiced.

3 TB. olive oil

1 large onion, peeled and diced

3 garlic cloves, peeled and minced

1 celery stalk, trimmed and sliced

1 red bell pepper, seeds and ribs removed, diced

1 yellow bell pepper, seeds and ribs removed, diced

1½ cups long-grain rice

1 (28-oz.) can diced tomatoes in tomato purée, drained with liquid reserved

1 to 1½ cups tomato juice

1 TB. fresh thyme or 1 tsp. dried

1 TB. fresh chopped oregano or 1 tsp. dried

1 bay leaf

Salt and cayenne to taste

1½ lb. large (21 to 30 per lb.) raw shrimp, peeled, deveined, rinsed, and patted dry with paper towels

1. Heat oil in a large skillet over medium-high heat. Add onion, garlic, celery, red bell pepper, and yellow bell pepper. Cook, stirring frequently, for 3 minutes or until onion is translucent. Stir in rice and cook, stirring frequently, for 2 minutes.

2. Add tomatoes to the skillet and add enough tomato juice to drained juices to measure 2¾ cups. Add thyme, oregano, and bay leaf to the skillet and season to taste with salt and cayenne.

3. Bring to a boil, cover the skillet, reduce heat to low, and simmer rice for 15 to 18 minutes or until rice is almost tender. Stir in shrimp, cover, and cook for an additional 3 to 5 minutes or until shrimp are pink and cooked through. Serve immediately.

Shrimp in Red Curry Sauce with Corn, Bok Choy, and Angel Hair Pasta

¾ lb. angel hair pasta, broken into 2-inch lengths

1 cup fish stock or bottled clam juice

1 TB. Thai red curry paste (available in the Asian section of most supermarkets, or at Asian grocery stores)

¼ cup soy sauce

2 TB. rice wine vinegar

2 TB. granulated sugar

2 TB. dry sherry

3 TB. vegetable oil

2 TB. grated fresh ginger

2 TB. minced garlic

6 scallions, trimmed and sliced into 1-inch lengths

1 small red onion, peeled, halved, and cut into ½-inch slices

¾ lb. bok choy, rinsed and patted dry on paper towels, trimmed, and cut into ½-inch slices, including leaves

1½ lb. large (21 to 30 per lb.) raw shrimp, peeled, deveined, rinsed, and patted dry with paper towels

1 (10-oz.) pkg. frozen corn, thawed

1 TB. cornstarch, mixed with 2 TB. cold water

Serves: 6 to 8
Prep time: 15 minutes
Cook time: 20 minutes

1. Bring a large pot of salted water to a boil. Cook angel hair pasta according to the package directions. Drain and set aside. Combine fish stock, curry paste, soy sauce, rice wine vinegar, sugar, and sherry in a small bowl and stir well to dissolve sugar. Set aside.

2. Heat oil in a large skillet over medium-high heat. Add ginger and garlic and cook, stirring constantly, for 30 seconds. Add scallions, red onion, and bok choy. Cook, stirring constantly, for 2 minutes. Add sauce mixture to the skillet, increase heat to high, and cover. Cook for 3 minutes or until crisp-tender.

3. Add shrimp and corn to the skillet. Cook for 2 minutes or until shrimp are pink and cooked through. Add cornstarch mixture and simmer, stirring constantly, for 1 minute or until lightly thickened. Add angel hair pasta and heat until pasta is hot. Serve immediately.

 Half Baked

Mixing cornstarch with cold water is essential to gaining a smooth sauce that is lightly thickened. Although this step might seem unnecessary, cornstarch added directly into a boiling liquid forms instant lumps that cannot be stirred away.

Shrimp, Crab, and Okra Gumbo with Rice

Serves: 6 to 8
Prep time: 15 minutes
Cook time: 1 hour

½ cup vegetable oil

¾ cup all-purpose flour

2 TB. (¼ stick) butter

1 large onion, peeled and diced

1 large green bell pepper, seeds and ribs removed, diced

2 celery stalks, trimmed and diced

5 garlic cloves, peeled and minced

4 cups fish stock or bottled clam juice

1 TB. fresh thyme or 1 tsp. dried

2 bay leaves

1 lb. okra, stems and tips trimmed, thinly sliced

1 (14-oz.) can diced tomatoes, undrained

½ to 1 tsp. hot red pepper sauce such as Tabasco

Salt and freshly ground black pepper to taste

1 lb. large (21 to 30 per lb.) raw shrimp, peeled, deveined, rinsed, and patted dry with paper towels

½ lb. lump crabmeat, picked over to discard shell fragments

3 TB. chopped fresh parsley

3 cups cooked long-grain rice, hot

Ellen on Edibles

Roux (pronounced *ROO*, like in kangaroo) is a mixture of fat and flour used as a thickening agent for soups and sauces. The first step in all roux preparation is to cook the flour. For white sauces, this is done over low heat and the fat used is butter. Many Creole and Cajun dishes, such as gumbo, use a fuller-flavored brown roux made with oil or drippings and cooked to a deep brown.

1. Preheat oven to 450°F. Combine oil and flour in an ovenproof Dutch oven and place in the oven. Bake *roux* for 20 to 30 minutes or until walnut brown. While roux is baking, melt butter in a large skillet over medium-high heat. Add onion, green bell pepper, celery, and garlic. Cook for 3 minutes or until onion is translucent. Set aside.

2. Place roux on the stove over medium heat. Add fish stock and whisk constantly until mixture comes to a boil and thickens. (You can do this a day in advance and refrigerate, tightly covered. Before continuing, bring mixture back to a simmer.)

3. Add vegetable mixture, thyme, bay leaves, okra, and tomatoes. Season to taste with hot red pepper sauce, salt, and pepper. Bring to a boil, cover, and cook over low heat for 35 to 40 minutes or until okra is very tender. Add shrimp, crabmeat, and parsley. Return to a boil, cover and remove from heat, and allow to sit for 5 minutes. Remove and discard bay leaves. To serve, place rice in bottom of soup bowls and ladle gumbo on top.

Skillet Scallops with Creamed Leeks, Bacon, and Brown Rice

2 TB. (¼ stick) butter

8 leeks, white parts only, trimmed, thinly sliced, and well rinsed

2 garlic cloves, peeled and minced

2 cups heavy cream

½ lb. bacon, cut into 1-inch pieces

3 cups cooked brown rice

Salt and freshly ground pepper to taste

1½ lb. fresh bay scallops or sea scallops cut into quarters, rinsed, and patted dry with paper towels

Serves: 6 to 8	
Prep time: 15 minutes	
Cook time: 25 minutes	

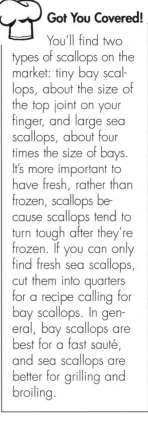

Got You Covered!

You'll find two types of scallops on the market: tiny bay scallops, about the size of the top joint on your finger, and large sea scallops, about four times the size of bays. It's more important to have fresh, rather than frozen, scallops because scallops tend to turn tough after they're frozen. If you can only find fresh sea scallops, cut them into quarters for a recipe calling for bay scallops. In general, bay scallops are best for a fast sauté, and sea scallops are better for grilling and broiling.

1. Melt butter in a large skillet over low heat. Add leeks and garlic, cover, and cook, stirring occasionally, for 10 minutes. Add cream, increase heat to medium, and cook, stirring occasionally, until mixture is reduced in volume by ⅔.

2. While sauce is cooking, fry bacon in a large skillet until crisp. Remove bacon with a slotted spoon and set aside. Discard all but 2 tablespoons bacon fat. When sauce is reduced, add bacon to it, along with cooked rice. Season to taste with salt and pepper. (You can do this a day in advance and refrigerate rice mixture, tightly covered. Before continuing, reheat mixture over low heat, stirring frequently. Refrigerate 2 tablespoons bacon fat also and reheat in a clean skillet when ready to continue.)

3. Heat reserved bacon fat in a skillet over high heat and when it begins to smoke, add scallops. Cook, stirring frequently, for 2 minutes. Season scallops with salt and pepper. To serve, divide leek mixture among 6 plates and top with scallops.

Skillet Oyster Stew

Serves: 6 to 8
Prep time: 15 minutes
Cook time: 15 minutes

4 TB. (½ stick) butter

1 large onion, peeled and diced

2 celery stalks, trimmed and sliced

2 carrots, peeled and sliced

½ red bell pepper, seeds and ribs removed, cut into ½-inch dice

2 pt. shucked oysters, drained, with liquor reserved

2 (8-oz.) bottles clam juice

3 large boiling potatoes, scrubbed and cut into ½-inch dice

3 TB. chopped fresh parsley

1 TB. fresh thyme or 1 tsp. dried

1 bay leaf

3 TB. all-purpose flour

1 cup half-and-half

Salt and freshly ground black pepper to taste

Half Baked

It's easy to over-cook oysters, and they will become tough and lose flavor as well as texture if they're subjected to that fate. But it's easy to cook them right. When they are cooked properly, the edges curl and they become firm to the touch. Depending on size, that only takes between 1 to 2 minutes, so watch carefully.

1. Melt 2 tablespoons butter in a large skillet over medium-high heat. Add onion, celery, carrots, and red bell pepper. Cook, stirring frequently, for 3 minutes or until onion is translucent.

2. Add oyster liquor, clam juice, potatoes, parsley, thyme, and bay leaf to the skillet. Bring to a boil, reduce heat to medium, and simmer, partially covered, for 10 minutes or until potatoes are tender.

3. While vegetables are cooking, melt remaining butter over low heat in a small saucepan. Stir in flour and cook, stirring constantly, for 2 minutes. Whisk in half-and-half, increase heat to medium, and bring to a boil, whisking frequently. Reduce heat to low, simmer 2 minutes, and remove the saucepan from heat.

4. Add oysters to the skillet and bring to a boil over medium-high heat. Cook for 1 to 2 minutes or until oysters curl at the edges; then stir in sauce and cook for 1 minute. Remove and discard bay leaf and season to taste with salt and pepper. Serve immediately.

Shrimp, Chicken, and Sausage with Yellow Rice (Jambalaya)

3 TB. olive oil

½ lb. boneless, skinless chicken breast, rinsed and patted dry with paper towels, cut into 1-inch pieces

⅓ lb. andouille or other smoked sausage, cut into ¼-inch slices

1 large onion, peeled and diced

3 garlic cloves, peeled and minced

½ red bell pepper, seeds and ribs removed, diced

2 celery stalks, trimmed and sliced

2 (5-oz.) pkg. yellow rice

3 cups chicken stock

1 TB. fresh thyme or 1 tsp. dried

1 bay leaf

Salt and freshly ground black pepper to taste

¾ lb. large (21 to 30 per lb.) raw shrimp, peeled, deveined, rinsed, and patted dry with paper towels

1 (10-oz.) pkg. frozen peas, thawed

Serves: 6 to 8	
Prep time: 15 minutes	
Cook time: 25 minutes	

1. Heat 1 tablespoon olive oil in a large skillet over medium-high heat. Add chicken and sausage and cook, stirring often, for 3 minutes or until chicken is opaque. Remove chicken and sausage from the pan and set aside.

2. Add remaining olive oil to the skillet and add onion, garlic, red bell pepper, and celery. Cook, stirring frequently, for 3 minutes or until onion is translucent. Stir in yellow rice and cook 1 minute.

3. Return chicken and sausage to the skillet and add chicken stock, thyme, and bay leaf. Bring to a boil, cover, reduce heat to low, and cook for 15 minutes or until rice is almost tender. Season to taste with salt and pepper and add shrimp and peas to the skillet. Cook for 3 to 5 minutes or until shrimp are pink and cooked through. Serve immediately.

 **Bake Lore**

Jambalaya is a staple of Louisiana cooking, where culinary traditions of France, Spain, Italy, Africa, the New World, and other cultures blended. Jambalaya was the local adaptation of the Spanish rice dish paella and became a favorite among the Cajuns, French transplants who settled in the Louisiana bayous.

Part 4

From the Coops

A chicken in every pot—along with turkey in some—summarizes the recipes in Part 4. But you might be surprised: within this panoply of poultry is a broad range of options.

In Chapter 7, you find dishes made from whole, uncooked chicken parts. Which parts you use is up to you, so you can personalize the recipes to suit your taste. Boneless, skinless chicken breasts are the most popular type of chicken, due to their lean nutritional profile and short cooking time. You get new ways to use them in Chapter 8.

And then there are recipes for cooked poultry, the reruns of the food world. The recipes in Chapter 9 provide needed variety after a day or two of plain poultry and can stretch the leftovers to create an exciting dinner for another night.

Chapter 7

The Sum of Its Parts: One-Dish Chicken Meals

In This Chapter

- ◆ Homey international comfort classics
- ◆ Enticing and exotic Asian options
- ◆ Make-ahead dishes

For the past two decades, chicken consumption has been on the rise, with the figure in 2004 topping 80 pounds per capita. Almost 100 percent of American households eat chicken at least once a week, and about half that number of folks triple the figure.

So there's always room for new chicken recipes or new ways to look at old classics. And that's what you'll find when cooking the dishes in this chapter.

Choosing Your Chicken

Chickens fall into several classifications, depending on their age and size when sent to market. The 3- to 4-pound chickens specified in this chapter are referred to as "broiler fryers" in chicken lingo. They're about 2½ months old and feed between 4 and 6 people.

Be sure to look for chickens marked USDA "Grade A," and look for packages that do not have an accumulation of liquid in the bottom. That can be a sign that the chicken has been frozen and defrosted. This is especially important if you might be freezing some of the chicken after you purchase it, because more than one freezing and defrosting can really damage the flavor and texture of the bird.

Store chicken in the coldest part of your refrigerator (40°F or below), sealed as it comes from the market, and use it within 2 or 3 days. If you need to keep it longer, freeze it. Although freezing can reduce flavor, moisture, and tenderness, it will preserve freshness.

To freeze chicken, rinse it under cold running water and pat the pieces dry with paper towels. Wrap each piece individually in plastic wrap, and place the pieces in a heavy resealable plastic bag. To defrost, place the frozen chicken on a plate in the refrigerator or thaw it in the microwave, following the manufacturer's instructions. After it's thawed, cook it as soon as possible, especially if you defrosted it in the microwave.

Better Birds

It was only after World War II, when modern mass-production came into being, that chickens were anything but "free range." Nowadays, these birds, slightly larger than broiler fryers, are the elite of the coop.

As the name implies, free-range chickens have the freedom to roam outdoors, and most chefs agree that this develops a fuller flavor—at a much fuller price. While many free-range chickens are fed a vegetarian diet that is usually free of antibiotics and growth hormones, "free-range" is not synonymous with "organic." The organic label, as specified by the U.S. Department of Agriculture, ensures that birds are fed a diet of organic foods and are not given any supplemental antibiotics or hormones.

For Safety's Sake

After you remove chicken from the wrapper, rinse it under cold running water. It should have absolutely no aroma. If it has any off smells, discard it or return it to the supermarket.

Illness-causing bacteria such as salmonella can grow in high-protein, low-acid foods like poultry, so always take care when handling raw chicken or turkey.

Never eat chicken raw. After cutting or working with raw chicken, thoroughly wash all utensils, cutting tools, cutting boards, and your hands. Never put cooked chicken on the same platter that held it raw, especially after browning it. That's when the contamination can occur the fastest. Don't pour uncooked marinades over cooked chicken.

Cooking Correctly

The rules have been changing for cooking pork in the past few years, but chicken must still be cooked to an internal temperature of 160°F for white meat and 180°F for dark meat to ensure there's no chance for microorganisms to survive.

The best way to test this is to use an instant-read meat thermometer. When the thickest part of the chicken is probed, the reading should be 180°F. If you don't want to take the temperature of every piece of chicken, recognize these visual signals: the chicken should be tender when poked with the tip of a paring knife, there should not be a hint of pink (even near the bones), and the juices should run clear.

Always test the dark meat before the white meat. Dark meat takes slightly longer to cook, so if the thighs are the proper temperature, you know the breasts will be fine.

The Do-It-Yourself Option

It is far more economical to purchase a whole chicken and cut it up yourself than to buy one already cut. Start by breaking back the wings until the joints snap; then use a boning knife to cut through the ball joints and detach the wings. While holding the chicken on its side, you will see a natural curve outlining the boundary between the breast and the leg/thigh quarters. Use sharp kitchen shears to cut along this line.

Cut the breast in half by scraping away the meat from the breast bone, and use a small paring knife to remove the wishbone. Cut away the breast bone using the shears and save it for stock. Divide the thigh/leg quarters by turning the pieces over and finding the joint. Cut through the joint and sever the leg from the thigh.

Healthful Habits

The skin is where all the saturated fat comes from. It is not advised to use boneless, skinless breasts or any boneless piece for the recipes in this chapter because the cooking time required for breasts is far shorter than those in the recipes here. But feel free to remove the skin (or buy the pieces skinless) for any of these recipes.

Braised Chicken with Bacon, Lettuce, Peas, and New Potatoes

Serves: 4 to 6
Prep time: 20 minutes
Cook time: 40 minutes

1 (3- to 4-lb.) chicken, cut into serving pieces, or 4 to 6 chicken pieces of your choice (breasts, thighs, legs), rinsed and patted dry with paper towels

Salt and freshly ground black pepper to taste

½ cup all-purpose flour

¼ lb. bacon, cut into 1-inch pieces

2 shallots, peeled and diced

2 garlic cloves, peeled and minced

2½ cups chicken stock

1 lb. new potatoes, scrubbed and halved

1 TB. chopped fresh rosemary or 1 tsp. dried

1 TB. chopped fresh chervil or 1 tsp. dried

1 TB. fresh thyme or 1 tsp. dried

2 (10-oz.) pkg. frozen pearl onions and peas, thawed

3 heads bibb lettuce, rinsed, trimmed, and cut into quarters

1. Preheat the oven to 350°F. Sprinkle chicken with salt and pepper, dust with flour (shaking off any excess) and set aside.

2. Place bacon in an ovenproof Dutch oven over medium-high heat. Cook, stirring often, until bacon is crisp. Remove bacon with a slotted spoon and set aside.

3. Add chicken pieces to the Dutch oven in a single layer and brown well on all sides, turning gently with tongs and being careful not to crowd the Dutch oven. Remove chicken and discard all but 1 tablespoon fat. Return the Dutch oven to the stove and add shallots and garlic. Cook, stirring often, for 3 minutes or until onions are translucent.

4. Add chicken and bacon and then add chicken stock, new potatoes, rosemary, chervil, and thyme. Bring to a boil and transfer to the oven. Bake, covered, for 20 minutes. Add pearl onions and peas and lettuce. Bake for an additional 15 to 20 minutes or until chicken is tender and no longer pink. (You can make this dish up to 2 days in advance and refrigerate, tightly covered. Reheat in a 350°F oven for 15 to 25 minutes or until hot.) Serve immediately.

 Half Baked

The moisture from cold food becomes steam when the food is placed into a hot pan. So if the pan is crowded with food, the food merely steams rather than developing a brown crust. Keep at least 1 inch of space around the pieces in the pan. This is true for meats as well as poultry.

Chicken with Potatoes, Mushrooms, and Onions in Red Wine Sauce (*Coq au Vin*)

1 (3- to 4-lb.) chicken, cut into serving pieces, or 4 to 6 chicken pieces of your choice (breasts, thighs, legs), rinsed and patted dry with paper towels

Salt and freshly ground black pepper to taste

½ cup all-purpose flour

¼ lb. bacon, cut into 1-inch pieces

3 garlic cloves, peeled and minced

1 lb. small white mushrooms, trimmed, wiped with a damp paper towel, and cut in half if larger than 1 inch in diameter

2 cups dry red wine

1 cup chicken stock

¼ cup chopped fresh parsley

1 TB. fresh thyme or 1 tsp. dried

1 bay leaf

1 lb. small new potatoes, scrubbed and quartered

½ (16-oz.) pkg. frozen pearl onions, thawed

Serves: 4 to 6
Prep time: 20 minutes
Cook time: 40 minutes

1. Preheat the oven to 350°F. Sprinkle chicken with salt and pepper, dust with flour (shaking off any excess), and set aside.

2. Place bacon in an ovenproof Dutch oven over medium-high heat. Cook, stirring often, until bacon is crisp. Remove bacon from the Dutch oven with a slotted spoon and set aside. Add chicken pieces in a single layer and brown well on all sides. Remove chicken and discard all but 2 tablespoons fat. Return the Dutch oven to the stove and add garlic and mushrooms. Cook, stirring often, for 3 to 5 minutes or until mushrooms are lightly browned. Add red wine and bring to a boil over high heat. Cook for 2 minutes; then add chicken stock, parsley, thyme, and bay leaf. Bring to a boil and reduce. Add bacon, chicken pieces, and potatoes.

3. Cover the Dutch oven, place it in the oven, and bake for 30 minutes or until potatoes are almost tender and chicken is tender and no longer pink. Add onions, season with salt and pepper if necessary, and bake for an additional 10 minutes or until potatoes are tender. Remove and discard bay leaf and serve immediately. (You can make this up to 2 days in advance and refrigerate, tightly covered. Reheat in a 350°F oven for 20 minutes or until hot.)

 Half Baked

When cooking with wine or any other acid such as lemon juice, it's important to use a stainless-steel or coated steel pan rather than aluminum. When exposed to the wine or acid, an aluminum pan can impart a metallic taste to the dish.

Old-Fashioned Chicken and Dumplings with Mixed Vegetables

Serves: 4 to 6
Prep time: 25 minutes
Cook time: 45 minutes

1 (3- to 4-lb.) chicken, cut into serving pieces, or 4 to 6 chicken pieces of your choice (breasts, thighs, legs), rinsed and patted dry with paper towels

Salt and freshly ground black pepper to taste

7 TB. butter

2 TB. olive oil

3 leeks, white part only, trimmed, thinly sliced, and well rinsed

2 garlic cloves, peeled and minced

2 carrots, peeled and cut into ¼-inch slices

2 celery stalks, trimmed and cut into ¼-inch slices

3 cups chicken stock

3 TB. chopped fresh parsley

1 TB. chopped fresh rosemary or 1 tsp. dried

1 TB. fresh thyme or 1 tsp. dried

1 bay leaf

1 cup all-purpose flour

1½ tsp. baking powder

Pinch of salt

½ tsp. dried thyme

½ tsp. dried rosemary

⅓ cup milk

½ lb. sugar snap peas, rinsed and stemmed

1. Sprinkle chicken with salt and pepper. Heat 2 tablespoons butter and oil in a large skillet over medium-high heat until butter is melted. Add chicken pieces to the skillet in a single layer and brown well on all sides, turning gently with tongs and being careful not to crowd the skillet. Remove chicken and set aside. Discard fat.

2. Return the skillet to the stove and melt remaining butter over medium-low heat. Add leeks, toss to coat, cover, and cook for 5 minutes without stirring. Uncover the skillet and add garlic, carrots, and celery. Cook, stirring occasionally, for 5 minutes. Return chicken to skillet and add chicken stock, parsley, rosemary, thyme, and bay leaf. Cover and cook chicken for 20 to 30 minutes or until chicken is tender and no longer pink. (You can do this 1 day in advance and refrigerate, tightly covered. Before continuing, reheat over medium heat to a simmer, stirring occasionally. Do not make dumpling dough until just prior to serving.)

3. While chicken is simmering, prepare dumpling dough. Combine flour, baking powder, salt, thyme, and rosemary in a mixing bowl. Cut in remaining butter using a pastry blender, two knives, or your fingertips until mixture resembles coarse crumbs. Add milk and stir to blend. *Knead* dough gently on a lightly floured counter; then cut into 12 equal parts.

4. Stir sugar snap peas into chicken mixture and place dough on top of chicken. Cover and cook for 15 minutes or until dumplings are puffed and cooked through. Do not uncover pan while dumplings are steaming. Serve immediately.

Ellen on Edibles _____

Kneading is the process of working dough to make it pliable so it will hold the gas bubbles from the leavening agent and expand when heated. Kneading is done with a pressing-folding-turning action. Press down into the dough with the heels of both hands, then push your hands away from your body. Fold the dough in half, and give it a quarter turn; then repeat the process. Yeast-risen bread dough must be kneaded for upward of 10 minutes, but light dumpling dough requires just a brief kneading.

Skillet Chicken with Mexican Rice and Peas (*Arroz con Pollo*)

Serves: 4 to 6
Prep time: 20 minutes
Cook time: 30 minutes

1 (3- to 4-lb.) chicken, cut into serving pieces or 4 to 6 chicken pieces of your choice (breasts, thighs, legs), rinsed and patted dry with paper towels

Salt and freshly ground black pepper to taste

3 TB. olive oil

1 large onion, peeled and diced

3 garlic cloves, peeled and minced

1 cup long-grain rice

1 (14.5-oz.) can diced tomatoes, drained

1 (4-oz.) can diced mild green chilies, drained

1¾ cups chicken stock

1 tsp. dried oregano, preferably Mexican

1 bay leaf

¼ cup chopped fresh cilantro

¼ cup sliced pimientos

1 (10-oz.) pkg. frozen peas, thawed

Half Baked

Be very careful when placing a can of chilies into your shopping cart. More than one cook has been calling out for pizza after discovering too late that the innocuous can was fiery jalapeño peppers rather than mild green chilies.

1. Sprinkle chicken with salt and pepper. Heat olive oil in a large, deep skillet over medium-high heat. Add chicken pieces to the skillet in a single layer and brown well on all sides, turning gently with tongs and being careful not to crowd the pan. Remove chicken and set aside.

2. Add onion and garlic to the skillet and cook, stirring frequently, for 3 minutes or until onion is translucent. Add rice and cook for 1 minute, stirring constantly.

3. Add tomatoes, green chilies, chicken stock, oregano, and bay leaf and bring to a boil over high heat, stirring frequently. Add chicken pieces, cover, reduce heat to medium-low, and cook for 25 to 35 minutes or until chicken is tender and no longer pink and almost all liquid has been absorbed.

4. Stir in cilantro, pimientos, and peas. Cover and cook for 2 to 3 minutes or until hot and remaining liquid is absorbed. Remove and discard bay leaf and serve immediately.

Spiced Chicken with Rice and Dried Currants (Country Captain)

1 (3- to 4-lb.) chicken, cut into serving pieces, or 4 to 6 chicken pieces of your choice (breasts, thighs, legs), rinsed and patted dry with paper towels

Salt and freshly ground black pepper to taste

3 TB. olive oil

1 large onion, peeled and diced

3 garlic cloves, peeled and minced

1 red bell pepper, seeds and ribs removed, diced

2 TB. curry powder

½ tsp. ground ginger

½ tsp. ground allspice

½ tsp. dried thyme

1 cup long-grain rice

1 (14.5-oz.) can diced tomatoes, drained

¼ cup dry sherry

1½ cups chicken stock

⅔ cup dried currants

Serves: 4 to 6	
Prep time: 20 minutes	
Cook time: 30 minutes	

1. Sprinkle chicken with salt and pepper. Heat olive oil in a large, deep skillet over medium-high heat. Add chicken pieces to the skillet in a single layer and brown well on all sides, turning gently with tongs and being careful not to crowd the pan. Remove chicken and set aside.

2. Add onion, garlic, and red bell pepper to the skillet and cook, stirring frequently, for 3 minutes or until onion is translucent. Add curry powder, ginger, allspice, thyme, and rice and cook for 1 minute, stirring constantly.

3. Add tomatoes, sherry, chicken stock, and currants and bring to a boil over medium-high heat, stirring frequently.

4. Add chicken pieces, cover, reduce heat to medium-low, and cook for 25 to 35 minutes or until chicken is tender and no longer pink and all liquid has been absorbed. Season with salt and pepper if necessary and serve immediately.

 **Bake Lore**

Country Captain is a chicken dish that dates back to Colonial times. Some food historians say it originated in Savannah, Georgia, a major port for the spice trade. Other sources say a British captain brought the curry-flavored dish back from India.

Braised Indian Chicken with Basmati Rice, Vegetables, and Toasted Cashews

Serves: 4 to 6
Prep time: 15 minutes, plus at least 4 hours for marinating
Cook time: 35 minutes

1 (8-oz.) container plain yogurt

4 garlic cloves, peeled and minced

2 TB. grated fresh ginger

1 TB. curry powder

1 TB. ground turmeric

1 tsp. ground cardamom

½ tsp. ground cinnamon

¼ to ½ tsp. cayenne

1 (3- to 4-lb.) chicken, cut into serving pieces, or 4 to 6 chicken pieces of your choice (breasts, thighs, legs), rinsed and patted dry with paper towels

1½ cups roasted cashew nuts

1 cup chicken stock

3 TB. olive oil

1 large onion, peeled and chopped

1 carrot, peeled and sliced

1 (10-oz.) pkg. frozen mixed vegetables, thawed

Salt and freshly ground black pepper to taste

2 to 3 cups cooked basmati rice, hot

Ellen on Edibles

Tumeric has a bitter, pungent flavor and gives foods a vibrant, intense yellow-orange color. Very popular in Indian cooking, it is always found in its dried and powdered form in supermarkets.

1. Combine yogurt, garlic, ginger, curry powder, turmeric, cardamom, cinnamon, and cayenne in a heavy plastic bag and mix well. Add chicken pieces, zip the bag, and turn to coat chicken pieces evenly. Marinate, refrigerated, for at least 4 hours, preferably overnight. Remove chicken from marinade, scrape off marinade, and reserve marinade.

2. Grind ¾ cup cashews with ¼ cup chicken stock in a food processor fitted with a steel blade or in a blender. Set aside. Coarsely chop remaining cashews and set aside. Heat oil in a large skillet over medium-high heat. Add chicken pieces to the skillet in a single layer and brown well on all sides. Remove chicken and set aside. Add onion and cook, stirring frequently, for 3 minutes or until onion is translucent. Add carrot, nut purée, remaining chicken stock, and reserved marinade and bring to a boil.

3. Add chicken, cover, reduce heat to medium-low, and cook for 25 to 35 minutes or until chicken is tender and no longer pink. Stir in mixed vegetables, season to taste with salt and pepper, and cook an additional 5 minutes. Serve chicken over rice and sprinkle with remaining cashews.

Mexican Chicken in Jalapeño Beer Sauce with Beans and Rice

1 (3- to 4-lb.) chicken, cut into serving pieces, or 4 to 6 chicken pieces of your choice (breasts, thighs, legs), rinsed and patted dry with paper towels

Salt and freshly ground black pepper to taste

2 TB. olive oil

1 large onion, peeled and diced

3 garlic cloves, peeled and minced

1 cup long-grain rice

1 (14.5-oz.) can diced tomatoes, drained

1 cup dark beer, preferably Mexican

¾ cup chicken stock

2 tsp. dried oregano, preferably Mexican

3 pickled jalapeño peppers, thinly sliced and drained, with liquid reserved

1 (15-oz.) can kidney beans, drained and rinsed

Serves: 4 to 6
Prep time: 15 minutes
Cook time: 30 minutes

1. Sprinkle chicken with salt and pepper. Heat olive oil in a large, deep skillet over medium-high heat. Add chicken pieces to the skillet in a single layer and brown well on all sides, turning gently with tongs and being careful not to crowd the pan. Remove chicken and set aside.

2. Add onion and garlic to the skillet and cook, stirring frequently, for 3 minutes or until onion is translucent. Add rice and cook, stirring constantly, for 1 minute.

3. Stir in tomatoes, beer, chicken stock, oregano, sliced jalapeños with 2 tablespoons reserved liquid, and beans.

4. Add chicken pieces, cover, reduce heat to medium-low, and cook for 25 to 35 minutes or until chicken is tender and no longer pink and rice is soft. Season to taste with salt and pepper and serve immediately.

 **Got You Covered!**

The amount of liquid specified in these recipes differs from the amount listed on a box when cooking rice or grains because foods such as chicken give off juices as they cook. So the amount of liquid needed to be added to cook the rice is less than if you were just cooking rice or grains alone.

Moroccan Chicken with Couscous, Chickpeas, and Artichoke Hearts

Serves: 4 to 6
Prep time: 20 minutes
Cook time: 35 minutes

1 (3- to 4-lb.) chicken, cut into serving pieces, or 4 to 6 chicken pieces of your choice (breasts, thighs, legs), rinsed and patted dry with paper towels

Salt and freshly ground black pepper to taste

2 TB. olive oil

1 large onion, peeled and diced

3 garlic cloves, peeled and minced

2 carrots, peeled and sliced

3 TB. sweet paprika, preferably Hungarian

2 TB. ground cumin

1 TB. ground coriander

2½ cups chicken stock

¼ cup balsamic vinegar

1 (15-oz.) can chickpeas, drained and rinsed

1 (10-oz.) pkg. frozen artichoke hearts, thawed and cut into wedges

2 cups couscous

 Bake Lore

Although we credit President Herbert Hoover with the quote about "a chicken in every pot," it was first said by King Henry IV of France, born in Navarre in 1553. At his coronation, he said he hoped that every peasant could afford a "chicken every Sunday," because chicken was deemed such a luxury in those days.

1. Sprinkle chicken with salt and pepper. Heat olive oil in a large, deep skillet over medium-high heat. Add chicken pieces to the skillet in a single layer and brown well on all sides, turning gently with tongs and being careful not to crowd the pan. Remove chicken and set aside.

2. Add onion and garlic and cook, stirring frequently, for 3 minutes or until onion is translucent. Reduce heat to low and add carrots, paprika, cumin, and coriander. Cook, stirring constantly, for 1 minute.

3. Add chicken stock and balsamic vinegar and bring to a boil over medium heat, stirring occasionally. Add chicken pieces, cover, reduce heat to medium-low, and cook for 25 to 35 minutes or until chicken is tender and no longer pink. Add chickpeas and artichoke hearts and simmer for 5 minutes or until artichoke hearts are tender.

4. Remove chicken and keep warm, reserving vegetables and sauce in the skillet. Stir couscous into the skillet, cover, and allow couscous to sit 5 minutes. Fluff couscous with fork, season with salt and pepper if necessary, and serve couscous with chicken.

Chicken with Carrots and Linguine in Asian Saffron Ginger Sauce

1 lb. linguine

¼ tsp. saffron threads

¼ cup boiling water

1 (3- to 4-lb.) chicken, cut into serving pieces, or 4 to 6 chicken pieces of your choice (breasts, thighs, legs), rinsed and patted dry with paper towels

Salt and freshly ground black pepper to taste

½ cup all-purpose flour

3 TB. vegetable oil

4 carrots, peeled and thinly sliced

1 bunch fresh chives, cut into ½-inch sections

2 garlic cloves, peeled and minced

1½ cups half-and-half

1 cup dry white wine

3 TB. Chinese oyster sauce (available in the Asian section of supermarkets and in Asian grocery stores)

1 tsp. Chinese chili sauce

Serves: 4 to 6	
Prep time: 20 minutes	
Cook time: 30 minutes	

1. Bring a large pot of salted water to a boil. Add linguine and cook according to package directions until al dente. Drain and set aside. Crush saffron threads with a mortar and pestle or heavy spoon and pour boiling water over them. Set aside.

2. Sprinkle chicken with salt and pepper and dust with flour, shaking off any excess. Heat oil in a large skillet over medium-high heat. Add chicken pieces to the skillet in a single layer and brown well on all sides, turning gently with tongs and being careful not to crowd the pan. Remove chicken and set aside.

3. Add carrots, ½ chives, and garlic to the skillet. Cook 30 seconds. Add half-and-half, white wine, oyster sauce, chili sauce, and saffron. Bring to a boil over high heat, stirring frequently. Add chicken, cover, reduce heat to low, and simmer 25 to 35 minutes or until chicken is tender and no longer pink. Remove chicken and vegetables and keep warm, reserving sauce in the skillet.

4. Increase heat to medium-high and boil until sauce is reduced in volume by ½ and is thick enough to lightly coat a spoon. Add linguine to sauce and heat through. Serve chicken and vegetables on top of linguine and sprinkle with remaining chives.

 Bake Lore

Saffron is—pound for pound—the most expensive food item in the world. These yellow-orange stigmas from tiny purple crocus must be hand-picked, and it takes more than 14,000 of these to make up a single ounce of saffron. In centuries past, saffron was used as a medicine and a dye for cloth with its characteristic vivid yellow color. The threads need to be crushed and soaked in hot liquid before using.

Chicken with Peppers, Rice, and Olives

Serves: 4 to 6
Prep time: 15 minutes
Cook time: 40 minutes

1 (3- to 4-lb.) chicken, cut into serving pieces, or 4 to 6 chicken pieces of your choice (breasts, thighs, legs), rinsed and patted dry with paper towels

Salt and freshly ground black pepper to taste

2 TB. olive oil

1 large onion, peeled and diced

3 garlic cloves, peeled and minced

1 red bell pepper, seeds and ribs removed, diced

1 yellow or orange bell pepper, seeds and ribs removed, diced

1 cup long-grain rice

1 (14.5-oz.) can diced tomatoes, drained

1 cup chicken stock

¾ cup lager beer

½ cup sliced green olives with pimiento

Ellen on Edibles

Lager, a light-colored beer, is what Americans generally think of as beer, but the genre of beverages brewed from malted barley and flavored with hops also includes darker cousins like ale, stout, and porter. Beer adds character to many cooked dishes, including breads and stews.

1. Preheat the oven to 350°F. Sprinkle chicken with salt and pepper. Heat olive oil in a large, deep ovenproof skillet or Dutch oven over medium-high heat. Add chicken pieces to the skillet in a single layer and brown well on all sides, turning gently with tongs and being careful not to crowd the pan. Remove chicken and set aside.

2. Add onion and garlic to the pan and cook, stirring frequently, for 3 minutes or until onion is translucent. Add red bell pepper, yellow bell pepper, and rice and cook, stirring constantly, for 1 minute.

3. Add tomatoes, chicken stock, beer, and olives. Stir well and bring to a boil over high heat. Add chicken, cover and bake for 25 to 30 minutes or until chicken is tender and no longer pink and rice has absorbed liquid. Serve immediately.

Chicken with Wild Mushrooms, Shallots, and Jasmine Rice in Asian Cream Sauce

¼ cup macadamia nuts

10 shallots, peeled

4 garlic cloves, peeled

½-inch piece fresh ginger, peeled

3 TB. soy sauce

2 TB. firmly packed dark brown sugar

½ to ¾ tsp. red pepper flakes

1 (14-oz.) can light coconut milk

1 (3- to 4-lb.) chicken, cut into serving pieces

Salt and freshly ground black pepper to taste

3 TB. Asian sesame oil

½ lb. fresh shiitake mushrooms, stems removed, wiped with a damp paper towel, and sliced

½ cup chicken stock

¼ cup chopped fresh cilantro

2 to 3 cups cooked jasmine rice

Serves: 4 to 6	
Prep time: 20 minutes	
Cook time: 40 minutes	

1. Combine macadamia nuts, 3 shallots, garlic, ginger, soy sauce, brown sugar, red pepper flakes, and ½ cup coconut milk in a food processor fitted with a steel blade or in a blender. Purée until smooth and set aside. Thinly slice remaining shallots and set aside.

2. Sprinkle chicken with salt and pepper. Heat sesame oil in a large, deep skillet over medium-high heat. Add chicken pieces and brown well on all sides. Remove chicken and set aside. Add sliced shallots and shiitake mushrooms and cook, stirring frequently, for 3 minutes or until shallots are translucent. Remove with a slotted spoon and set aside.

3. Add puréed macadamia mixture to the skillet and cook over high heat, stirring constantly, for 3 minutes. Add remaining coconut milk and chicken stock and bring to a boil. Add chicken and shiitake mushrooms and bring to a boil. Simmer, covered, for 25 to 35 minutes or until chicken is tender and no longer pink.

4. Remove chicken and keep warm. Boil sauce over high heat for 5 minutes or until reduced in volume by ⅓. Stir in cilantro and rice, adjust seasoning with salt and pepper, and cook until rice is hot. Serve immediately.

Got You Covered!

Although not used extensively in American cooking, nuts are used in many Asian and Latin American cuisines as a thickening agent for sauces and gravies. High in protein as well as in fat, nuts give sauces a creamy appearance without the presence of a dairy product.

Fast and Fit: Meals Using Boneless, Skinless Chicken Breasts

In This Chapter

◆ One-dish dinners that are on the table in minutes

◆ Recipes from cuisines around the globe

◆ Fork-only recipes great for entertaining

Boneless chicken breasts are the definition of scratch cooking with speed. They take to myriad forms of preparation that are drawn from a United Nations of countries, as you'll see when cooking the recipes in this chapter.

These dishes are also perfect for entertaining because the boneless breasts can be cut up into bite-size pieces. That means your guests need only a fork when dining from a plate on their lap.

Boning Up

Although boneless, skinless chicken breasts are now available in all supermarkets, the price per pound for the edible meat is still less if you bone the bird yourself. In addition, your cache of bones and skin for making chicken stock is always replenished.

If possible, buy the chicken breasts whole rather than split. Pull off the skin with your fingers, and then make an incision on either side of the breast bone, cutting down until you feel the bone resisting the knife. Working one side at a time, place the blade of your boning knife against the carcass, and scrape away the meat. You will then have two pieces: the large fillet and the small tenderloin.

To trim the fillet, cut away any fat, and pound the meat gently between two sheets of plastic wrap to an even thickness. To trim the tenderloin, secure the tip of the tendon that will be visible with your free hand. Using a paring knife, scrape down the tendon, and the meat will push away.

If you buy boneless, skinless breasts, go over them carefully. Because they are boned by machine, chances are that stray bones or part of the breast bone will still be attached. You will also have to trim the tenderloin.

Pounding to Perfection

Some recipes will tell you to pound the breast to an even thickness so it will cook evenly and quickly. To do so, place the breast between two sheets of wax paper and pound with the smooth side of a meat mallet or the bottom of a small, heavy skillet or saucepan. However, don't do this unless instructed.

After you have boned and pounded the chicken breasts, you can keep a supply frozen. They defrost in a matter of minutes and can be quickly cooked for a sautéed supper. Wrap each breast separately in plastic wrap and then lay the wrapped breasts flat in a heavy resealable plastic bag. When they're frozen, you can easily separate the individual breasts and defrost only the number required for a recipe.

Stocking Up

Not only do you save money when you bone your own chicken breasts, but you also save money (and gain great flavor) from making homemade stock with the bones and skin. Keep a gallon plastic bag for bones and skin in your freezer, and when it's full and you've got a couple hours at home, it's time to start up the simmer.

The easiest way to make stock is to place the trimmings into a large stockpot and cover them with water. Then add an envelope of vegetable soup mix and perhaps a bay leaf and a teaspoon or so dried thyme. Bring it to a boil over high heat and when it comes to a boil, reduce the heat to low so it's just simmering. Or you can cook it the classic way. Add carrots, onion, celery, salt, and pepper to the trimmings. If you do so, you can throw the vegetables into the pot peeled but whole.

When it first starts to simmer, you'll see some foam on the surface. Skim off the "scum" (and that's what it's really called) and throw it out. Simmer the stock for 3 hours; then strain it through a colander and discard the solids. When it's cool, freeze it in 1-cup batches in heavy freezer bags or tightly sealed plastic containers, and you've got up to 4 months to use it.

It's also a good idea to measure the capacity of your ice cube tray with a tablespoon, and freeze some stock as cubes. This is really useful when a recipe calls for less than ½ cup stock.

Cutting with Cunning

The smaller the piece of chicken, the faster it will cook. Whole boneless breasts require the longest amount of cooking time, followed by pounded breasts and then cubes and slices.

The best way to cut a breast into slices or cubes is against—rather than with—the grain. The grain on a chicken breast goes horizontally, from the thickest part to the narrowest. Holding the breast in front of you, start slicing from the narrow end. If you're making slices, you're done. If you're making cubes, cut each slice into cubes. If you want to make a dish that specifies whole breasts for a buffet dinner so guests can eat with a fork alone, feel free to cut the breasts into 1-inch cubes.

Extending the Options

You can substitute turkey cutlets for boneless, skinless chicken breasts in any recipe, and the dish will probably have a richer flavor as a result. Although you can bone turkey breasts as outlined earlier, they are way too thick to cook whole. Slice them into cutlets down the side as if you were carving a roasted turkey.

You can also substitute veal scallops for pounded chicken breasts. They will be as delicate, and the meal will be more elegant. Sauté them for just 2 to 3 minutes on a side.

Skillet Chicken and Rice with Dried Fruit and Apricot Mustard Sauce

---

Serves: 6 to 8

Prep time: 15 minutes

Cook time: 25 minutes

1½ lb. boneless, skinless chicken breast halves, rinsed and patted dry with paper towels and cut into 1-inch cubes

Salt and freshly ground black pepper to taste

2 TB. vegetable oil

1 small onion, peeled and minced

3 garlic cloves, peeled and minced

1 red bell pepper, seeds and ribs removed, thinly sliced

1½ cups long-grain rice

2 cups apricot nectar

¾ cup chicken stock

3 TB. *Dijon mustard*

⅓ cup chopped dried apricots

¼ cup raisins, preferably golden raisins

¼ cup dried currants (or additional raisins)

1 (10-oz.) pkg. frozen cut green beans, thawed

Ellen on Edibles

Dijon mustard, known for its clean, sharp flavor, was actually invented in Dijon, France. It is made from a combination of brown and black mustard seeds, and the essential ingredients are white wine and unfermented grape juice. Grey Poupon is the best-known brand in America, but there are dozens of French producers, many of which also flavor their mustard.

1. Sprinkle chicken with salt and pepper. Heat oil in a large, deep skillet over medium-high heat. Add chicken pieces to the skillet in a single layer and cook, stirring frequently, for 2 minutes or until chicken is opaque. Remove chicken and set aside.

2. Add onion and garlic to the skillet and cook, stirring frequently, for 3 minutes or until onion is translucent. Add red bell pepper and rice and cook, stirring frequently, for 2 minutes. Add chicken, apricot nectar, chicken stock, Dijon mustard, dried apricots, raisins, and dried currants. Bring to a boil, stirring occasionally. Cover, reduce heat to low, and simmer for 15 minutes.

3. Stir in green beans, cover the skillet again, and cook for 3 to 5 minutes or until chicken is tender and no longer pink and rice has absorbed all liquid. Serve immediately.

Lemongrass Chicken Curry with Linguine, Coconut, and Bean Sprouts

1 small onion, peeled and diced

3 garlic cloves, peeled

½-inch slice fresh ginger

⅓ cup roasted peanuts

1½ cups chicken stock

3 TB. vegetable oil

3 TB. curry powder

½ tsp. Chinese five-spice powder

2 (14-oz.) cans light coconut milk

¼ cup thinly sliced lemongrass

2 TB. soy sauce

5 plum tomatoes, cored, seeded, and diced

1½ lb. boneless, skinless chicken breast halves, rinsed and patted dry with paper towels and cut into 1-inch cubes

Salt and freshly ground black pepper to taste

¾ lb. linguine, broken into 2-inch lengths and cooked

½ lb. mung bean sprouts, rinsed

Serves: 6 to 8	
Prep time: 25 minutes	
Cook time: 40 minutes	

1. Combine onion, garlic, ginger, peanuts, and ¼ cup chicken stock in a food processor fitted with a steel blade or in a blender. Purée until smooth, scraping sides as necessary. Set aside.

2. Heat 1 tablespoon oil in a saucepan over medium-high heat. Add curry powder and Chinese five-spice powder and cook, stirring constantly, for 1 minute. Add purée and cook for 2 minutes, stirring constantly. Add coconut milk, remaining 1¼ cups chicken stock, lemongrass, and soy sauce. Bring to a boil, reduce heat to medium, and simmer sauce for 15 minutes, stirring occasionally. Add tomatoes and simmer for an additional 15 minutes. (You can do this a day in advance and refrigerate, tightly covered. Before continuing, return to a simmer over low heat, stirring occasionally.)

3. While sauce is simmering, heat remaining oil in a skillet over medium-high heat. Sprinkle chicken with salt and pepper and add chicken to the skillet in a single layer. Cook, stirring constantly, for 2 minutes. Add chicken to sauce and return to a boil. Simmer, uncovered, for 5 to 7 minutes. Add linguine and bean sprouts and stir to combine. Cook for 2 minutes or until pasta is hot. Serve immediately.

 **Got You Covered!**

Lemongrass, technically an herb and used in Thai and Vietnamese cooking, is characterized by a strong citrus flavor with a spicy finish similar to that of ginger. Fresh lemongrass is sold by the grayish green stalk that looks like a fibrous, woody scallion. Cut the lower bulb 5 to 8 inches from the stalk, discarding the fibrous upper part. Trim off the outer layers as you would peel an onion; then bruise the stem to release the flavor.

Chicken with Buckwheat Kasha and Wild Mushrooms in Brown Gravy

Serves: 6 to 8
Prep time: 25 minutes
Cook time: 20 minutes

½ oz. dried wild mushrooms, such as porcini or morels

½ cup boiling water

1½ lb. boneless, skinless chicken breast halves, rinsed and patted dry with paper towels and cut into 1-inch cubes

Salt and freshly ground black pepper to taste

2 TB. vegetable oil

2 TB. (¼ stick) butter

1 medium onion, peeled and diced

2 garlic cloves, peeled and minced

2 celery stalks, trimmed and thinly sliced

1 carrot, peeled and thinly sliced

½ lb. fresh shiitake mushrooms, stems removed, wiped with a damp paper towel, and sliced

1 TB. fresh thyme or 1 tsp. dried

1½ cups chicken stock

1 cup coarse-grain *kasha*, prepared according to package directions

1 (1.1-oz.) pkg. mushroom gravy mix, prepared according to package directions

1. Place dried mushrooms in a small bowl and pour boiling water over them. Allow mushrooms to sit in liquid for 10 minutes and then drain, reserving soaking water. Remove and discard stems, finely chop mushrooms, and strain soaking liquid. Set aside.

2. Sprinkle chicken with salt and pepper. Heat oil in a large, deep skillet over medium-high heat. Add chicken to the skillet in a single layer and cook, stirring frequently, for 2 to 3 minutes or until chicken is lightly browned. Remove chicken with a slotted spoon and set aside.

3. Add butter to the skillet and allow it to melt. And add onion and garlic and cook, stirring frequently, for 3 minutes or until onion is translucent. Add celery, carrot, and fresh shiitake mushrooms. Cook, stirring frequently, for 3 minutes or until mushrooms are soft. Add dried mushrooms, mushroom liquid, chicken, thyme, and chicken stock. Bring to a boil, reduce heat to low, and simmer, uncovered, for 5 to 7 minutes or until chicken is tender and no longer pink. Add kasha to chicken mixture and return to a boil. Simmer for 5 minutes, covered, or until liquid is absorbed. Serve immediately, drizzled with prepared mushroom gravy.

Ellen on Edibles

Kasha (pronounced *KAH-shuh*) is roasted buckwheat groats that are popular in traditional Eastern European cooking. They are usually found in the Kosher food section of supermarkets, and the grain takes on a nutty flavor when toasted and cooked.

Mexican Chicken with Vegetables and Crispy Corn Tortilla Topping

6 to 8 boneless, skinless chicken breast halves, rinsed and patted dry with paper towels

Salt and freshly ground black pepper to taste

2 TB. olive oil

1 large onion, peeled and diced

3 garlic cloves, peeled and minced

1 red bell pepper, seeds and ribs removed, thinly sliced

1 TB. chili powder

2 tsp. ground cumin

1 tsp. dried oregano, preferably Mexican

1 (14.5-oz.) can diced tomatoes, undrained

1 (10-oz.) pkg. frozen corn, thawed

1 (15-oz.) can red kidney beans, drained and rinsed

6 (6-in.) corn tortillas, cut into 1-inch strips

Vegetable oil spray

Serves: 6 to 8	
Prep time: 15 minutes	
Cook time: 20 minutes	

1. Preheat the oven to 350°F. Grease a 10×14-inch baking pan. Sprinkle chicken breasts with salt and pepper. Heat oil in a large skillet over medium-high heat. Add chicken breasts to the skillet in a single layer and cook for 2 minutes per side or until browned, turning gently with tongs. Remove chicken and set aside.

2. Add onion, garlic, and red bell pepper to the skillet. Cook, stirring frequently, for 3 minutes or until onion is translucent. Stir in chili powder, cumin, and oregano. Cook, stirring constantly, for 1 minute. Add tomatoes, corn, and kidney beans and bring to a boil. Scrape mixture into the prepared baking pan and top with chicken breasts. Cover with aluminum foil and bake for 20 minutes or until chicken is tender and no longer pink.

3. Cover a baking sheet with aluminum foil. Place tortilla strips on the baking sheet and spray strips with vegetable oil spray. Bake tortilla strips for 10 to 15 minutes or until crisp. Remove from the oven and set aside.

4. To serve, divide chicken and vegetables onto plates and top with tortilla strips.

Got You Covered!

If you want to shortcut the preparation time for this dish, crush some bagged yellow tortilla chips instead of spending the time baking fresh strips. The strips look nice, but the flavor will be the same.

Chicken, Mushrooms, and Linguine in Garlicky Marsala Sauce

Serves: 6 to 8
Prep time: 15 minutes
Cook time: 20 minutes

1 lb. linguine, broken into 2-inch lengths

6 to 8 boneless, skinless chicken breast halves, rinsed and patted dry with paper towels

Salt and freshly ground black pepper to taste

½ cup all-purpose flour

3 TB. olive oil

6 garlic cloves, peeled and minced

2 shallots, peeled and minced

½ lb. white mushrooms, trimmed, wiped with a damp paper towel, and sliced

1 cup dry Marsala wine

½ cup chicken stock

¼ cup chopped fresh parsley

1 tsp. Italian seasoning

1. Bring a large pot of salted water to a boil. Add linguine and cook according to package directions until al dente. Drain and set aside.

2. Sprinkle chicken with salt and pepper. *Dredge* chicken in flour (shaking off any excess) and set aside. Heat oil in a large, deep skillet over medium-high heat. Add chicken to the skillet in a single layer and cook for 2 minutes per side or until lightly browned, turning gently with tongs. Remove chicken with tongs and set aside. Add garlic, shallots, and mushrooms to the skillet and cook, stirring frequently, for 3 minutes or until shallots are translucent.

3. Add chicken, Marsala, chicken stock, parsley, and Italian seasoning. Bring to a boil over medium-high high heat, stirring occasionally. Reduce heat to low, cover, and cook for 10 to 12 minutes or until chicken is tender and no longer pink. Stir in linguine and cook for 2 minutes to heat through. Serve immediately.

Ellen on Edibles

To **dredge** is to coat raw food lightly with a milled grain or other ground or powdered carbohydrate prior to pan-frying or browning. The food is most often coated with flour, but you can also coat with cornmeal, cornstarch, or breadcrumbs.

Sweet-and-Sour Chicken with Pineapple, Scallions, Snow Peas, and Jasmine Rice

1½ lb. boneless, skinless chicken breast halves, rinsed and patted dry with paper towels and sliced into ½-inch thick slices against the grain

Freshly ground black pepper to taste

1 TB. cornstarch

2 TB. soy sauce

3 TB. vegetable oil

12 scallions, trimmed and cut into 2-inch pieces, including green tops

1 red bell pepper, seeds and ribs removed, thinly sliced

¾ cup applesauce

1 (8-oz.) can pineapple chunks packed in pineapple juice, drained with juice reserved, halved

3 TB. firmly packed dark brown sugar

3 TB. cider vinegar

⅓ lb. snow peas, rinsed and stemmed

2 to 3 cups cooked jasmine rice

Serves: 6 to 8	
Prep time: 15 minutes	
Cook time: 12 minutes	

1. Season chicken to taste with pepper and place in a mixing bowl. Stir cornstarch into soy sauce, pour mixture over chicken, and toss lightly to coat. Set aside.

2. Heat oil in a large, deep skillet over medium-high heat. Add chicken, scallions, and red bell pepper. Cook, stirring constantly, for 3 minutes or until chicken is opaque. Add applesauce, pineapple with juice, brown sugar, and cider vinegar. Bring to a boil and simmer, uncovered, for 3 to 5 minutes or until chicken is tender and cooked through. Add snow peas, cover, and simmer for 2 minutes or until snow peas are crisp-tender. Stir rice into the skillet and cook for 2 minutes or until rice is hot. Serve immediately.

 Got You Covered!

Sweet and sour is a classic taste combination popular around the world, and it's very easy to increase the complexity to transform this dish—or any other Asian sweet-and-sour one—into sweet and hot. Just add 1 to 2 tablespoons Chinese chili sauce and omit the vinegar. Chili sauce contains vinegar in addition to fiery peppers.

Chicken Cacciatore with Orzo

Serves: 6 to 8
Prep time: 25 minutes
Cook time: 25 minutes

1 oz. dried porcini mushrooms

1 cup boiling chicken stock

6 to 8 boneless, skinless chicken breast halves, rinsed and patted dry with paper towels

Salt and freshly ground black pepper to taste

⅓ cup olive oil

¼ lb. prosciutto, finely chopped

1 large onion, peeled and chopped

4 garlic cloves, peeled and minced

½ lb. white mushrooms, trimmed, wiped with a damp paper towel, and sliced

2 cups orzo

1 (28-oz.) can diced tomatoes, undrained

3 TB. chopped fresh parsley

1 tsp. Italian seasoning

1 bay leaf

1. Preheat the oven to 350°F. Grease a 10×14-inch baking pan. Place dried porcini mushrooms in a small bowl and pour boiling chicken stock over them. Allow mushrooms to sit in liquid for 10 minutes; then drain, reserving chicken stock. Remove and discard mushroom stems and finely chop mushrooms. Strain stock through paper coffee filter or paper towel. Reserve mushrooms and liquid.

2. Sprinkle chicken with salt and pepper. Heat ½ olive oil in a large skillet over medium-high heat. Add chicken to the skillet in a single layer and cook for 2 minutes per side or until lightly browned, turning gently with tongs. Remove chicken with tongs and set aside. Add remaining olive oil to the skillet and add prosciutto, onion, and garlic. Cook, stirring frequently, for 3 minutes or until onion is translucent. Add white mushrooms and orzo and cook for 2 minutes, stirring frequently.

3. Add chopped porcini, chicken stock, tomatoes, parsley, Italian seasoning, and bay leaf. Bring to a boil and cook over low heat, covered, for 5 minutes. Scrape mixture into the prepared baking dish. Arrange chicken breasts on top and cover with aluminum foil.

4. Bake for 15 to 20 minutes or until chicken is tender and no longer pink and orzo is al dente. Remove and discard bay leaf and serve immediately.

 Bake Lore

Cacciatore is Italian for "hunter's style." A number of dishes from chicken to beef to veal use cacciatore as a handle, but all it means is that the dish is cooked with tomatoes. The rest of the ingredients are up to the cook.

Baked Chicken and Asparagus Risotto

1 lb. fresh asparagus, rinsed

4 cups chicken stock

3 fresh parsley sprigs

2 sprigs fresh thyme or 1 tsp. dried

1 bay leaf

6 boneless, skinless chicken breast halves, rinsed, patted dry with paper towels and cut into 1-inch cubes

Salt and freshly ground black pepper to taste

3 TB. butter

1 large onion, peeled and chopped

3 garlic cloves, peeled and chopped

2 cups Arborio rice

½ cup dry white wine

¾ cup grated Parmesan cheese

Serves: 6 to 8
Prep time: 20 minutes
Cook time: 30 minutes

1. Preheat the oven to 400°F. Grease a 10×14-inch baking pan.

2. Break off woody stems from asparagus, reserve spears, and place stems in a saucepan with chicken stock, parsley, thyme, and bay leaf. Bring to a boil over high heat, reduce heat to low, and simmer, uncovered, for 10 minutes. Strain and discard solids and return stock to the saucepan. While stock is simmering, slice asparagus spears on the diagonal into 1-inch pieces and set aside.

3. Sprinkle chicken with salt and pepper. Melt butter in a large skillet over medium-high heat. Add chicken to the skillet in a single layer and cook, stirring frequently, for 2 minutes or until chicken is opaque. Remove chicken with a slotted spoon and set aside. Add onion and garlic and cook, stirring frequently, for 3 minutes until onion is translucent. Add Arborio rice and cook for 2 minutes, stirring constantly.

4. Add white wine, increase heat to high, and cook, stirring constantly, for 3 minutes or until wine is almost evaporated. Add chicken stock and chicken and bring to a boil. Scrape mixture into the prepared baking pan, cover with aluminum foil, and bake for 10 minutes. Remove foil, stir in asparagus, and bake for an additional 15 to 20 minutes or until rice is soft and has absorbed liquid. Stir in Parmesan cheese and serve immediately.

Ellen on Edibles

Risotto is a traditional Italian rice dish that dates back to the Renaissance. The key ingredient is Arborio rice, which is a short, fat-grained Italian rice with a high starch content. Stirring it in stock creates a creamy matrix when this starch is released.

Skillet Chicken with Broccoli, Orzo, and Cheddar

Serves: 6 to 8
Prep time: 15 minutes
Cook time: 25 minutes

6 to 8 boneless, skinless chicken breast halves, rinsed and patted dry with paper towels

Salt and freshly ground black pepper to taste

3 TB. butter

1 large onion, peeled and chopped

3 garlic cloves, peeled and chopped

2 cups orzo

3 cups chicken stock

1 TB. chopped fresh tarragon or 1 tsp. dried

2 (10-oz.) pkg. frozen broccoli spears, thawed and sliced into 1-inch pieces

1½ cups grated mild or sharp cheddar cheese

 Half Baked

It's important to not stir cheese into a dish until the very end of the cooking time. The dairy solids in cheese cause it to scorch very quickly, and that flavor can ruin an entire dish. Unless otherwise directed, add cheese as the final ingredient, right before you serve the dish.

1. Sprinkle chicken breasts with salt and pepper. Heat butter in a large, deep skillet over medium-high heat. Add chicken breasts to the skillet in a single layer, working in 2 batches if necessary. Cook for 2 minutes per side or until chicken is opaque, turning gently with tongs. Remove chicken with tongs and set aside.

2. Add onion, garlic, and orzo to the skillet and cook, stirring frequently, for 3 minutes or until onion is translucent. Add chicken stock and tarragon. Bring to a boil, reduce heat to low, and cook for 5 minutes. Stir in broccoli and arrange chicken breasts on top. Cover and cook for 10 minutes. Turn chicken breasts gently with tongs and cook for an additional 5 to 7 minutes or until chicken is tender and no longer pink and orzo is soft.

3. Remove chicken from the skillet and cover chicken with aluminum foil to keep warm. Stir cheese into the skillet and cook, stirring occasionally, for 2 minutes or until cheese is melted. Serve immediately with chicken on top of orzo.

Moroccan-Spiced Chicken with Spinach and Pasta

¾ lb. spaghetti, broken into 2-inch lengths

⅓ cup olive oil

1 cup raisins, preferably golden

½ cup pine nuts

1 TB. granulated sugar

½ tsp. ground cardamom

½ tsp. ground cinnamon

1 TB. grated lemon zest

2 (10-oz.) pkg. frozen chopped spinach, thawed

¼ cup dry sherry

1 cup chicken stock

1 TB. lemon juice

2 TB. (¼ stick) butter

6 boneless, skinless chicken breast halves, rinsed and patted dry with paper towels and cut into 1-inch cubes

Salt and freshly ground black pepper to taste

Serves: 6 to 8
Prep time: 15 minutes
Cook time: 25 minutes

1. Preheat the oven to 350°F. Grease a 10×14-inch baking pan. Bring a large pot of salted water to a boil over high heat. Cook spaghetti according to the package directions until al dente. Drain and place in the prepared baking pan.

2. Heat olive oil in a large skillet over medium heat. Add raisins, pine nuts, sugar, cardamom, cinnamon, and lemon zest. Cook, stirring constantly, for 2 minutes or until pine nuts are browned.

3. Place spinach in a colander and press with the back of a spoon to extract as much liquid as possible. Add spinach and cook, stirring constantly, for 2 minutes. Add sherry and cook 1 minute. Add chicken stock and lemon juice and cook for 2 minutes. Scrape mixture into the baking pan with spaghetti.

4. Return the skillet to the stove, add butter, and allow it to melt. Sprinkle chicken with salt and pepper and add to the skillet in a single layer. Cook, stirring frequently, for 3 to 5 minutes or until chicken is opaque. Scrape chicken into the baking pan and stir with other ingredients. Cover with aluminum foil and bake for 15 minutes or until chicken is tender and no longer pink. Serve immediately.

Half Baked

The amount of water that will come out of a thawed package of frozen spinach is amazing. It's important to press it as hard as possible, or the spinach will be soupy and not sauté well.

Chicken Parmesan with Herbed Tomato Sauce and Pasta

Serves: 6 to 8
Prep time: 10 minutes for sauce and 15 minutes for dish
Cook time: 30 minutes for sauce and 15 minutes for chicken

Sauce:

3 TB. olive oil

1 medium onion, peeled and diced

3 garlic cloves, peeled and minced

1 tsp. dried oregano

1 tsp. dried basil

1 (28-oz.) can crushed tomatoes in tomato purée

¼ cup dry red wine

Salt and crushed red pepper flakes to taste

Chicken:

1 lb. spaghetti, broken into 2-inch lengths

6 to 8 boneless, skinless chicken breast halves, rinsed, patted dry with paper towels, and pounded to an even ½-inch thickness

Salt and freshly ground black pepper to taste

1 cup milk

1 cup all-purpose flour

4 large eggs, lightly beaten

4 cups Italian breadcrumbs

¾ cup olive oil

2 cups grated mozzarella cheese

⅓ cup grated Parmesan cheese

1. For sauce, heat olive oil in a saucepan over medium-high heat. Add onion, garlic, oregano, and basil. Cook, stirring frequently, for 3 minutes or until onion is translucent. Add tomatoes and red wine and season to taste with salt and crushed red pepper flakes. Bring to a boil, stirring occasionally. Reduce heat to low and simmer, uncovered, stirring occasionally, for 30 minutes. (You can do this up to 2 days in advance and refrigerate, tightly covered. Or freeze sauce for up to 3 months.)

2. Bring a large pot of salted water to a boil. Add spaghetti and cook according to package directions until al dente. Drain and set aside.

3. Sprinkle chicken with salt and pepper. Place milk, flour, eggs, and breadcrumbs into individual shallow bowls. Dip chicken breasts into milk and then into flour, shaking off any excess. Then dip chicken into egg and finally into breadcrumbs, pressing into breadcrumbs to make them adhere. (You can do this a day in advance and refrigerate, tightly covered. But do not cook breasts until just before serving.)

4. Preheat the oven broiler, placing oven rack 8 to 10 inches from the broiler element, and grease a 10×14-inch baking pan. Heat olive oil in a large skillet over medium-high heat. Add chicken breasts to the skillet in a single layer, being careful not to crowd the pan and working in 2 batches if necessary. Cook for 3 to 4 minutes per side, until golden brown, turning gently with tongs. Remove chicken with tongs to paper towels and pat with towels.

5. To serve, arrange warm pasta in the bottom of the prepared baking pan and spread with 1 cup tomato sauce. Arrange chicken breasts on top, overlapping them if necessary. Coat with remaining sauce and sprinkle top with mozzarella and Parmesan cheeses. Broil for about 5 minutes or until cheese is melted and browned. Serve immediately.

Got You Covered!

You can shortcut this dish considerably by using purchased sauce. It can be ready for baking in a matter of 15 minutes. Or make a double or triple batch of this easy sauce and freeze it for future use.

The Second Time Around: Dishes with Cooked Poultry

In This Chapter

- ◆ Recipes that create an exciting ending for leftover turkey and chicken
- ◆ Old-fashioned American classics
- ◆ Dishes that can also be made into vegetarian options

Leftovers are the re-runs of the food world. And although the first viewing may have been riveting, the ending is predictable the second time around. Just ask any American the Monday morning after Thanksgiving if they'd like some turkey for dinner.

To the rescue come the recipes in this chapter. They are fast to make and are drawn from a variety of cuisines. And because the poultry is already cooked, it becomes just another ingredient rather than central to the cooking process. You can even transform some of these dishes into vegetarian fare without sacrificing any flavor.

Poultry Pointers

Some of these recipes are written for chicken and others for turkey, but use the different birds interchangeably. If you have leftovers and don't plan to use them within a few days, cut them up and freeze them. Frozen cooked poultry can be used for up to 3 months.

It's very quick to defrost cut cooked poultry in a microwave oven, or you can toss the contents of the freezer bag into a dish frozen if there's a sauce simmering in which it can thaw.

Although these recipes are designed for cooked poultry that is a neutral ingredient, if you have poultry that was cooked in a sauce, such as any of the dishes in Chapter 7, they can still earn a second life here. Remove all skin and discard any of the meat that is clearly colored and flavored by the sauce.

Fast Fixings

Let's say you're craving a recipe in this chapter but don't have any cooked poultry on hand. Don't fret. A supermarket rotisserie chicken yields about 3 to 4 cups of shredded meat, so you're all set.

In addition to rotisserie chickens, many supermarkets also carry preroasted chickens and turkey breasts in the poultry refrigerator cases. Many also carry precooked, presliced chicken.

Alternately, you can purchase boneless raw chicken and cook it quickly either by poaching it in chicken stock or putting it in a microwave oven. The same rules apply. Cook the chicken or turkey to an internal temperature of 180°F, and until it is no longer pink.

These recipes are very tolerant of substitutions, but keep one important caveat in mind: do not use raw chicken or turkey in any of these recipes. They were not formulated to cook the poultry sufficiently to make it safe, and because raw poultry gives off liquid into a dish, you will not be happy with the soupy results.

Cutting Up

You'll see that some of these recipes specify shredded poultry while others have you cutting it into cubes. There is a rationale for this. In some dishes, the smaller shreds are preferable because they better absorb the sauce, and if a dish is layered, you can't see the difference. Shredding, because you can do it with your (clean, freshly washed) hands, is also faster.

But there are times, such as in the Chicken Pot Pie, that the pieces are more visible in the finished dish. So to make it more aesthetically pleasing, these recipes call for you to dice or cube the poultry. But if you're low on time, shredding will be just fine.

Chicken, Vegetable, and Pasta Bake with Spicy Puttanesca Sauce

1 lb. linguine, broken into 2-inch lengths and prepared according to package directions

4 TB. olive oil

1 large onion, peeled and diced

4 garlic cloves, peeled and minced

1 (28-oz.) can crushed tomatoes in tomato purée

¼ cup dry red wine

½ cup chopped pitted kalamata olives

¼ cup capers, drained and rinsed

2 TB. chopped fresh basil

1 tsp. Italian seasoning

Salt and crushed red pepper flakes to taste

2 small zucchini, trimmed and thinly sliced

1 red bell pepper, seeds and ribs removed, thinly sliced

3 cups shredded cooked chicken

1 (15-oz.) can chickpeas, drained and rinsed

½ cup grated Parmesan cheese

¼ cup Italian breadcrumbs

Serves: 6 to 8
Prep time: 15 minutes
Cook time: 25 minutes

1. Preheat the oven to 350°F. Grease a 10×14-inch baking pan. Place pasta into prepared baking pan.

2. Heat 2 tablespoons olive oil in a saucepan over medium-high heat. Add onion and garlic. Cook, stirring occasionally, for 3 minutes or until onion is translucent. Stir in tomatoes, red wine, olives, capers, basil, and Italian seasoning. Season with salt and crushed red pepper to taste. Bring to a boil, reduce heat to medium, and simmer, uncovered, for 10 minutes.

3. While sauce is simmering, heat remaining olive oil in a large skillet over medium heat. Add zucchini and red bell pepper and cook, stirring frequently, for 5 to 10 minutes.

4. Add sauce, cooked vegetables, chicken, and chickpeas to linguine and stir well. Cover with aluminum foil and bake for 10 minutes. Remove the foil and sprinkle Parmesan cheese and breadcrumbs over top. Bake for an additional 15 minutes or until bubbly. Serve immediately.

 Bake Lore

It's the fragrance of this spicy Italian sauce that earned it it's slightly off-color name. *Puttana* is the Italian word for "whore," and *alla puttanesca* signifies a dish served with this sauce with olives and capers. It has been said that the aroma was like the perfume of an exotic woman.

Old-Fashioned American Chicken Pot Pie

Serves: 6 to 8
Prep time: 30 minutes
Cook time: 35 minutes

4 TB. (½ stick) butter

2 TB. olive oil

4 shallots, peeled and minced

2 garlic cloves, peeled and minced

½ lb. white mushrooms, trimmed, wiped with a damp paper towel, and sliced

1 cup chicken stock

1 large carrot, peeled and thinly sliced

2 celery stalks, trimmed and thinly sliced

1 (10-oz.) Russet potato, peeled and cut into ½-inch dice

1 TB. fresh chopped tarragon or 1 tsp. dried

2 tsp. fresh thyme or ½ tsp. dried

1 bay leaf

1 cup frozen peas, not thawed

3 TB. all-purpose flour

1 cup half-and-half

Salt and freshly ground black pepper to taste

3 cups cooked chicken, cut into ½-inch dice

1 sheet frozen puff pastry (½ of a 17-oz. pkg.), thawed

1 large egg

1 TB. milk

1. Preheat the oven to 375°F. Grease a 9×13-inch baking pan. Heat 2 tablespoons butter and olive oil in a medium skillet over medium-high heat until butter is melted. Add shallots and garlic and cook, stirring frequently, for 3 minutes or until shallots are translucent.

2. Add mushrooms to the skillet and cook for 2 minutes or until mushrooms begin to soften. Add chicken stock, carrot, celery, potato, tarragon, thyme, and bay leaf. Bring to a boil, reduce heat to low, and simmer, uncovered, for 8 to 10 minutes or until potato is tender. Add peas and cook 2 minutes. Strain mixture, reserving stock. Remove and discard bay leaf and transfer vegetables to the prepared baking pan.

3. Heat remaining butter in a saucepan over low heat. Stir in flour and stir constantly for 2 minutes. Whisk in reserved stock and bring to a boil over medium-high heat, whisking constantly. Add half-and-half and simmer 2 minutes. Season to taste with salt and pepper. Add chicken to the baking pan with vegetables and stir in sauce. (You can do this a day in advance and refrigerate, tightly covered. Before continuing, reheat in a microwave oven or in a saucepan over low heat, stirring frequently.)

4. Roll puff pastry into an 11×15-inch rectangle. Beat egg lightly with milk. Brush egg mixture around outside edge of the baking pan. Place pastry on top of the pan and crimp the edges, pressing to seal pastry to the sides of the pan. Brush pastry with egg mixture and cut in 6 (1-inch-long) vents in pastry to allow steam to escape.

5. Bake for 35 minutes or until pastry is golden brown. Serve immediately.

Half Baked

The purpose of an egg wash is to give pastry a browned and shiny crust. But it's important to brush the crust before cutting the steam vents because the egg wash can clog the vents, which will create a soggy crust.

Chicken in Creamy Mustard Dill Sauce with Vegetables and Orzo

Serves: 6 to 8
Prep time: 15 minutes
Cook time: 25 minutes

2 cups orzo

5 TB. butter

1 small onion, peeled and diced

4 celery stalks, trimmed and thinly sliced

2 carrots, peeled and thinly sliced

2 TB. all-purpose flour

2 cups chicken stock

½ cup heavy cream

2 TB. Dijon mustard

2 TB. coarse-grain mustard

Salt and freshly ground black pepper to taste

¼ cup chopped fresh dill

3 cups shredded cooked chicken

Half Baked

There are two related foods on the market that could not be more different: dill *weed* and dill *seed*. The weed has bright-green feathery leaves and a delicate flavor. The seed is actually the dried fruit from the herb and is much stronger and more pungent. It is the seed that flavors dill pickles. Dill weed is now about as common as parsley in markets, and like parsley, the dried form has virtually no flavor, so buy it fresh.

1. Preheat the oven to 375°F. Grease a 9×13-inch baking pan. Bring a large pot of salted water to a boil. Add orzo and cook for 5 minutes. Drain and set aside.

2. Heat 3 tablespoons butter in a skillet over medium-high heat. Add onion, celery, and carrots. Cook, stirring frequently, for 3 minutes or until onion is translucent. Reduce heat to low, cover, and cook for 7 to 10 minutes or until vegetables are soft. Set aside.

3. While vegetables are cooking, melt remaining butter in a small saucepan over low heat. Stir in flour and stir constantly for 2 minutes. Whisk in chicken stock and bring to a boil over medium-high heat, whisking constantly. Add cream, Dijon mustard, and coarse-grain mustard and simmer for 2 minutes. Season to taste with salt and pepper. Add dill and chicken to the skillet with vegetables and stir in sauce and orzo.

4. Cover with aluminum foil and bake for 25 minutes or until orzo is soft. Serve immediately.

Crispy Nacho-Topped Southwest Chicken and Vegetable Casserole

¼ cup olive oil

1 small onion, peeled and diced

3 garlic cloves, peeled and minced

1 TB. chili powder

1 tsp. ground cumin

1 tsp. dried oregano, preferably Mexican

4 cups frozen hash brown potatoes, thawed

1 (10-oz.) pkg. frozen corn, thawed

1 (14.5-oz.) can diced tomatoes with Mexican seasoning, undrained

2 canned *chipotle chilies in adobo sauce*, finely chopped

3 cups shredded chicken

1 (15-oz.) can red kidney beans, drained and rinsed

Salt and freshly ground black pepper to taste

2 cups crushed corn chips

1 cup grated Monterey Jack cheese

Serves: 6 to 8
Prep time: 15 minutes
Cook time: 25 minutes

1. Preheat the oven to 350°F. Grease a 9×13-inch baking pan. Heat oil in a large skillet over medium-high heat. Add onion and garlic. Cook, stirring frequently, for 3 minutes or until onion is translucent. Stir in chili powder, cumin, and oregano. Stir constantly for 1 minute.

2. Stir in potatoes and cook for 5 to 8 minutes or until potatoes are lightly browned. Stir in corn, tomatoes, chipotle peppers, chicken, and kidney beans. Season to taste with salt and pepper. Scrape mixture into the prepared baking pan and level top with a rubber spatula.

3. Cover with aluminum foil and bake for 10 minutes. Remove the foil and sprinkle with crushed corn chips and grated Monterey Jack cheese. Bake for an additional 15 minutes or until cheese is melted and dish is hot. Serve immediately.

Ellen on Edibles

Chipotle chilies in adobo sauce are a canned Mexican product, and both the peppers, which are smoked jalapeños, and the rich, dark red sauce are used to flavor dishes. The sauce also contains herbs and vinegar, so it's similar to a hot red pepper sauce but with a more complex, richer flavor.

Tarragon Chicken, Spinach, Noodle, and Ricotta Casserole

Serves: 6 to 8
Prep time: 10 minutes
Cook time: 35 minutes

12 oz. medium-width egg noodles

1 TB. butter

4 scallions, trimmed with all but 2 inches of green tops discarded, thinly sliced

3 cups shredded cooked chicken

1 (10-oz.) pkg. frozen chopped spinach, thawed and squeezed in a colander to extract as much water as possible

1 (15-oz.) container low-fat ricotta cheese

⅓ cup chicken stock

¼ cup milk

2 TB. chopped fresh tarragon or 2 tsp. dried

1 cup grated mozzarella cheese

Salt and freshly ground black pepper to taste

 **Got You Covered!**

This recipe is equally successful made vegetarian, served either as an entrée or as a side dish. Omit the chicken and substitute vegetable stock for the chicken stock. As a side dish, this will serve 8 to 12 people.

1. Preheat the oven to 375°F. Grease a 10×14-inch baking pan. Bring a large pot of salted water to a boil and cook egg noodles according to the package directions until al dente. Drain and place in the prepared pan.

2. Melt butter in a small skillet over medium heat. Add scallions and cook, stirring frequently, for 2 minutes or until scallions are soft. Scrape scallions into the pan, along with chicken, spinach, ricotta, chicken stock, milk, tarragon, and mozzarella cheese. Season to taste with salt and pepper and stir well.

3. Cover with aluminum foil and bake for 15 minutes. Remove the foil and bake for an additional 20 minutes or until bubbly. Serve immediately.

Chicken and Mango with Rice, Sugar Snap Peas, and Toasted Almonds

3 TB. vegetable oil

2 shallots, peeled and minced

2 garlic cloves, peeled and minced

1½ cups long-grain rice

½ tsp. ground ginger

½ tsp. ground coriander

½ tsp. ground cinnamon

1½ cups chicken stock

1½ cups mango nectar

½ cup slivered almonds

3 cups diced cooked chicken

2 ripe mangoes, peeled, pitted, and cut into ½-inch dice

¾ lb. sugar snap peas, rinsed and stemmed

Salt and freshly ground black pepper to taste

Serves: 6 to 8
Prep time: 15 minutes
Cook time: 20 minutes

1. Heat oil in a saucepan over medium-high heat. Add shallots and garlic and cook, stirring frequently, for 3 minutes or until shallots are translucent. Stir in rice, ginger, coriander, and cinnamon. Cook, stirring constantly, for 1 minute. Add chicken stock and mango nectar. Bring to a boil, reduce heat to low, and simmer, covered, for 15 minutes.

2. While mixture is simmering, preheat oven to 350°F. Place almonds on a baking sheet and toast in the oven for 3 to 5 minutes or until lightly browned. Remove from the oven and set aside.

3. Stir chicken, mangoes, and sugar snap peas into the saucepan. Return to a boil and simmer, covered, for 5 minutes or until rice is tender and sugar snaps are crisp-tender. Season to taste with salt and pepper and serve garnished with toasted almonds.

Got You Covered!

Due to their elliptical shape, mangoes are very hard to peel. Begin by cutting a small slice off one end and then stand the mango flat on the cut surface. Using a vegetable peeler or sharp paring knife, peel the mango from the top down. After it is peeled, locate the flat pit and slice away the flesh on one side. Repeat on the other side, and then slice the flesh still clinging to the sides of the pit.

Turkey Tetrazzini

Serves: 6 to 8
Prep time: 25 minutes
Cook time: 30 minutes

1 lb. spaghetti, broken into 2-inch lengths and cooked according to pkg. directions

4 TB. (½ stick) butter

2 TB. olive oil

2 shallots, peeled and minced

2 garlic cloves, peeled and minced

2 celery stalks, trimmed and thinly sliced

½ lb. white mushrooms, trimmed, wiped with a damp paper towel, and sliced

3 TB. all-purpose flour

½ cup medium dry sherry

1 cup turkey stock or chicken stock

1½ cups half-and-half

3 to 4 cups shredded turkey

1 cup frozen peas, thawed

1 cup grated Parmesan cheese

Salt and freshly ground black pepper to taste

½ cup breadcrumbs

1. Preheat the oven to 350°F. Grease a 10×14-inch baking pan. Drain pasta and place in the prepared baking pan.

2. Heat 2 tablespoons butter and olive oil in a large skillet over medium-high heat until butter is melted. Add shallots, garlic, and celery and cook, stirring frequently, for 3 minutes or until shallots are translucent. Add mushrooms and cook for 3 minutes or until mushrooms are soft. Add to the baking pan with spaghetti.

3. Heat remaining butter in a saucepan over low heat. Stir in flour and stir constantly for 2 minutes. Whisk in sherry and bring to a boil over medium-high heat, whisking constantly. Simmer for 3 minutes; then add turkey stock and half-and-half and simmer for 2 minutes.

4. Stir in turkey, peas, and ¾ cup Parmesan cheese and season to taste with salt and pepper. Add mixture to pasta and vegetables in the baking pan. (You can do this a day in advance and refrigerate, tightly covered. Add 15 minutes to initial bake time.)

5. Cover the baking pan with aluminum foil and bake for 15 minutes. Combine remaining ¼ cup Parmesan cheese with breadcrumbs. Remove the foil, sprinkle breadcrumb mixture on top, and bake for an additional 15 to 20 minutes or until bubbly and top is browned. Serve immediately.

 **Bake Lore**

This grand-mother of all leftover poultry casseroles was named for Italian singer Luisa Tetrazzini, who was the toast of the American opera circuit in the early 1900s. Where the dish was created, and by whom, is not known.

Mexican Turkey Lasagna with Corn Tortillas and Pinto Beans

2 TB. vegetable oil

1 large onion, peeled and diced

2 garlic cloves, peeled and minced

1 TB. chili powder

1 tsp. ground cumin

1 tsp. dried oregano, preferably Mexican

1 (14.5-oz.) can diced tomatoes, drained

1 (8-oz.) can tomato sauce

1 (15-oz.) can pinto beans, drained and rinsed

3 cups shredded cooked turkey

Salt and freshly ground black pepper to taste

1½ cups ricotta cheese

2 large eggs, lightly beaten

1 (4-oz.) can diced mild green chilies, drained

3 TB. chopped fresh cilantro

12 (6-in.) corn tortillas

1½ cups grated Monterey Jack cheese

Serves: 6 to 8	
Prep time: 15 minutes	
Cook time: 35 minutes	

1. Preheat the oven to 375°F. Grease a 9×13-inch baking pan. Heat oil in a medium skillet over medium-high heat. Add onion and garlic. Cook, stirring frequently, for 3 minutes or until onion is translucent. Stir in chili powder, cumin, and oregano. Cook, stirring constantly, for 1 minute. Add tomatoes, tomato sauce, pinto beans, and turkey. Bring to a boil and simmer for 2 minutes. Season to taste with salt and pepper and set aside.

2. Combine ricotta, eggs, green chilies, and cilantro in a mixing bowl. Season to taste with salt and pepper and stir well.

3. Place ½ turkey mixture in the bottom of the prepared pan. Top with 6 tortillas, overlapping them to cover filling. Spread ricotta cheese mixture on top and sprinkle with ½ cup Monterey Jack cheese. Arrange remaining tortillas on top, then spread with remaining turkey mixture, and sprinkle with remaining Monterey Jack cheese.

4. Cover the pan with aluminum foil and bake for 15 minutes. Remove the foil and bake for an additional 20 minutes or until bubbly and cheese is melted. Allow to sit for 5 minutes.

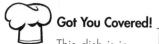 **Got You Covered!**

This dish is incredibly versatile and can easily be turned into a vegetarian dish by omitting the turkey. It will still have a rich flavor, and if you want to compensate for the volume, substitute 2 small zucchini or yellow squash, sautéed in olive oil, for the turkey.

Turkey and Vegetables in Mole Sauce with Polenta Topping

Serves: 6 to 8
Prep time: 30 minutes
Cook time: 35 minutes

2 cups turkey stock or chicken stock

1 medium green pepper, seeds and ribs removed, diced

1 large tomato, cored, seeded, and diced

2 garlic cloves, peeled

½ small onion, peeled and diced

½ cup breadcrumbs

¼ cup blanched almonds

½ oz. (½ square) unsweetened baking chocolate, broken into pieces

3 TB. raisins

3 TB. all-purpose flour

½ to 1 tsp. cayenne

½ tsp. ground cinnamon

¼ tsp. ground cloves

Salt to taste

3 cups shredded cooked turkey

1 (15-oz.) can red kidney beans, drained and rinsed

1 (10-oz.) pkg. frozen mixed vegetables, thawed

1 (18-oz.) roll prepared polenta, sliced 1-inch thick

 Bake Lore

Mole is one of the oldest sauces in North America, dating back to the Aztec Indians of Mexico centuries before Columbus landed in America. Its most salient feature is the inclusion of some sort of bitter chocolate, which adds richness to the dark, reddish-brown sauce without adding sweetness.

1. Combine 1 cup turkey stock with green bell pepper, tomato, garlic, onion, breadcrumbs, almonds, chocolate, raisins, flour, cayenne, cinnamon, cloves, and salt in a food processor fitted with a steel blade or in a blender. Purée until smooth and scrape mixture into a saucepan. Stir in remaining turkey stock and bring to a boil over medium-high heat, stirring frequently. Reduce heat to low and simmer sauce, uncovered, stirring occasionally, for 30 minutes. (You can do this up to 2 days in advance and refrigerate, tightly covered. You can also freeze sauce for up to 3 months. Before continuing, reheat sauce to a simmer.)

2. Preheat the oven to 375°F. Grease a 9×13-inch baking pan. Combine sauce, turkey, kidney beans, and mixed vegetables in the prepared pan and stir well. Arrange polenta slices on top and cover with aluminum foil. Bake for 15 minutes; then remove the foil and bake for an additional 20 to 30 minutes or until bubbly and polenta is browned. Serve immediately.

Turkey Gratin with Ham, Tomatoes, and Asparagus in Cheddar Sauce

3 TB. butter

3 TB. all-purpose flour

1½ cups half-and-half

2 cups grated sharp or mild cheddar cheese

Salt and cayenne to taste

6 slices thick white bread, toasted

⅓ lb. smoked ham, sliced

3 cups shredded cooked turkey

3 large tomatoes, cored, seeded, and sliced

1 (10-oz.) pkg. asparagus spears, thawed

¼ cup grated Parmesan cheese

Serves: 6 to 8
Prep time: 15 minutes
Cook time: 25 minutes

1. Preheat the oven to 400°F. Grease a 9×13-inch baking pan. Melt butter in a saucepan over low heat. Stir in flour and stir constantly for 2 minutes. Whisk in half-and-half and bring to a boil. Simmer, stirring frequently, for 2 minutes. Stir in cheddar cheese until it is melted and season to taste with salt and cayenne. Set aside.

2. Place bread in the bottom of the prepared pan and layer with ham, turkey, and tomatoes. Ladle ¾ sauce on top and cover with aluminum foil. Bake for 10 minutes. Remove the foil and arrange asparagus on top. Top with remaining sauce and sprinkle with Parmesan cheese. Bake for 15 minutes or until bubbly and top is browned. Serve immediately.

Got You Covered!

You can use any number of vegetables in this recipe to make it a balanced dish. Try broccoli spears, cut green beans, or cauliflower florets. Precook the sturdier vegetables, but put string beans in raw.

Part 5

From the Butcher Shop

Call them stews. Call them pot roasts. Or call them braises. One benefit uniting the recipes in Part 5 is that they're all made from the least-expensive cuts of meat. That's economical, yes, but also delicious, as those cuts become meltingly tender when they're slowly cooked with liquid.

Part 5 begins with Chapter 10, recipes to expand your options for ground meat, primarily ground beef, a family-meal stalwart if ever there was one. Chapter 11 focuses on beef as well, this time in larger pieces for stews and roasts.

But there's more in the butcher shop than beef. Chapter 12 features recipes for pork, "the other white meat," as well as a few ways to cook with ham and pork sausages. And Chapter 14 contains recipes for those other grazing greats—lamb and veal.

Chapter **10**

International Helpers for Hamburger

In This Chapter

- ◆ New looks at old friends like chili
- ◆ Ground meat dishes made with healthful vegetables
- ◆ Ways to make hamburger *haute*

There's always a place for lighting the grill and filling the air with the aroma of grilled burgers or steaks. But ground beef isn't limited to summer cookouts, and there's always room for expanding your repertoire of ways to prepare it. That's what you'll find in this chapter.

An advantage of all these recipes is that the beef is thoroughly cooked, so there's no risk of food-borne bacteria in these dishes. And it's just as delicious as that juicy burger, too.

The Daily Grind

Generally, ground beef is made from the less-tender and less-popular cuts of beef, although it sometimes includes trimmings from more tender cuts like steak. Grinding tenderizes the meat, and the fat on these bargain cuts reduces its dryness and improves the flavor of hamburgers or any dish.

The cut of meat from which it is made and the amount of fat incorporated into the mix determine the price of ground beef. High-fat mixtures are less costly but will shrink more when cooked.

The least expensive product, made from the shank and brisket, is sold as ground beef and can contain up to 30 percent fat. Moderately priced ground chuck is the next category. Because it contains enough fat (about 15 to 20 percent) to give it flavor and make it juicy, yet not enough to cause excess shrinkage, ground chuck is a good choice for these recipes.

The Tiffany of hamburger, boasting 10 percent fat or less, are ground round and ground sirloin. Because these are extremely lean cuts, there is little fat to remove after browning the meat.

Safety First

Any food of animal origin can harbor bacteria. Ground beef can contain a number of invisible, odor-free, illness-causing bacteria, including *salmonella* and *E coli*. Other families of bacteria can cause spoilage, with food developing a bad odor or feeling sticky on the outside. However, these are not as potentially dangerous because you can detect them.

Ground meat is more prone to these problems than larger cuts. When meat is ground, the microorganisms residing on its surface can get mixed into it, so more of the meat is exposed to the harmful bacteria. Bacteria multiply rapidly in the "danger zone"—temperatures between 40° and 140°F. To keep bacterial levels low, store ground beef at 40°F or less and use within 2 days or freeze. To destroy harmful bacteria, cook ground beef to 160°F.

Seeing liquid in the bottom of a tray of ground meat does not signal a potential problem. When making ground beef, some retail stores grind the meat while it is still frozen. Ice crystals in the frozen meat break down the cell walls, and the meat releases some of its juices during cooking. The same thing happens after you freeze ground meat at home.

Thoughtful Thawing

The best way to safely thaw ground beef is in the refrigerator. Keeping meat cold while it is defrosting is essential to prevent the growth of bacteria. Cook or refreeze it within 1 or 2 days after thawing.

To defrost ground beef more rapidly, you can defrost it in the microwave oven or in cold water. If you're using the microwave, cook the ground beef immediately because some areas may begin to cook during the defrosting. To defrost in cold water, put the meat in a watertight plastic bag and submerge. Change the water every 30 minutes. Cook immediately. Do not refreeze ground meat thawed in cold water or in the microwave oven.

Meaty Matters

Although most of these recipes list lean ground beef as the key ingredient, others specify ground lamb and Italian sausage. These different meats add their own flavor to the recipe, but you can always use ground beef in their stead. Ground pork and ground veal are not as hearty as beef or lamb, so they should not be substituted.

Dishes such as raw steak tartare have dropped in popularity over the past few decades, but the underlying principle held dear by tartare devotees holds true for ground beef: the only way to ensure really fresh ground meat is to grind it yourself. You can do this easily by purchasing low-cost cuts of beef, trimming off the visible white fat, and chopping it in a food processor fitted with a steel blade using the pulsing action. It's also easier if the meat is partially frozen. To freeze, place cubes on a baking sheet and freeze them for 20 to 30 minutes.

Basic Browning

There is very little technical knowledge needed to make dishes with ground meat. The one major principle to follow is the initial browning of the meat.

Browning means to cook quickly over moderately high heat, which causes the surface of the food to brown. In the case of cubes of beef for stew, browning seals in the juices and keeps the interior moist. For ground meats, the browning gives food an appetizing color, allows you to drain off some of the inherent fat, and also gives the dish a rich flavor as the sugars caramelize.

You can brown larger pieces under an oven broiler, but brown most ground meats in a skillet. Crumble the meat in a skillet over medium-high heat. Break up the lumps with a meat fork or the back of a spoon as the meat browns; then stir it around frequently until all the lumps are brown and no pink remains. At that point, it's easy to remove it from the pan with a slotted spoon and discard the fat. You can then use the pan again without washing it for any precooking of other ingredients. The residue from browning will give whatever you're cooking more flavor.

Stuffed Cabbage with Apples, Rice, and Raisins in Sweet-and-Sour Tomato Sauce

Serves: 6 to 8
Prep time: 30 minutes
Cook time: 2 hours

1 (3-lb.) head green cabbage

1½ lb. ground beef

1½ cups cooked rice

1 onion, peeled and grated

2 garlic cloves, peeled and minced

Salt and freshly ground black pepper to taste

3 Golden Delicious apples, peeled, cored, and diced

¾ cup raisins

1 (15-oz.) can tomato sauce

¾ cup cider vinegar

¾ cup dark brown sugar

1. Preheat the oven to 375°F. Grease a 10×14-inch baking pan. Bring a large pot of water to a boil. Remove and discard broken outer leaves of cabbage. Core cabbage by cutting around all 4 sides of the core with a heavy, sharp knife. Discard core and spear cabbage in center with a meat fork.

2. Hold cabbage in boiling water and pull off leaves with tongs as they become pliable. Continue until you have 12 to 18 leaves separated. Reserve these leaves, remove cabbage head from water, and shred 3 cups cabbage from it. Scatter shredded cabbage in the bottom of the prepared pan.

3. Combine beef, rice, onion, garlic, salt, and pepper in a mixing bowl and mix well. Place 1 cabbage leaf on a work surface in front of you and scoop ⅓ cup meat mixture into the large end. Fold sides over meat and roll leaf. Place in baking pan, seam side down, and repeat with remaining leaves and meat.

4. Scatter apples and raisins over cabbage rolls. Combine tomato sauce, cider vinegar, and brown sugar in a mixing bowl and stir well. Pour mixture over cabbage rolls.

5. Cover with aluminum foil and bake for 1½ hours. Remove the foil and bake for an additional 30 minutes or until lightly browned. Serve immediately. (You can make this up to 2 days in advance and refrigerate, tightly covered. Reheat covered with foil at 350°F for 25 to 30 minutes or until hot.)

 **Got You Covered!**

After the cabbage has been submerged in the boiling water, some of the inner leaves will be hot and blanched, and the central core will still be cold and crisp. Shred the cabbage from the exterior in and save the cold inner core for coleslaw.

Italian Stuffed Peppers Parmesan with Beef and Cheese

6 to 8 large (8-oz.) red bell peppers

2 TB. olive oil

2 large onions, peeled and chopped

3 garlic cloves, peeled and minced

6 TB. chopped fresh parsley

1 TB. Italian seasoning

Salt and freshly ground black pepper to taste

¾ cup Italian breadcrumbs

¼ cup milk

¾ cup grated mozzarella cheese

2 cups jarred marinara sauce

2 large eggs, lightly beaten

1½ lb. lean ground beef

½ cup grated Parmesan cheese

Serves: 6 to 8	
Prep time: 15 minutes	
Cook time: 45 minutes	

1. Preheat the oven to 375°F. Grease a 10×14-inch baking pan. Cut off top ½ inch of red bell peppers and reserve. Scoop out seeds and ribs with your hands. Discard stems and chop pepper tops.

2. Heat oil in a large, heavy skillet over medium-high heat. Add onions, garlic, and chopped pepper pieces. Cook, stirring frequently, for about 5 minutes or until onions soften. Transfer to a large bowl. Mix in parsley, Italian seasoning, salt, pepper, breadcrumbs, milk, mozzarella cheese, ½ cup marinara sauce, eggs, and beef and stir to combine.

3. Fill pepper cavities with beef mixture. Stand peppers up in the prepared baking pan and pour remaining 1½ cups marinara sauce over them. Cover with aluminum foil and bake for 25 minutes. Remove foil, *baste* peppers with sauce in the pan, and sprinkle with Parmesan cheese. Bake for an additional 20 minutes. Serve immediately, spooning sauce over top of peppers.

 Ellen on Edibles

Basting is the process of brushing or spooning sauce or fat over food as it cooks. The purpose of basting is to keep food moist as well as to add flavor and color.

Chili Con Carne with Vegetables on Cheddar Biscuits

Serves: 6 to 8
Prep time: Chili 20 minutes, biscuits 5 minutes
Cook time: Chili 1 hour, biscuits 15 minutes

¼ cup vegetable oil

2 large onions, peeled and diced

6 garlic cloves, peeled and minced

2 carrots, peeled and thinly sliced

1½ lb. lean ground beef

3 TB. chili powder

1 TB. ground cumin

1 TB. dried oregano, preferably Mexican

Salt and cayenne to taste

2 (8-oz.) cans tomato sauce

1 cup beef stock

2 TB. cider vinegar

2 (15-oz.) cans red kidney beans, drained and rinsed

1½ cups all-purpose flour

2 tsp. baking powder

½ teaspoon baking soda

Salt to taste

2 TB. (¼ stick) cold butter, cut into small pieces

1 cup grated sharp cheddar cheese

1 cup sour cream

1. Heat oil in a Dutch oven or a large saucepan over medium-high heat. Add onion, garlic, and carrots. Cook, stirring frequently, for 3 minutes or until onion is translucent. Remove with a slotted spoon and set aside. Add beef to the Dutch oven and cook until browned, breaking up lumps with a fork. Drain fat off beef and return vegetable mixture to the Dutch oven. Stir in chili powder, cumin, oregano, salt, and cayenne. Cook, stirring constantly, for 1 minute. Stir in tomato sauce, beef stock, and cider vinegar. Bring to a boil, stirring occasionally. Reduce heat to low, cover, and simmer mixture for 45 minutes. Add beans and simmer an additional 15 minutes. (You can make chili up to 2 days in advance and refrigerate, tightly covered. Reheat it over low heat, stirring occasionally, or in a microwave oven until hot.)

2. While chili is simmering, make biscuits. Preheat the oven to 425°F. Sift flour, baking powder, baking soda, and salt together into a bowl. Cut in butter using a pastry blender, two knives, or your fingertips until the mixture resembles coarse meal. Add cheddar cheese and sour cream and stir until it forms a soft but not sticky dough. Knead dough gently on a lightly floured surface, roll or pat it out ½-inch thick, and cut out 6 to 8 rounds with a floured cookie cutter. Bake biscuits on an ungreased baking sheet for 15 to 17 minutes or until golden. (You can make biscuits up to 3 hours in advance and keep at room temperature.)

3. To serve, cut biscuits in half. Place bottom halves on individual plates, top with chili, and top with remaining biscuit halves.

Got You Covered!

If you don't have a large selection of round biscuit cutters, don't fret. Save a juice can or use a small glass instead. They'll both cut out perfect rounds.

Whipped Potato–Topped Shepherd's Pie

Serves: 6 to 8
Prep time: 45 minutes
Cook time: 15 minutes

2 lb. lean ground lamb or ground beef

8 TB. (1 stick) butter

3 TB. olive oil

½ lb. fresh shiitake mushrooms, stems removed, wiped with a damp paper towel, and sliced

2 onions, peeled and diced

4 garlic cloves, peeled and minced

2 cups dry red wine

1 (1.1-oz.) pkg. mushroom gravy mix

2 TB. chopped fresh rosemary leaves or 2 tsp. dried

1 TB. fresh thyme or 1 tsp. dried

2 lb. red-skinned potatoes, scrubbed and cut into 1-inch dice

½ cup heavy cream

2 cups grated sharp cheddar cheese

Salt and freshly ground black pepper to taste

1 (1-lb.) pkg. frozen mixed vegetables

1. Preheat the oven to 400°F. Grease a 9×13-inch baking pan.

2. For filling, heat a large skillet over medium-high heat. Add lamb and cook until well browned, breaking up lumps with a fork. Remove lamb with a slotted spoon and set aside in a bowl. Drain fat from the skillet.

3. Heat 2 tablespoons butter and 1 tablespoon oil in the same skillet over medium-high heat until butter is melted. Add mushrooms and cook, stirring constantly, for 3 minutes or until mushrooms are soft. Scrape mushrooms into the bowl with lamb.

4. Heat remaining butter and remaining oil in the skillet over medium heat. Add onion and garlic and cook, stirring constantly, for 3 minutes or until onion is translucent. Add lamb and mushrooms, red wine, mushroom gravy mix, rosemary, and thyme. Bring to a boil, reduce heat to low, and simmer, uncovered, for 30 minutes or until thickened. Tilt the pan to spoon off as much fat as possible. (You can do this up to 2 days in advance and refrigerate, tightly covered. Before continuing, reheat over low heat, stirring occasionally, until hot.)

5. While lamb is simmering, prepare topping. Place potatoes in a saucepan, cover with salted water, and bring to a boil over high heat. Reduce heat to medium and boil potatoes, uncovered, for 12 to 15 minutes or until soft. Drain potatoes and set aside in a bowl. Heat cream, remaining butter, and cheddar cheese in the saucepan over medium heat until cheese is melted, stirring occasionally. Return potatoes to saucepan and mash well with a potato masher. Season with salt and pepper to taste and set aside.

6. Add mixed vegetables to lamb and return to a boil. Simmer for 3 minutes; then scrape mixture into the prepared baking dish. Spoon potatoes on top of lamb, smoothing them into an even layer. (Do this up to 4 hours in advance and keep at room temperature, if you want. Add 5 to 10 minutes to baking time if lamb is not hot.)

7. Bake for 15 minutes or until lamb is bubbly and potatoes are lightly browned. Serve immediately.

 Bake Lore

Shepherd's Pie is a classic served at pubs in Great Britain that dates back to the eighteenth century. It was originally created as an economical way to use up the leftovers from the traditional "Sunday joint," which was a leg of lamb served with potatoes and vegetables.

Chili Relleño Bake

Serves: 6 to 8
Prep time: 15 minutes
Cook time: 45 minutes

1½ lb. lean ground beef

2 TB. olive oil

1 medium onion, peeled and diced

1 garlic clove, peeled and minced

2 tsp. ground cumin

1 tsp. dried oregano, preferably Mexican

1 (16-oz.) can refried beans

2 (4-oz.) cans diced mild green chilies, drained

Salt and freshly ground black pepper to taste

8 oz. Monterey Jack cheese, shredded

1½ cups milk

3 large eggs

¼ cup yellow cornmeal

Hot pepper sauce (such as Tabasco) to taste

1. Preheat the oven to 350°F. Grease a 9×13-inch baking pan. Heat a large skillet over medium-high heat. Add beef and cook until browned, breaking up lumps with a fork. Remove beef from the skillet with a slotted spoon and set aside in a bowl. Drain fat from the skillet.

2. Heat oil in the skillet and add onion and garlic. Cook, stirring frequently, for 3 minutes or until onion is translucent. Add cumin and oregano and cook, stirring constantly, for 1 minute. Remove from heat; add beef, refried beans, and green chilies. Season to taste with salt and pepper, stir, and set aside.

3. Spread ½ beef mixture onto the bottom of the prepared baking pan and sprinkle ½ Monterey Jack cheese over top. Repeat with remaining beef mixture and cheese.

4. In a medium-size mixing bowl, whisk together milk, eggs, cornmeal, and hot sauce until well blended and pour over casserole. Cover with aluminum foil and bake for 15 minutes. Remove the foil and bake for an additional 30 minutes. Allow to sit for 5 minutes; then serve immediately.

 **Got You Covered!**

This versatile dish is much faster to make than traditional chili relleño, which requires labor-intensive stuffing of individual peppers. To make this into a vegetarian dish, substitute 1 (15-ounce) can kidney beans and 2 small zucchini for the ground beef.

Italian Pasta, Beef, and Bean Casserole (*Pasta Fazool*)

1 lb. mostaccioli or penne pasta

1 lb. bulk hot or sweet Italian sausage or link sausage with casings discarded

½ lb. lean ground beef

2 TB. olive oil

1 large onion, peeled and chopped

4 garlic cloves, peeled and minced

1 tsp. dried oregano

½ tsp. dried thyme

1 (28-oz.) can diced tomatoes, drained

2 TB. tomato paste

1 (15-oz.) can kidney beans, drained and rinsed

Salt and freshly ground black pepper to taste

½ cup grated Parmesan cheese

¼ cup chopped fresh parsley

1 cup grated fontina or provolone cheese

Serves: 6 to 8	
Prep time: 20 minutes	
Cook time: 30 minutes	

1. Preheat the oven to 400°F. Grease a 10×14-inch baking pan. Bring a large pot of salted water to a boil. Boil mostaccioli according to the package directions until al dente. Drain and place in prepared baking pan.

2. Heat a large skillet over medium-high heat. Add sausage and beef and cook until well browned, breaking up lumps with a fork. Remove sausage and beef with a slotted spoon and set aside in a bowl. Drain fat from the skillet.

3. Heat olive oil in the skillet and add onion and garlic. Cook, stirring frequently, for 3 minutes or until onion is translucent. Add oregano and thyme and cook, stirring constantly, for 1 minute. Add tomatoes, tomato paste, and kidney beans and simmer for 5 minutes. Season to taste with salt and pepper. Stir in Parmesan cheese and parsley and stir mixture into pasta in the baking pan.

4. Cover with aluminum foil and bake for 15 minutes. Remove the foil, sprinkle with fontina cheese, and bake for an additional 15 minutes or until bubbly and cheese is melted. Serve immediately.

 Bake Lore

Although the names of Italian pasta shapes might sound romantic, they are merely the translation of the word for the look of the pasta. *Penne* means "quills" or "pens," while *mostaccioli* means "small mustaches." *Rotelle* are "wheels," and *farfalle* are "butterflies."

Provençale Beef Balls with Herbed Potatoes in Red Wine Sauce with Gruyère Cheese

Serves: 6 to 8
Prep time: 25 minutes
Cook time: 45 minutes

1 cup breadcrumbs

¾ cup milk

1½ lb. lean ground beef

2 large eggs, lightly beaten

1 medium onion, peeled and finely chopped

3 garlic cloves, peeled and minced

3 TB. chopped fresh parsley

Salt and freshly ground black pepper to taste

3 large Russet potatoes, peeled and thinly sliced

1¼ cups dry red wine

3 TB. tomato paste

1 cup beef stock

1 TB. herbes de Provence

1 cup grated Gruyère cheese

1. Preheat the broiler and line a broiler pan with aluminum foil. Grease a 9×13-inch baking pan.

2. Combine breadcrumbs and milk in a mixing bowl and stir well. Add ground beef, eggs, onion, garlic, and parsley. Season to taste with salt and pepper. Form mixture into meatballs the size of a walnut and place on the aluminum foil. Brown meatballs under the broiler for about 5 minutes, turning once with tongs.

3. Place potatoes in the prepared baking pan. Top with meatballs. Combine wine, tomato paste, beef stock, and herbes de Provence in a mixing bowl and whisk well. Season to taste with salt and pepper and pour mixture over meatballs.

4. Cover with aluminum foil and bake for 30 minutes. Remove the foil, sprinkle with Gruyère cheese, and bake for an additional 15 minutes or until potatoes are tender and dish is bubbly. Serve immediately.

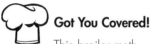 **Got You Covered!**

This broiler method of browning is far more efficient for small items such as meatballs because it's like mass production. Alternately, you can brown meatballs in a skillet over medium-high heat in a few tablespoons oil. Turn them gently with tongs as they brown.

Easy Lasagna

1½ lb. lean ground beef or bulk Italian sausage or some mixture of the two

3 TB. olive oil

1 large onion, peeled and diced

3 garlic cloves, peeled and minced

½ lb. white mushrooms, trimmed, wiped with a damp paper towel, and sliced

1 (26-oz.) jar thick spaghetti sauce or marinara sauce

1½ cups water

¼ cup chopped fresh basil

1 TB. Italian seasoning

Salt and freshly ground black pepper to taste

1 (1-lb.) box no-boil lasagna noodles

1 (15-oz.) container part-skim ricotta cheese

½ lb. grated mozzarella cheese

1 cup grated Parmesan cheese

Serves: 6 to 8	
Prep time: 25 minutes	
Cook time: 1 hour	

1. Preheat the oven to 350°F. Grease a 9×13-inch baking pan. Heat a large skillet over medium-high heat. Add beef and cook until well browned, breaking up lumps with a fork. Remove beef with a slotted spoon and set aside in a bowl. Drain fat from the skillet.

2. Heat oil in the skillet and add onion and garlic. Cook, stirring frequently, for 3 minutes or until onion is translucent. Add mushrooms and cook for 3 minutes or until mushrooms are soft.

3. Combine spaghetti sauce, water, basil, and Italian seasoning and season mixture to taste with salt and pepper. Spread 1½ cups sauce mixture in the prepared baking pan. Arrange ⅓ noodles, slightly overlapping if necessary, over sauce. Spread ½ ricotta over noodles. Sprinkle with ½ mozzarella cheese, ½ beef mixture, and ¼ cup Parmesan cheese. Top with 1½ cups sauce. Repeat layering with lasagna noodles, ricotta, mozzarella, beef, and ¼ cup Parmesan cheese. Arrange remaining lasagna noodles over top. Spoon remaining sauce over lasagna, covering them completely. Sprinkle with remaining ½ cup Parmesan. Cover tightly with aluminum foil and place on a baking sheet.

4. Bake for 1 hour or until noodles are tender and dish is bubbly. (You can make this up to a day in advance and refrigerate, tightly covered. Reheat in 350°F oven for 30 to 40 minutes.) Allow to stand 5 minutes; then serve immediately.

Half Baked

Be sure to buy the right lasagna noodles for this dish. The precooked noodles are fairly new to the market, and they are what they say: noodles that are partially cooked to rid them of some of the starch and then dehydrated. Regular lasagna noodles will not cook as well in this kind of dish.

Tex-Mex Beef and Vegetable Pie (Tamale Pie)

Serves: 6
Prep time: 15 minutes
Cook time: 50 minutes

1½ lb. lean ground beef

3 TB. olive oil

1 large onion, peeled and chopped

2 celery stalks, trimmed and sliced

½ red bell pepper, seeds and ribs removed, chopped

1 jalapeño chili, seeds and ribs removed, finely chopped

6 garlic cloves, peeled and minced

2 TB. *chili powder*

1 tsp. ground cumin

¼ tsp. ground cinnamon

1 (14.5-oz.) can diced tomatoes, undrained

1 (8-oz.) can tomato sauce

½ cup golden raisins

Salt and freshly ground black pepper to taste

2 large eggs, lightly beaten

½ cup milk

2 TB. all-purpose flour

1 (10-oz.) pkg. frozen corn kernels, thawed and drained

4 scallions, trimmed with all but 2 inches of green tops discarded and chopped

2 TB. chopped fresh cilantro

Ellen on Edibles

Chili powder is a spice blend you can make yourself. Combine 2 tablespoons ground red chili, 2 tablespoons paprika, 1 tablespoon ground coriander, 1 tablespoon garlic powder, 1 tablespoon onion powder, 2 teaspoons ground cumin, 2 teaspoons ground red pepper or cayenne, 1 teaspoon ground black pepper, and 1 teaspoon dried oregano.

1. Preheat the oven to 350°F. Grease a 9×13-inch baking pan. Heat a large skillet over medium-high heat. Add beef and cook until well browned, breaking up lumps with a fork. Remove beef with a slotted spoon and set aside in a bowl. Drain fat from the skillet.

2. Heat oil in the skillet and add onion, celery, red bell pepper, jalapeño, and garlic. Cook, stirring frequently, for 3 minutes or until onion is translucent. Stir in chili powder, cumin, and cinnamon and stir 1 minute. Add tomatoes, tomato sauce, and raisins and season to taste with salt and pepper. Bring to a boil and simmer, uncovered, for 15 minutes. Spread mixture in the prepared baking pan.

3. Whisk eggs, milk, and flour and season to taste with salt and pepper. Stir in corn, scallions, and cilantro. Spoon evenly over beef mixture. Cover with aluminum foil and bake, for 20 minutes. Remove foil and bake for an additional 30 minutes or until top is browned. Serve immediately.

Here's the Beef: Easy and Economical Entrées

In This Chapter

- ◆ Hearty stews with potatoes, vegetables, rice, and pasta
- ◆ Slowly braised dishes using less-expensive cuts of meat
- ◆ Beef entrées flavored with myriad herbs and spices

Some would say Americans have transferred their eating loyalty from the cow to the chicken, but beef is still an important part of our diet, and there's a whole world out there beyond the burger.

In this chapter are a number of ways to create delicious one-dish meals, primarily from less-expensive cuts of meat. Although these are not "fast food," they are all "do-ahead food."

The Benefits of Braising

Most of these dishes—and the ones that follow in the chapters for pork, lamb, and veal—fall under the generic category of "braised" food. No cuisine or culture can claim braising, although we've borrowed our English word from the French. These dishes are *sand pots* in China, *ragouts* in France, and *stews* in North America; every culture has less-tender cuts of meat—which are also usually less expensive—that are simmered in aromatic liquid for many hours until they're tender. That's what braising is all about—tenderness. And the amount of time it takes to reach the descriptive state of "fork tender" depends on each individual piece of meat. No hard-and-fast rules exist.

The process is referred to as *braising* when you're dealing with a large roast and *stewing* when the meat is in smaller cubes. *Stew* also implies that vegetables are added somewhere along the way.

Braising is a low-heat method because the meat is the same temperature as the simmering liquid, 212°F. This simmering converts the collagen of the meat's connective tissue to gelatin, so the meat is tender. There's no fear that the outside will dry out, as in high heat dry roasting, because the food is covered in the pan, which contains liquid that produces a moist heat. That's also why it takes almost as long to cook a stew, with the meat cut in small pieces, as it does to braise a large roast. The only difference is the time the meat takes to reach the same temperature as the liquid.

The tougher the piece of meat, the more connective tissue it has, so the more tender it will become while braising. Conversely, if an innately tender cut of meat such as a tenderloin or rib roast is braised, it will become tough because there is no collagen to convert.

There are a few exceptions to the rule in this chapter, and those recipes utilize sirloin tips. These ends of the sirloin steak are perfect for a quick sauté followed by a short cooking time.

Cutting the Calories

In addition to its lower cost, another benefit of braising meats is that it's possible to remove a great percentage of the saturated fat from the dish. It's easy to find and discard this "bad fat," both before and after cooking.

Fat is easy to spot on raw meat. It's the white stuff around the red stuff. Cut it off with a sharp paring knife, and you're done.

Although some fat remains in the tissue, the cooking process releases much of the saturated fat. To discard the fat …

- ◆ If you're cooking in advance and then going to refrigerate a dish, you're in luck. All the fat rises to the top and hardens when chilled. Just scrape it off and throw it away.

- ◆ The same principle of fat rising to the surface is true when food is hot, but it's a bit harder to eliminate it. Tilt the pan so the fat forms a puddle on the lower side. Then scoop it off with a soup ladle. When you're down to too little to scoop off, level the pan and blot the top with paper towels. You'll get even more fat off with this process.

Gradations of Grading

The best beef, in terms of both flavor and texture, comes from cows 18 to 24 months old. The U.S. Department of Agriculture grades beef in the United States as "prime," "choice," or "select," based on the age, color, texture, and *marbling* of the meat. Prime is the most marbled and contains the most fat, and it's usually reserved for restaurants. You'll find choice and select in your supermarket.

When you're looking at beef in the supermarket meat case, seek deep red, moist meat generously marbled with white fat. Yellow fat is a tip-off to old age. Beef is purple after it's cut, but it quickly "blooms" to bright red when it's exposed to the air. Well-aged beef is dark and dry.

To avoid paying for waste, have the meat thoroughly trimmed by a butcher. Otherwise, a low per pound price can translate into a higher cost for the edible portion.

Ellen on Edibles

Marbling is the thin streaks of fat—reminiscent of veins in marble—that run through pieces of red meat. They enhance the flavor and tenderness, but the fat is saturated. Much of it can be removed after beef is cooked.

Choice Cuts

When you go into the market, chances are you'll head for the packages of already-cut meat labeled "stewing beef." The market has done the cutting for you, but it's still a good idea to look over the meat and discard any large pieces of fat. Also, check the recipes. Because the size cubes listed in the recipes and the size you buy might be different, the meat might require additional cutting for the cooking time to remain accurate.

You can usually save money by cutting the meat into cubes yourself. The general guideline is that if the meat is less expensive, it's the cut you want, but here are some specifics:

♦ *Chuck* is the beef taken from between the neck and shoulder blades. Some chuck roasts also contain a piece of the blade bone, but it's easy to cull the meat from a chuck roast.

♦ *Round* is the general name for the large quantity of beef from the hind leg extending from the rump to the ankle. The eye of the round and the bottom round are the two least tender cuts. Reserve the top round for roasting.

♦ *Brisket* comes from the breast section under the first five ribs. The leaner piece is called the flat cut, and the fattier piece is the point cut. Brisket makes a succulent pot roast, but it's not recommended for cutting into cubes for stewing because the fibers are distinct and the meat can become stringy if cubed.

Skillet Beef Stroganoff with Mushrooms and Noodles

Serves: 6 to 8
Prep time: 15 minutes
Cook time: 20 minutes

8 oz. egg noodles

2 lb. sirloin tips, cut into 1-inch pieces, rinsed, and patted dry with paper towels

Salt and freshly ground black pepper to taste

2 TB. vegetable oil

2 TB. (¼ stick) butter

2 large shallots, peeled and diced

2 garlic cloves, peeled and minced

½ lb. white mushrooms, trimmed, wiped with a damp paper towel, and sliced

2 TB. paprika

2 TB. tomato paste

1 cup beef stock

½ cup water

2 TB. Dijon mustard

1 (1.2-oz.) pkg. dehydrated mushroom gravy mix

½ cup sour cream

Bake Lore

Beef Stroganoff was named for a nineteenth-century Russian diplomat, Count Paul Stroganoff. It was one of the dishes that became a hallmark of what Americans called "continental cuisine" many years ago.

1. Bring a large pot of salted water to a boil. Cook noodles according to the package directions. Drain and set aside.

2. Season beef with salt and pepper to taste. Heat oil in a large covered skillet over medium-high heat. Add sirloin pieces to the skillet in a single layer and cook, turning sirloin pieces with tongs, until browned on all sides. Remove sirloin pieces with a slotted spoon and set aside.

3. Melt butter in the skillet; then add shallots and garlic. Cook, stirring frequently, for 3 minutes or until shallots are translucent. Add mushrooms and cook for 3 minutes or until mushrooms are soft. Add paprika and cook, stirring constantly, for 1 minute.

4. Add tomato paste, beef stock, water, Dijon mustard, and mushroom gravy mix. Bring to a boil, whisking often. Add sirloin pieces and simmer, covered, for 5 minutes. Add sour cream and cooked noodles and cook, stirring occasionally, for 1 minute. Serve immediately.

Cuban Pot Roast in Orange Sherry Sauce with Carrots, Potatoes, and Onions

Serves: 6 to 8
Prep time: 15 minutes
Cook time: 2½ hours

3 lb. chuck roast or beef brisket, rinsed and patted dry with paper towels

Salt and freshly ground black pepper to taste

¼ cup all-purpose flour

⅓ cup olive oil

2 large onions, peeled and sliced

5 garlic cloves, peeled and minced

1 tsp. dried oregano

1 cup dry sherry

½ cup orange juice

¼ cup lime juice

1 (14.5-oz.) can beef stock

2 bay leaves

3 carrots, peeled and cut into 1-inch chunks

4 large boiling potatoes, scrubbed and cut into 1-inch dice

1. Preheat the oven to 350°F. Sprinkle roast with salt and pepper and rub it with flour, shaking off any excess.

2. Heat oil in an ovenproof Dutch oven over medium-high heat. Add chuck roast and cook, turning with tongs, until browned on all sides. Remove chuck roast with tongs and set aside.

3. Add onion and garlic to the Dutch oven. Cook, stirring frequently, for 3 minutes or until onion is translucent. Stir in oregano and cook, stirring constantly, for 1 minute. Return chuck roast to the pan and add sherry, orange juice, lime juice, beef stock, and bay leaves. Bring to a boil, cover, and place in the oven.

4. Bake for 1 hour; then turn chuck roast. Add carrots and potatoes and bake for an additional 1½ hours or until meat is tender. (You can do this up to 2 days in advance and refrigerate, tightly covered. Reheat in a 350°F oven for 30 to 40 minutes or until hot.)

5. Spoon as much grease as possible off the top of the pan, remove and discard bay leaves, transfer roast to a cutting board or serving platter, and slice. Season sauce to taste with salt and pepper. Serve immediately with sauce.

 **Got You Covered!**

Here's a tip from traditional Spanish cooking: add a wine cork or two to a braised meat dish before cooking. The cork releases enzymes that help the meat become tender.

Braised Beef with Asian Vegetables, Rice, and Spiced Chutney Sauce

Serves: 6 to 8
Prep time: 20 minutes
Cook time: 2¼ hours

2 lb. lean stewing beef, cut into 1-inch cubes, rinsed, and patted dry with paper towels

Salt and freshly ground black pepper to taste

¼ cup vegetable oil

1 onion, peeled and diced

3 garlic cloves, peeled and minced

2 tsp. curry powder

½ tsp. ground ginger

½ cup jarred mango *chutney*

⅓ cup raisins

2 (14.5-oz.) cans beef stock

1½ cups long-grain converted rice

2 carrots, peeled and cut into ⅓-inch slices on the diagonal

2 celery stalks, trimmed and cut into ⅓-inch slices on the diagonal

1 (8-oz.) can sliced water chestnuts, drained and rinsed

¼ lb. snow peas, stemmed and rinsed

3 scallions, trimmed and thinly sliced

1. Preheat the oven to 350°F. Season beef cubes with salt and pepper. Heat oil in a Dutch oven over medium-high heat. Add beef cubes to the Dutch oven in a single layer and cook, turning pieces with tongs, until browned on all sides. Remove beef cubes with a slotted spoon and set aside.

2. Add onion and garlic to the Dutch oven and cook, stirring frequently, for 3 minutes or until onion is translucent. Stir in curry powder and ginger and cook, stirring constantly, for 1 minute. Stir in chutney, raisins, and beef stock. Return beef to the pan, bring to a boil, cover, and place in the oven.

3. Bake for 1½ hours. (You can make this a day in advance and refrigerate, tightly covered. Before continuing, reheat to boiling on top of stove.)

4. Remove the Dutch oven from the oven and stir in rice, carrots, celery, and water chestnuts. Cover and bake for an additional 25 to 30 minutes or until rice is tender and liquid is absorbed. Stir in snow peas and bake for an additional 10 minutes or until snow peas are crisp-tender. Sprinkle dish with scallions and serve immediately.

Ellen on Edibles

Chutney, from the Hindi word *chatni*, is a spicy Indian condiment containing some sort of fruit or vegetable, vinegar, and spices. It's always used as an accompaniment to curried dishes, but you can also use it with many foods to add a fat-free flavor accent.

Beef Goulash with Vegetables and Egg Noodles in Hearty Paprika Sauce

2 lb. lean stewing beef, cut into 1-inch cubes, rinsed, and patted dry with paper towels

Salt and freshly ground black pepper to taste

½ cup all-purpose flour

2 TB. olive oil

2 TB. (¼ stick) butter

1 large onion, peeled and diced

3 garlic cloves, peeled and minced

5 TB. *paprika*, preferably Hungarian

2 TB. tomato paste

1 (14.5-oz.) can beef stock

2 tsp. caraway seeds

2 carrots, peeled and cut into 1-inch chunks

1 (10-oz.) pkg. frozen cut green beans, thawed

1 cup sour cream

8 oz. medium egg noodles, cooked according to package directions

3 TB. chopped fresh dill

Serves: 6 to 8	
Prep time: 15 minutes	
Cook time: 2 hours	

1. Season beef cubes with salt and pepper. Pour flour into a resealable plastic bag, add beef cubes, seal, and toss to coat. Remove beef cubes and shake off any excess. Heat oil and butter in a Dutch oven over medium-high heat until butter is melted. Add beef cubes to the Dutch oven in a single layer and cook, turning pieces with tongs, until browned on all sides. Remove beef cubes with a slotted spoon and set aside.

2. Add onion and garlic to the Dutch oven and cook, stirring frequently, for 3 minutes or until onion is translucent. Stir in paprika and cook for 1 minute, stirring constantly. Stir in tomato paste, beef stock, and caraway seeds. Bring to a boil, stirring occasionally, over medium-high heat.

3. Return beef to Dutch oven and add carrots. Cover pan and simmer beef for 1 hour 50 minutes or until beef is tender. Add green beans and simmer for an additional 10 minutes. Stir in sour cream and allow mixture to heat, but do not let liquid boil. To serve, spoon beef on top of hot noodles and sprinkle with dill.

Ellen on Edibles

Paprika is a powder made by grinding aromatic sweet red pepper pods several times. The color can vary from deep red to bright orange, and the flavor can range from mild to pungent and hot. Hungarian cuisine is characterized by paprika as a flavoring, and Hungarian paprika is considered the best of all paprika products.

Beef, Wild Mushroom, and Barley Casserole

Serves: 6 to 8
Prep time: 25 minutes
Cook time: 2 hours

2 (14.5-oz.) cans beef stock

½ oz. dried porcini or other wild European mushroom

2 lb. lean stewing beef, cut into 1-inch cubes, rinsed, and patted dry with paper towels

Salt and freshly ground black pepper to taste

3 TB. olive oil

1 onion, peeled and diced

2 garlic cloves, peeled and minced

½ lb. fresh crimini mushrooms, stems removed, wiped with a damp paper towel, and sliced

½ lb. fresh portobello mushrooms, stems removed, peeled with gills scraped out and caps diced

1 carrot, peeled and diced

3 TB. chopped fresh parsley

1 TB. fresh thyme or 1 tsp. dried

1 bay leaf

1 cup pearl *barley*, rinsed well

¼ cup grated Parmesan cheese

Ellen on Edibles

Barley is the grain that is malted to make beer and whiskey and dates back to the Stone Age. For cooking, the barley has been refined to pearl barley, which has had the husk removed and been steamed and polished. It comes in coarse, medium, and fine sizes, all of which cook at about the same rate. Be sure to rinse the barley before cooking.

1. Preheat the oven to 350°F. Bring beef stock to a boil in a small saucepan over high heat. Add dried mushrooms and remove from heat. Allow mushrooms to sit in liquid for 15 minutes; then drain, reserving beef stock. Finely chop mushrooms. Set aside mushrooms and stock.

2. Season beef cubes with salt and pepper. Heat oil in an oven-proof Dutch oven over medium-high heat. Add beef cubes to the Dutch oven and cook until browned on all sides. Remove beef cubes and set aside.

3. Add onion and garlic to the Dutch oven and cook, stirring frequently, for 3 minutes or until onion is translucent. Add crimini mushrooms, portobello mushrooms, and carrot. Cook, stirring frequently, for 3 minutes. Add beef cubes, reserved beef stock and dried porcini mushrooms, parsley, thyme, and bay leaf. Bring to a boil, cover, place in the oven, and bake for 1 hour.

4. Remove the Dutch oven from the oven and stir in pearl barley. Bake for an additional 1 to 1¼ hours or until beef and barley are tender and liquid has been absorbed. Remove and discard bay leaf, stir in Parmesan cheese, and season to taste with salt and pepper.

Beef Braised in Red Wine with Potatoes and Vegetables (Boeuf Bourguignon)

2 lb. lean stewing beef, cut into 1-inch cubes, rinsed, and patted dry with paper towels

Salt and freshly ground black pepper to taste

½ cup all-purpose flour

¼ cup olive oil

2 TB. (¼ stick) butter

1 large onion, peeled and diced

3 garlic cloves, peeled and minced

½ lb. small white mushrooms, trimmed, wiped clean with a damp paper towel, and halved, if large

2 cups dry red wine

1 cup beef stock

2 TB. tomato paste

2 TB. chopped fresh parsley

2 tsp. herbes de Provence

1 bay leaf

2 carrots, peeled and cut into 1-inch chunks

1½ lb. baby red potatoes, scrubbed, or small red potatoes, scrubbed and cut into quarters

Serves: 6 to 8
Prep time: 25 minutes
Cook time: 2 hours

1. Preheat the oven to 350°F. Season beef cubes with salt and pepper. Pour flour into a resealable plastic bag, add beef cubes, seal, and toss to coat. Remove beef and shake off any excess. Heat oil and butter in a Dutch oven over medium-high heat until butter is melted. Add beef to the Dutch oven in a single layer and cook, turning pieces with tongs, until browned on all sides. Remove beef with a slotted spoon and set aside.

2. Add onion and garlic to the Dutch oven and cook, stirring frequently, for 3 minutes or until onion is translucent. Add white mushrooms and cook for 2 minutes more. Add red wine, beef stock, tomato paste, parsley, herbes de Provence, and bay leaf. Stir well, add beef cubes, and bring to a boil. Cover, place in the oven, and bake for 1 hour.

3. Remove the Dutch oven from the oven, add carrots and potatoes, and cook for an additional 1½ hours or until beef and potatoes are tender. Spoon off as much fat as possible from the surface, remove and discard bay leaf, and serve immediately. (You can do this up to 2 days in advance and refrigerate, tightly covered. Reheat in a 350°F oven for 30 minutes or until hot.)

Got You Covered!

Coating food with flour before browning it accomplishes a number of purposes. On one hand, it creates a thin brown skin, and the frying cooks the flour particles. The finished sauce is also lightly thickened from the flour, but with no lingering "flour-y" taste.

Indonesian Short Ribs of Beef with Root Vegetables and Basmati Rice

Serves: 6 to 8
Prep time: 20 minutes
Cook time: 3 hours

6 lb. meaty short ribs of beef, cut into 3-inch lengths, rinsed, and patted dry with paper towels

Salt and freshly ground black pepper to taste

¼ cup vegetable oil

3 large onions, peeled and roughly diced

4 garlic cloves, peeled and minced

1 large jalapeño chili, seeds and ribs removed, finely chopped

3 TB. fresh grated ginger

2 TB. ground coriander

1 TB. ground turmeric

2 stalks fresh lemongrass, trimmed to 3 inches and crushed

3 cups light coconut milk

2 cups beef stock

2 carrots, peeled and cut into 1-inch chunks

2 parsnips, peeled and cut into 1-inch chunks

1 celery root, peeled and cut into 1-inch dice

3 cups cooked basmati rice

Half Baked

It's important to pat meat very dry with paper towels because wet—or even overly damp—meat will not brown properly. Also, as is the case with chicken, it's important not to crowd the pan with too much food at once.

1. Preheat the oven to 350°F. Sprinkle short ribs with salt and pepper. Heat oil in a Dutch oven over medium-high heat. Add short ribs to the Dutch oven in a single layer and cook, turning pieces with tongs, until browned on all sides. Remove short ribs with tongs and set aside.

2. Add onion, garlic, and jalapeño chili to the Dutch oven and cook, stirring frequently, for 3 minutes or until onion is translucent. Add ginger, coriander, and turmeric and cook, stirring constantly, for 1 minute. Add short ribs, lemongrass, coconut milk, and beef stock. Bring to a boil, cover, place in the oven, and bake for 1 hour.

3. Remove the Dutch oven from the oven and add carrots, parsnips, and celery root. Bake for an additional 1¾ hours or until short ribs and vegetables are tender. Remove and discard lemongrass and spoon as much fat as possible off the surface of the dish. (You can do this up to 2 days in advance and refrigerate, tightly covered. Reheat in a 350°F oven for 30 minutes or until hot.) Stir in rice and bake for 15 to 20 minutes. Serve immediately.

Reuben Sandwich Bake with Sauerkraut and Swiss Cheese

1 (2-lb.) pkg. sauerkraut

5 TB. butter

1 small onion, peeled and diced

2 tsp. caraway seeds

3 cups shredded Swiss cheese

1⅓ cups bottled Thousand Island salad dressing

1 lb. thinly sliced cooked corned beef, coarsely chopped

6 slices rye bread, cut horizontally into 1-inch strips

Serves: 6 to 8
Prep time: 10 minutes
Cook time: 35 minutes

1. Preheat the oven to 375°F. Grease a 9×13-inch baking pan. Place sauerkraut in a colander and press with the back of a spoon to extract as much liquid as possible. Rinse sauerkraut under cold running water for 2 minutes. Then place sauerkraut in a large mixing bowl and fill bowl with cold water. Soak sauerkraut for 5 minutes.

2. While sauerkraut is soaking, heat butter in a small skillet over medium-high heat until melted. Pour off and reserve 3 tablespoons butter.

3. Add onion to remaining butter and cook, stirring frequently, for 3 minutes. Drain sauerkraut in a colander again, pressing with the back of a spoon to extract as much liquid as possible. Place sauerkraut in the prepared baking pan and top with onions and caraway seeds.

4. Layer with ½ Swiss cheese, ½ Thousand Island dressing, and corned beef. Then layer with remaining Thousand Island dressing and Swiss cheese. (You can make this up to 2 days in advance and refrigerate, tightly covered. Add 10 minutes to initial bake time if chilled.) Brush bread strips with reserved melted butter. Place bread strips on top of Swiss cheese.

5. Cover with aluminum foil and bake for 10 minutes. Remove foil and bake for an additional 25 minutes or until bread is browned and cheese is melted. Serve immediately.

 Bake Lore

Although now defunct, Reuben's Delicatessen was a New York institution that opened in the late 1890s. Legend has it that owner Arthur Reuben invented the Reuben sandwich there in 1914 for the cast of a Charlie Chaplin film. It contains sauerkraut, corned beef, Swiss cheese, and Russian dressing, and it's served grilled on seeded rye bread.

Caribbean Beef with Vegetables, Rice, and Toasted Peanuts in Spiced Rum Sauce

Serves: 6 to 8
Prep time: 15 minutes
Cook time: 30 minutes

2 lb. sirloin tips, cut into 1-inch pieces, rinsed, and patted dry with paper towels

Salt and freshly ground black pepper to taste

1 tsp. ground ginger

4 TB. vegetable oil

1 large onion, peeled and chopped

4 garlic cloves, peeled and minced

1 red bell pepper, seeds and ribs removed, cut into thin slices

1 green bell pepper, seeds and ribs removed, cut into thin slices

1 yellow bell pepper, seeds and ribs removed, cut into thin slices

1 large jalapeño pepper, seeds and ribs removed, finely chopped

1½ cups long-grain rice

2 TB. minced fresh ginger

3 TB. tomato paste

1 TB. molasses

2 (14.5-oz.) cans beef stock

¼ cup pimiento-stuffed olives, sliced

3 medium tomatoes, cored, seeded, and cut into ¾-inch dice

3 TB. fresh lime juice

½ cup dark rum

½ cup chopped fresh cilantro

½ cup coarsely chopped salted peanuts (not dry roasted)

Got You Covered!

Green bell peppers are always available and most always are cheaper than colored bell peppers. The green bell peppers are merely immature peppers picked before they turn color. They are less expensive because they are not as perishable in this young condition and are easier to transport. The flavor is not as sweet, however.

1. Sprinkle sirloin pieces with salt, pepper, and ground ginger. Heat oil in a large skillet over medium-high heat. Add sirloin pieces and cook until browned on all sides. Remove sirloin pieces and set aside.

2. Add onion, garlic, red bell pepper, green bell pepper, yellow bell pepper, and jalapeño pepper and cook, stirring frequently, for 3 minutes or until onion is translucent. Add rice and cook for 2 minutes, stirring frequently.

3. Stir in fresh ginger, tomato paste, molasses, beef stock, olives, tomatoes, lime juice, and rum. Bring to a boil, cover, reduce heat to low, and simmer, stirring occasionally, for 15 minutes or until rice is almost tender.

4. Stir in sirloin pieces and simmer for 10 minutes or until beef is medium-rare. Season to taste with salt and pepper and arrange mixture on plates. Sprinkle with cilantro and peanuts and serve immediately.

Mexican Beef with Black Beans, Corn, and Rice in Chipotle Sauce

Serves: 6 to 8	
Prep time: 15 minutes	
Cook time: 2 hours	

2 lb. lean stewing beef, cut into 1-inch cubes, rinsed, and patted dry with paper towels

Salt and freshly ground black pepper to taste

¼ cup olive oil

1 large onion, peeled and diced

3 garlic cloves, peeled and minced

1 tsp. ground cumin

1 tsp. dried oregano, preferably Mexican

1 to 2 chipotle chilies in adobo sauce, finely chopped, sauce reserved

2 (14.5-oz.) cans beef stock

1 (14-oz.) can diced tomatoes, undrained

1½ cups long-grain rice

1 (15-oz.) can black beans, drained and rinsed

1 (10-oz.) pkg. frozen corn, thawed

¼ cup sliced pimientos, drained and rinsed

1. Preheat the oven to 350°F. Season beef cubes with salt and pepper. Heat oil in an ovenproof Dutch oven over medium-high heat. Add beef cubes to the Dutch oven in a single layer and cook, turning pieces with tongs, until browned on all sides. Remove beef cubes with a slotted spoon and set aside.

2. Add onion and garlic to the pan and cook, stirring frequently, for 3 minutes or until onion is translucent. Add cumin and oregano and cook, stirring constantly, for 1 minute. Add beef cubes, chipotles and 1 tablespoon reserved adobo sauce, beef stock, and tomatoes. Bring to a boil, cover, and bake for 1½ hours. (You can do this a day in advance and refrigerate, tightly covered. Before continuing, reheat to boiling on top of stove.)

3. Remove the Dutch oven from the oven and stir in rice, beans, corn, and pimientos. Return the Dutch oven to the oven and cook for 30 to 35 minutes or until rice is tender and liquid is absorbed. Season to taste with salt and pepper and serve immediately.

 **Got You Covered!**

Mexican oregano is widely available in the Hispanic section of supermarkets and in Hispanic grocery stores. It has a more pungent aroma and flavor than its Mediterranean cousin, although both are part of the mint family. If using Mediterranean oregano, you might want to increase the amount by 20 percent to achieve the same vibrant flavor.

Porky Pleasures: Recipes Featuring Pork, Ham, and Sausage

In This Chapter

- ◆ One-dish cover and bake dinners from around the world
- ◆ Old-fashioned classics like pork and beans and macaroni and cheese with ham
- ◆ Leftover baked ham? No problem

One little piggy might have gone to market, but lots of little and big piggies end up in pans as stews each year, especially now that the "other white meat" has shed its bad rep of being fatty.

Pork is leaner and faster to cook than beef or lamb, and its delicate flavor offers countless flavoring options. Here, you'll discover many creative ways to utilize cuts of pork, as well as options for its first cousins, ham and sausage.

Pork's Updated Image

Fresh pork makes up only one third of the pork supply and comes primarily from the loin and front shoulder. The remaining two thirds is sold as prepared meats such as ham, bacon, hot dogs, and sausage.

All cuts of pork are relatively tender and have no official grading system as beef has. As of 1986, the U.S. Department of Agriculture (USDA) stopped inspecting fresh pork for *Trichinella spiralis* because none had been found for more than 50 years. A change resulting from no fear of bacteria is that although pork is cooked to a higher internal temperature than beef and lamb are, you no longer need to cook it to 180°F, at which time it goes beyond well done to dried out.

Recent studies of randomly selected pork cuts from leading supermarkets in 15 U.S. cities have shown that today's pork is 31 percent lower in fat, 17 percent lower in calories, and 10 percent lower in cholesterol than in 1983. In addition, more than 60 percent of the fat in pork is unsaturated. This compares favorably with beef and lamb, which are 52 percent and 44 percent unsaturated, respectively.

Professionals attribute the reduction of fat content, the other side of which is a higher protein count, in part to improvements in the breeding and feeding of pigs. Retailers are also trimming fat more closely from pork cuts, so consumers are getting more lean meat for their dollar.

Picking Pretty Pork

Look for pork that is a pale grayish-pink. It should feel firm and smooth and look fresh, and the bones should be red, rather than white. The whiter the bones, the older the animal from which the meat was taken.

A significant amount of liquid in the package indicates that a good deal of moisture has been lost and the meat may be dry and tough. Avoid meat that feels slimy or has an off color or unpleasant smell.

Parts to Ponder

Almost all cuts of pork are inherently tender, because pigs don't create tough muscles running around the prairies like cows and lambs do. So unlike a chuck roast that must be braised so the collagen in the muscles converts to gelatin, almost all cuts of pork can be dry-roasted if desired. One exception is the pork shoulder, which is more muscular and fatty than the loin, tenderloin, or leg. Shoulder roasts should always be cooked with liquid.

Pork has layers of fat that encircle the meat rather than marbling it. Leave some fat so the meat does not dry out when cooking.

With the exception of the tenderloin, which will become stringy if subjected to long, slow cooking, almost all cuts of pork are up for grabs. That's why you don't find precut pork for stews the way other animals' trimmings are packaged. Just choose pork that looks lean and is the least expensive.

One warning regarding spare ribs is in order: spare ribs are great on the grill, but use only the boneless country ribs for braised dishes because the percentage of bone to meat is so great that ribs require far too much liquid to cook.

Hamming It Up

Ham is actually a cut and not a type of meat. It comes from a hog's hind leg from the shank bone to the hip bone. Most ham, save fresh ham, is cured or smoked in some fashion. Such popular foods as Italian prosciutto or Virginia's prized Smithfield hams are not actually cooked at all. They are cured and their texture changes, like acidulating fish for ceviche.

Just as the recipes in Chapter 9 are a panacea for leftover poultry, in this chapter, you'll find some creative ways to use leftover baked ham that don't involve a pot of pea soup. But while turkey is still turkey after the skin is removed, depending on how the ham was treated, it might require some attention. If the ham has been baked with a brown sugar glaze, it's best to cut off the outside portion that's been flavored by the glaze. You can save it for baked beans.

The Sausage Solution

Sausage comes in many varieties, but they are all basically the same thing: ground meat and seasonings. The differences come from the kind of meat used, whether or not fat is added, and the kind of seasonings and other ingredients added as well. Sausages can be fresh, cured, or smoked, and also can be uncooked, partially cooked, or fully cooked. They can be in a casing or not, and they may or may not be frozen.

Braised Ribs with Asian Vegetables, Jasmine Rice, and Spicy Garlic Sauce

Serves: 6 to 8
Prep time: 10 minutes
Cook time: 1 hour, 25 minutes

Got You Covered!

You probably have noticed that recipes in this book take you to different stages of cooking before a dish can be successfully reheated. This is determined by which foods are sturdy and which foods are more delicate. In this case, the delicate vegetables would become colorless and devoid of texture if they were cooled and then reheated. That's what gives leftover Asian food its unappealing appearance. Vegetables such as potatoes and carrots can be reheated successfully after they're fully cooked; snow peas cannot.

5 TB. fermented black beans, not rinsed and finely chopped

10 garlic cloves, peeled and minced

¼ cup soy sauce

2 TB. firmly packed light brown sugar

1 (14.5-oz.) can chicken stock

3 TB. sesame oil

1 tsp. dried red pepper flakes

4 scallions, trimmed with all but 2 inches of green tops discarded, thinly sliced

2 lb. boneless country ribs, cut into 2-inch pieces, rinsed, and patted dry with paper towels

4 stalks bok choy, rinsed and patted dry on paper towels, trimmed and cut on the diagonal into ½-inch pieces

¼ lb. snow peas, stemmed and rinsed

1 red bell pepper, seeds and ribs removed, cut into thin strips

3 cups cooked jasmine rice

1. Combine fermented black beans, garlic, soy sauce, brown sugar, and chicken stock in a mixing bowl and stir well. Heat sesame oil in a large, deep skillet over medium-high heat. Add dried red pepper flakes and scallions and cook, stirring constantly, for 30 seconds. Add ribs to the skillet in a single layer and cook, turning pieces with tongs, until browned on all sides. Add black bean mixture and bring to a boil. Cover, reduce heat to low, and simmer ribs, stirring occasionally, for 1 to 1½ hours or until tender. (You can do this up to 2 days in advance and refrigerate, tightly covered. Before continuing, reheat over low heat until simmering.)

2. Add bok choy, snow peas, and red bell pepper and cook for 10 minutes or until vegetables are crisp-tender. Stir in rice and cook for 3 to 5 minutes or until rice is hot. Serve immediately.

Caribbean Braised Ribs with Mango, Pineapple, and Rice

2 lb. boneless country pork ribs, cut into 2-inch pieces, rinsed, and patted dry with paper towels

Salt and freshly ground black pepper to taste

4 TB. vegetable oil

1 small onion, peeled and diced

3 garlic cloves, peeled and minced

1 TB. curry powder

1½ cups pineapple juice

1 (14.5-oz.) can chicken stock

⅓ cup bottled mango chutney

½ cup long-grain rice

4 cups diced (½-inch) fresh pineapple

1 (10-oz.) pkg. frozen peas, thawed

Serves: 6 to 8
Prep time: 15 minutes
Cook time: 1½ hours

1. Preheat the oven to 350°F. Sprinkle ribs with salt and pepper. Heat oil in an ovenproof Dutch oven over medium-high heat. Add ribs in a single layer and cook, turning pieces with tongs, until browned on all sides. Remove ribs with a slotted spoon and set aside.

2. Add onion and garlic to the Dutch oven and cook, stirring frequently, for 3 minutes or until onion is translucent. Stir in curry powder and cook, stirring constantly, for 1 minute. Add ribs, pineapple juice, chicken stock, and mango chutney and bring to a boil. Cover, place in the oven, and bake for 1 hour.

3. Add rice and pineapple. Bake for an additional 20 minutes or until rice has almost absorbed liquid. Add peas and bake an additional 10 minutes. Serve immediately.

Half Baked

This recipe specifies fresh pineapple because it is the most tender and has not been processed. Canned pineapple is acceptable, but only if the pineapple is packed in juice and not syrup. The syrup would make this dish overly sweet.

Pork Chops with Braised Red Cabbage, Apples, and Onion

Serves: 6 to 8
Prep time: 15 minutes
Cook time: 40 minutes

1 (2-lb.) head red cabbage, cored and shredded

2 TB. red wine vinegar

2 TB. granulated sugar

6 to 8 boneless pork loin chops, trimmed of fat, rinsed, and patted dry with paper towels

Salt and freshly ground black pepper to taste

3 TB. butter

1 onion, peeled and chopped

2 McIntosh or Golden Delicious apples, peeled and sliced

1 cup dry red wine

1 cup chicken stock

1 (3-in.) cinnamon stick

1 bay leaf

⅓ cup red currant jelly

3 cups mashed potatoes, homemade or purchased

1. Place cabbage in a large bowl. Sprinkle with vinegar and sugar and toss.

2. Sprinkle pork chops with salt and pepper. Melt butter in a Dutch oven over medium-high heat. Add pork chops in a single layer and cook, turning with tongs, until browned on all sides. Remove pork chops with a slotted spoon and set aside.

3. Add onion and apples and cook, stirring frequently, for 3 minutes or until onion is translucent. Add red wine, chicken stock, cinnamon stick, and bay leaf. Bring to a boil and stir in cabbage with any juices from the bowl.

4. Add pork chops and cover them in cabbage, cover the Dutch oven, and cook over low heat for 30 to 45 minutes or until cabbage is tender. Remove pork chops and set aside. Remove and discard cinnamon stick and bay leaf and stir jelly into cabbage. Cook, uncovered, over medium heat for 10 minutes or until liquid reduces in volume and becomes syrupy. Return pork chops to the Dutch oven and heat through. (You can do this up to 2 days in advance and refrigerate, tightly covered. Reheat over low heat until simmering.) Serve chops and cabbage with mashed potatoes.

Bake Lore

Cabbage is one of the oldest vegetables in history, although its stature has ranged from lowly to esteemed, depending on the culture. Greek philosopher Diogenes remarked to a young man, "If you lived on cabbage, you would not be obliged to flatter the powerful." The young man's retort was, "If you flattered the powerful, you would not be obliged to live on cabbage."

Pork Chops, Pinto Beans, Corn, and Rice in Tomatillo Sauce

6 to 8 boneless pork loin chops, trimmed of fat, rinsed, and patted dry with paper towels

Salt and freshly ground black pepper to taste

6 *tomatillos*, husked, cored, and cut into chunks

1 (14.5-oz.) can chicken stock

3 TB. vegetable oil

1 onion, peeled and chopped

3 garlic cloves, peeled and minced

2 TB. chili powder

1 TB. ground cumin

1 (8-oz.) can tomato sauce

1 TB. granulated sugar

1½ cups long-grain rice

1 zucchini, trimmed and thinly sliced

1 (15-oz.) can pinto beans, drained and rinsed

1 (10-oz.) pkg. frozen corn, thawed

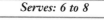

Serves: 6 to 8
Prep time: 15 minutes
Cook time: 1½ hours

1. Preheat the oven to 350°F. Sprinkle pork chops with salt and pepper. Combine tomatillos and chicken stock in a food processor fitted with a steel blade or in a blender. Purée until smooth and set aside.

2. Heat oil in an ovenproof Dutch oven over medium-high heat. Add pork chops in a single layer and cook, turning with tongs, until browned on all sides. Remove pork chops with a slotted spoon and set aside.

3. Add onion and garlic to the Dutch oven and cook, stirring frequently, for 3 minutes or until onion is translucent. Stir in chili powder and cumin and cook, stirring constantly, for 1 minute. Add tomatillo mixture, tomato sauce, and sugar and bring to a boil. Add pork chops, cover, place in the oven, and bake for 1 hour.

4. Remove the Dutch oven from the oven and add rice, zucchini, pinto beans, and corn. Bake for an additional 30 minutes or until rice has absorbed liquid. Serve immediately.

Ellen on Edibles

Tomatillos (pronounced *tohm-aah-TEE-os*), popular in Mexican and Southwestern cooking, are covered in a thin, parchmentlike husk that must be pulled off and discarded before cooking. You can use these raw in salsa, but their distinctive tangy flavor with hints of lemon and herbs is released when they are cooked. Choose firm tomatillos with tight-fitting husks and rinse them well before dicing or cooking.

Pork and Old-Fashioned Boston Baked Beans

Serves: 6 to 8
Prep time: 15 minutes, plus minimum of 1 hour for soaking beans
Cook time: 3½ hours

1 lb. dried small navy beans, rinsed and picked over to remove broken beans or pebbles

½ lb. bacon, cut into ½-inch pieces

1 lb. pork loin, cut into ½-inch cubes, rinsed, and patted dry with paper towels

Salt and freshly ground black pepper to taste

1 large red onion, peeled and diced

2 garlic cloves, peeled and minced

6 cups water

1 cup ketchup

⅓ cup pure maple syrup

¼ cup cider vinegar

¼ cup firmly packed dark brown sugar

3 TB. dried mustard powder

1. Place beans in a large saucepan and fill the pot with cold water. Soak beans for 8 to 12 hours; then drain and continue. Or bring beans to a boil, cover, and allow to sit for 1 hour and then drain. Whichever soaking method you use, begin cooking beans as soon as possible after soaking.

2. Preheat the oven to 350°F. Place bacon in an ovenproof Dutch oven over medium-high heat and cook until crisp. Remove bacon with a slotted spoon and set aside. Sprinkle pork cubes with salt and pepper. Add pork cubes in a single layer and cook, turning pieces with tongs, until browned on all sides. Remove pork cubes with a slotted spoon and set aside.

3. Add red onion and garlic to the Dutch oven and cook, stirring frequently, for 3 minutes or until onion is translucent. Add pork cubes, beans, water, ketchup, maple syrup, vinegar, brown sugar, and mustard powder. Bring to a boil, cover, place in the oven, and bake for 1 hour.

4. Uncover, stir, and bake for an additional 2½ to 3 hours or until beans are very tender and sauce is thickened. Serve immediately. (You can do this up to 2 days in advance and refrigerate, tightly covered. Reheat, covered, in a 350°F oven for 25 to 40 minutes or until hot.)

 Bake Lore

Boston baked beans are so interwoven into the city's history that the city is still known as "Beantown." During the Colonial era, the Puritans would bake beans on Saturday and serve them for dinner that night and again for lunch on Sunday because no cooking was allowed on the Sabbath.

Pork Chops with Carrots, Parsnips, and Citrus-Glazed Sweet Potatoes

6 to 8 boneless loin pork chops, trimmed, rinsed, and patted dry with paper towels

Salt and freshly ground black pepper to taste

2 TB. vegetable oil

3 to 4 large yams or sweet potatoes, peeled and cut into ½-inch slices

3 carrots, peeled and thinly sliced

2 parsnips, peeled and thinly sliced

¾ cup (1½ sticks) butter, melted

1½ cups firmly packed dark brown sugar

3 navel oranges, peeled and trimmed of white pith, seeded and thinly sliced

2 lemons, peeled and trimmed of white pith, seeded and thinly sliced

¼ cup Grand Marnier or Cointreau or other orange liqueur (optional)

Serves: 6 to 8
Prep time: 15 minutes
Cook time: 1½ hours

1. Preheat the oven to 400°F. Grease a 10×14-inch baking pan. Sprinkle pork chops with salt and pepper. Heat oil in a skillet over medium-high heat. Add pork chops in a single layer and cook, turning pieces with tongs, until browned on all sides. Remove pork chops with tongs and set aside.

2. Layer ½ yam, carrot, and parsnip slices in the prepared baking pan. Combine melted butter and brown sugar and set aside.

3. Spread vegetables with ½ butter mixture. Top with ½ orange and lemon slices. Top with remaining vegetables, butter mixture, and fruit. Arrange chops on top of second layer and pour Grand Marnier over top (if using).

4. Cover with aluminum foil and bake for 45 minutes. Remove foil, baste chops with juices from the pan, and bake for an additional 15 to 25 minutes or until vegetables can be easily pierced with a knife and liquid has thickened into a glaze. (You can do this up to 2 days ahead and refrigerate, tightly covered. Reheat, covered with foil, in a 350°F oven for 15 to 25 minutes or until hot.) Serve immediately.

 **Got You Covered!**

What's the difference between yams and sweet potatoes? For the sake of cooking, the two are almost identical. Yams have a higher moisture content than sweet potatoes, so if you're using sweet potatoes for this dish, you might want to add a few extra tablespoons orange juice. On the other hand, sweet potatoes are higher in vitamins A and C than yams.

New Mexican Pork and Hominy Stew (*Pozole*)

2 lb. lean pork, cut into 1-inch cubes, rinsed, and patted dry with paper towels

Salt and freshly ground black pepper to taste

3 TB. vegetable oil

1 large onion, peeled and diced

3 garlic cloves, peeled and minced

2 tsp. ground cumin

2 tsp. dried oregano, preferably Mexican

1 (14.5-oz.) can chicken stock

1 (14.5-oz.) can diced tomatoes, undrained

1 (4-oz.) can diced mild green chilies, drained

3 (15-oz.) cans yellow hominy, drained and rinsed well

1 (10-oz.) pkg. frozen corn, thawed

1 (10-oz.) pkg. frozen cut green beans, thawed

4 scallions, trimmed with all but 2 inches of green tops discarded and thinly sliced

¼ cup chopped fresh cilantro

Sour cream

Lime wedges

 **Got You Covered!**

Pork is much more delicate in flavor and lighter in color than beef or lamb, so use chicken stock rather than beef stock for pork dishes, because beef stock would darken the delicate color and overpower the subtle flavor. Pork is rarely, if ever, made into a stock on its own, although smoked ham bones can be used to flavor stocks and soups.

1. Preheat the oven to 350°F. Sprinkle pork cubes with salt and pepper. Heat oil in an ovenproof Dutch oven over medium-high heat. Add pork cubes in a single layer and cook, turning pieces with tongs, until browned on all sides. Remove pork cubes with tongs and set aside.

2. Add onion and garlic to the Dutch oven and cook, stirring frequently, for 3 minutes or until onion is translucent. Stir in cumin and oregano and cook, stirring constantly, for 1 minute. Add pork cubes, chicken stock, tomatoes, and green chilies. Bring to a boil, cover, place in the oven, and bake for 1 hour. Add hominy and bake for 30 minutes.

3. Add corn, green beans, and scallions and bake an additional 30 minutes or until pork is very tender. (You can do this up to 2 days ahead and refrigerate, tightly covered. Reheat, covered with foil, in a 350°F oven for 15 to 25 minutes or until hot.) Sprinkle with cilantro and serve immediately, passing bowls of sour cream and lime wedges.

Brazilian Mixed Pork Stew with Black Beans (*Feijoada*)

1 lb. dried black beans, rinsed and picked over to remove broken beans or pebbles

½ lb. kielbasa or other smoked sausage, cut into 1-inch pieces

½ lb. chorizo sausage, cut into 1-inch pieces

½ lb. bratwurst, cut into 1-inch slices

½ lb. ham steak, trimmed of fat and cut into 1-inch pieces

3 large onions, peeled and diced

5 garlic cloves, peeled and minced

1 red bell pepper, seeds and ribs removed, chopped

5 cups water

3 navel oranges, rinsed, 1 cut into quarters

3 bay leaves

Salt and freshly ground black pepper to taste

1 lb. shredded cabbage

2 TB. (¼ stick) butter

3 to 4 cups cooked rice, hot

Serves: 6 to 8
Prep time: 30 minutes plus a minimum of 1 hour for soaking beans
Cook time: 1½ hours

1. Place beans in a large saucepan and fill with cold water. Soak beans for 8 to 12 hours; then drain and continue. Or bring beans to a boil, cover, and allow to sit for 1 hour; then drain.

2. Place kielbasa, chorizo, bratwurst, and ham in a Dutch oven over medium-high heat. Cook, stirring frequently, until sausages are browned. Remove meat with a slotted spoon and set aside. Add onions, garlic, and red bell pepper. Cook, stirring frequently, for 3 minutes or until onion is translucent. Add beans and meats to the Dutch oven and add water, orange quarters, and bay leaves. Bring to a boil, cover, reduce heat, and simmer for 1½ hours or until beans are tender. Remove and discard orange quarters and bay leaves.

3. While stew is simmering, bring a large pot of salted water to a boil over high heat. Add cabbage and boil for 5 minutes. Drain, pressing with the back of a spoon to extract as much liquid as possible. Melt butter in a skillet over medium heat. Add cabbage and cook, stirring occasionally, for 5 to 10 minutes. Season to taste with salt and pepper and keep warm.

4. Transfer 1 cup beans and ½ cup cooking liquid to a food processor fitted with a steel blade or to a blender. Purée until smooth and stir mixture back into the Dutch oven. Season to taste with salt and pepper. Serve over rice with cabbage.

Half Baked

Start cooking beans as soon as they are done soaking because bacteria can grow in warm or even room-temperature water and the beans will begin to ferment. Also, be sure the beans are cooked to the proper consistency before adding any acidic ingredients, such as tomatoes or lemon. The acid prevents the beans from becoming tender.

Baked Macaroni and Cheese with Ham

Serves: 6 to 8
Prep time: 15 minutes
Cook time: 30 minutes

1 lb. elbow macaroni

4 TB. (½ stick) butter

4 TB. all-purpose flour

1 tsp. paprika

¼ tsp. cayenne

1 cup chicken stock

2 cups whole milk

1 lb. grated sharp cheddar cheese

1 TB. Dijon mustard

Salt and freshly ground black pepper to taste

1 lb. ham steak, trimmed of fat and cut into ½-inch cubes

1. Preheat the oven to 400°F. Grease a 10×14-inch baking pan. Bring a large pot of salted water to a boil. Add macaroni and cook according to package directions until al dente. Drain and set aside.

2. Melt butter in a saucepan over low heat. Stir in flour, paprika, and cayenne and stir constantly for 2 minutes. Whisk in chicken stock and bring to a boil over medium-high heat, whisking constantly. Reduce heat to low and simmer for 2 minutes. Stir in whole milk and all but ½ cup grated cheese, stirring until cheese is melted. Stir in mustard and season to taste with salt and pepper.

3. Stir ham and macaroni into sauce and transfer mixture to the prepared baking pan. Cover with aluminum foil and bake for 10 minutes. Remove foil, sprinkle with remaining cheese, and bake for an additional 15 to 20 minutes or until bubbly. Allow to sit for 5 minutes; then serve.

 **Got You Covered!**

You can vary this dish by substituting any cooked poultry for the ham. Or transform it into a vegetarian dish by omitting the ham. If you're serving this as a side dish, it will serve 8 to 10 people.

Ham, Potatoes, and Leek Gratin

2 TB. (¼ stick) butter

4 TB. all-purpose flour

1½ cups milk

1½ cups grated Gruyère cheese

Salt and freshly ground black pepper to taste

6 large russet potatoes, peeled and thinly sliced

2 leeks, trimmed with all but 1 inch of light green tops discarded, thinly sliced, and rinsed well

1 (2-oz.) jar sliced pimientos, drained

1 lb. thickly sliced smoked ham

Serves: 6 to 8
Prep time: 15 minutes
Cook time: 1 hour 5 minutes

1. Preheat the oven to 350°F. Grease a 10×14-inch baking pan. Melt butter in a saucepan over low heat. Stir in flour and stir constantly for 2 minutes. Whisk in milk and bring to a boil over medium-high heat, whisking constantly. Reduce heat to low and simmer for 2 minutes. Stir in 1 cup grated Gruyère cheese, stirring until cheese is melted. Season to taste with salt and pepper and set aside.

2. Arrange ⅓ potato slices in pan and top with ⅓ leeks and ⅓ pimientos. Add a layer of ½ ham slices and top with ⅓ sauce. Repeat with a second layer and end with a layer of just vegetables and sauce.

3. Cover with aluminum foil and bake 35 minutes. Remove the foil, sprinkle with remaining ½ cup Gruyère cheese, and bake for an additional 30 to 35 minutes or until potatoes are tender and liquid is thickened. Let stand 5 minutes before serving. (You can do this up to 2 days in advance and refrigerate, tightly covered. Reheat, covered with foil, in a 350°F oven for 20 to 30 minutes or until hot.)

Half Baked

When making a dish that contains ham, prosciutto, sausage, or any cured or spiced pork product, use salt sparingly, if at all, because all these foods have a high salt content. In a dish such as this one with potatoes, chances are you'll need to add additional salt, but that's not the case with most ham dishes.

Ham Hash with Caraway and Mustard

Serves: 6 to 8
Prep time: 15 minutes
Cook time: 35 minutes

1 small rutabaga, peeled and cut into ½-inch cubes

3 large red-skinned potatoes, scrubbed and cut into ½-inch cubes

3 TB. olive oil

1 large red onion, peeled and coarsely chopped

3 garlic cloves, peeled and minced

1 red bell pepper, seeds and ribs removed, cut into ¼-inch dice

1 lb. baked ham, thinly sliced and cut into ½-inch squares

2 TB. (¼ stick) butter

⅓ cup dry white wine

1½ tsp. *caraway seed*

1 tsp. Worcestershire sauce

Salt and freshly ground black pepper to taste

½ cup chopped fresh parsley

1 TB. grainy Dijon mustard

Ellen on Edibles

Caraway seed is best known as the flavoring of seeded rye bread. However, this aromatic seed with a nutty anise flavor is from an herb in the parsley family. Caraway seeds are used often in German, Austrian, and Hungarian cuisine.

1. Bring a large pot of salted water to a boil. Add rutabaga and potato cubes and cook for about 10 to 15 minutes or until crisp-tender. Drain and set aside.

2. Heat olive oil in a large skillet over medium-high heat. Add red onion, garlic, and red bell pepper and cook, stirring frequently, for 3 minutes or until onion is translucent. Stir in rutabaga, potatoes, ham, butter, and white wine. Add caraway seed and Worcestershire sauce and season to taste with salt and pepper. Cook over medium heat, stirring frequently, for 20 to 25 minutes or until all liquid has evaporated and mixture is lightly browned and crisp.

3. Stir in parsley and Dijon mustard and cook for 2 minutes more. Serve immediately.

Italian Sausage with Chickpeas and Spinach

2 lb. Italian sausage links

1 small red onion, peeled and finely chopped

2 garlic cloves, peeled and minced

2 (10-oz.) pkg. frozen chopped spinach, thawed

1 (15-oz.) can chickpeas, drained and rinsed

¾ cup evaporated milk

¾ cup grated Parmesan cheese

1 tsp. grated lemon zest

1 TB. lemon juice

¼ tsp. ground nutmeg

Salt and freshly ground black pepper to taste

⅓ cup fine dry breadcrumbs

2 TB. butter, melted

Serves: 6 to 8	
Prep time: 15 minutes	
Cook time: 35 minutes	

1. Preheat the oven to 375°F. Grease a 9×13-inch baking pan. Cook sausage in a large skillet over medium heat for about 8 minutes or until no pink remains, turning often with tongs. Drain on paper towels and slice into bite-size pieces.

2. Pour off all but 2 tablespoons fat from the skillet. Add red onion and garlic and cook, stirring frequently, for 3 minutes or until onion is translucent. Place spinach in a colander and press with the back of a spoon to extract as much liquid as possible.

3. Combine sausage, onion mixture, spinach, chickpeas, evaporated milk, ½ cup Parmesan cheese, lemon zest, lemon juice, and nutmeg in a mixing bowl. Season to taste with salt and pepper and spread mixture in the prepared baking pan.

4. For topping, in a small mixing bowl combine breadcrumbs, remaining ¼ cup Parmesan cheese, and butter. Sprinkle on top of casserole. Cover with aluminum foil and bake for 15 minutes. Remove the foil and bake for an additional 20 minutes or until bubbly. Serve immediately.

 **Got You Covered!**

To make this into a healthier dish, substitute any of the uncooked chicken or turkey sausages for the pork sausage, which is higher in fat. You can also make this dish spicier by using hot sausage, rather than mild.

Other Grazing Greats: Meals Starring Lamb and Veal

In This Chapter

- ◆ Hearty stews from luscious lamb
- ◆ Subtle dishes made with delicate veal
- ◆ Braised shanks cooked until meltingly tender

Americans don't eat as much rosy, flavorful lamb or tender, delicate veal as Europeans do, but these foods still have their fans. Lamb takes to hearty treatments, and veal is similar to chicken with its quick-cooking time frame and ability to absorb flavors.

I created the recipes in this chapter to showcase these alternatives to beef. I included stews and also recipes for shanks because these less-tender parts of the animals have been growing in popularity.

Who Had a Little Lamb?

Lamb is far more flavorful than beef and has a rosy richness that fills the house with a wonderful aroma as it cooks. Certain herbs, such as rosemary and thyme, complement lamb's inherent flavor, so I use them often in the lamb recipes in this chapter.

Smaller than cows or pigs, a full-grown lamb of about 8 months old rarely weighs more than 115 pounds. The meat is so tender that almost all cuts can be roasted, even when the animal is mature. What is termed "spring lamb" comes from young animals, less than 5 months old, and "lamb" is from animals less than 1 year old. "Mutton" is lamb that comes from animals 1 to 2 years old and should only be braised or stewed because all cuts will require some tenderizing.

When choosing lamb, let its color be your guide. Look for lamb with deep pink flesh that is finely grained with white marbling and fat, although the color of the fat may vary with the species of animal and what it was fed. Avoid meat that has a dry surface or looks dark red or brown.

Lamb shanks are cooked whole, and the cuts used most often for braised dishes are the shoulder and boneless leg.

Versatile Veal

Pork manufacturers have built a campaign about pork being the "other white meat," but veal is even more delicate and is a luxurious meat regardless of whether it is braised, sautéed, or roasted. Veal comes from calves up to 6 months old that weigh no more than 200 to 250 pounds.

To ensure tender, pink meat, the animal is fed its mother's milk rather than grain. Most milk-fed veal comes from 3- to 4-month-old calves, as older animals have usually started to eat grass and are on their way to becoming young cows. The meat of grass-fed veal is darker and coarser, with neither the full-flavored richness of beef nor the delicacy of milk-fed veal.

Because the meat is young, most cuts are tender, can be cooked in many ways, and will retain its delicate flavor. However, don't consider veal just a youthful version of beef; rather, treat it like chicken in the delicacy of the seasoning.

Although there is no such thing as inexpensive veal because the animals are so small, the recipes in this chapter do not require the investment of buying prized veal scallops. Like most animals, the shoulder and leg portions are the most economical. Unlike lamb shanks, veal shanks are cooked in crosswise slices, and generically called osso buco, although that is the name of a specific Italian method to prepare them. Veal breast is another option; however, the amount of fat and bone is rather high.

Lamb Stew with White Beans and Sausage (*Cassoulet*)

6 slices bacon, cut into ½-inch pieces

2 lb. lamb shoulder or boneless leg of lamb, cut into 1-inch cubes, rinsed, and patted dry with paper towels

Salt and freshly ground black pepper to taste

2 large onions, peeled and diced

4 garlic cloves, peeled and minced

2 cups dry white wine

2 cups beef stock

3 TB. tomato paste

1 TB. fresh thyme or 1 tsp. dried

1 TB. chopped fresh rosemary or 1 tsp. dried

½ lb. kielbasa or other smoked sausage, cut into ½-inch pieces

2 (15-oz.) cans white cannellini beans, drained and rinsed

1 (10-oz.) pkg. frozen baby lima beans, thawed

¼ cup olive oil

2 cups Italian breadcrumbs

¼ cup grated Parmesan cheese

2 TB. chopped fresh parsley

Serves: 6 to 8	
Prep time: 25 minutes	
Cook time: 2¼ hours	

1. Preheat the oven to 350°F. Place bacon in an ovenproof Dutch oven over medium-high heat. Cook until crisp; then remove bacon with a slotted spoon and set aside. Discard all but 2 tablespoons bacon fat.

2. Sprinkle lamb cubes with salt and pepper. Add lamb cubes to the Dutch oven and cook until browned on all sides. Remove lamb cubes and set aside.

3. Add onion and garlic and cook, stirring frequently, for 3 minutes or until onion is translucent. Add lamb cubes, white wine, beef stock, tomato paste, thyme, and rosemary. Stir well, bring to a boil, cover, and place in the oven.

4. Bake for 1 hour. Add kielbasa, cannellini beans, and lima beans and bake for an additional hour or until lamb is tender.

5. Increase the oven temperature to 400°F. Combine olive oil, breadcrumbs, Parmesan cheese, and parsley in a small bowl; mix well and sprinkle on top of *cassoulet*. Bake uncovered for 15 minutes or until top is browned. Serve immediately.

Ellen on Edibles

Cassoulet is a traditional dish from the Languedoc region in Southwestern France. The only constant to its preparation is the beans, and in France they use small green dried flageolet. Although some sort of sausage is usually used, the other meats can vary from cured duck or goose to pork or beef.

Moroccan Spiced Lamb Stew with Vegetables, Dried Fruit, Couscous, and Toasted Almonds

Serves: 6 to 8
Prep time: 20 minutes
Cook time: 2 hours

2 lb. lamb shoulder or boneless leg of lamb, cut into 1-inch cubes, rinsed, and patted dry with paper towels

Salt and freshly ground black pepper to taste

¼ cup olive oil

1 large onion, peeled and chopped

2 garlic cloves, peeled and minced

1 (14.5-oz.) can beef stock

1 tsp. ground ginger

¼ tsp. ground cinnamon

¾ cup pitted prunes, diced

½ cup dried apricots, diced

2 large carrots, peeled and cut into ½-inch slices

1 large sweet potato, peeled and cut into ¾-inch dice

1 medium yellow squash, cut into ¾-inch pieces

2 cups couscous

½ cup slivered blanched almonds, toasted in a 350° oven for 3 to 5 minutes

1. Sprinkle lamb cubes with salt and pepper. Heat oil in a Dutch oven over medium-high heat. Add lamb cubes to the Dutch oven in a single layer and cook, turning pieces with tongs, until browned on all sides. Remove lamb cubes with a slotted spoon and set aside.

2. Add onion and garlic and cook, stirring frequently, for 3 minutes or until onion is translucent. Add lamb cubes, beef stock, ginger, cinnamon, prunes, and dried apricots. Bring to a boil and simmer, covered, for 1½ hours. Add carrots and sweet potato and simmer for 20 minutes or until sweet potato and lamb are tender. Add yellow squash and cook for an additional 10 minutes.

3. Remove solids from the Dutch oven with a slotted spoon and keep warm. Measure pan juices and add or subtract so you have 2½ cups. If more, reduce in a saucepan over high heat until liquid measures 2½ cups. If less, add beef stock to reach the measurement.

4. Return juices to a boil and stir in couscous. Cover, remove from heat, and allow to sit for 5 minutes. Fluff couscous with a fork and serve stew on a bed of couscous with almonds sprinkled on top.

Got You Covered!

In addition to looking more appealing, toasted nuts have a crispier texture and more pleasing flavor. Toasting releases the nuts' fragrant and aromatic oils.

Lamb and Chorizo Pot Pie

1½ lb. lamb shoulder or boneless leg of lamb, cut into ½-inch pieces, rinsed, and patted dry with paper towels

Salt and freshly ground black pepper to taste

½ cup all-purpose flour

¼ cup olive oil

2 sweet onions (such as Vidalia or Maui), peeled, halved, and thinly sliced

1 red bell pepper, seeds and ribs removed, and thinly sliced

2 garlic cloves, peeled and minced

1 TB. paprika

2 tsp. dried oregano

1 (14.5-oz.) can beef stock

½ cup dry white wine

½ lb. sweet Spanish chorizo, casings removed, finely chopped

2 large boiling potatoes, scrubbed and cut into ½-inch dice

1 sheet frozen puff pastry (½ of a 17-oz. pkg.), thawed

1 large egg

1 TB. milk

Serves: 6 to 8
Prep time: 30 minutes
Cook time: 2½ hours

1. Sprinkle lamb pieces with salt and pepper. Pour flour into a resealable plastic bag, add lamb pieces, seal, and toss to coat. Remove lamb pieces and shake off any excess. Heat oil in a large skillet over medium-high heat. Add lamb pieces to the skillet in a single layer and cook, turning pieces with tongs, until brown on all sides. Remove lamb with a slotted spoon and set aside.

2. Add onion, red bell pepper, and garlic to the pan and cook, stirring frequently, for 3 minutes or until onion is translucent. Stir in paprika and oregano and cook, stirring constantly, for 1 minute. Add lamb, beef stock, white wine, and chorizo. Bring to a boil, reduce heat to low, and simmer, covered, for 1¼ hours. Add potatoes and simmer for 30 minutes or until potatoes and lamb are tender. (You can do this up to 2 days in advance and refrigerate, tightly covered. Before continuing, reheat over low heat until simmering.)

3. Preheat the oven to 375°F. Grease a 9×13-inch baking pan. Transfer lamb mixture into the prepared baking pan. Roll puff pastry into an 11×15-inch rectangle. Beat egg lightly with milk. Brush egg mixture around the outside edge of the prepared baking pan. Place pastry on top of lamb and crimp the edges, pressing to seal pastry to the sides of the pan. Brush top of pastry with egg mixture and cut 6 (1-inch) vents to allow steam to escape.

4. Bake for 35 minutes or until golden brown. Serve immediately.

Got You Covered!

An easy way to coat food with flour is to place the flour and food in a heavy plastic bag. Keep the air in the bag so the food can move around freely, and hold the top tightly closed with your hand. Shake the food around, and it will be evenly coated.

Herbed Lamb Shanks with Red Wine and Vegetables

Serves: 6 to 8
Prep time: 20 minutes
Cook time: 2½ hours

6 to 8 lamb *shanks*

Salt and freshly ground black pepper to taste

½ cup all-purpose flour

⅓ cup olive oil

1 large onion, peeled and diced

2 celery stalks, peeled and diced

2 large carrots, peeled and diced

4 garlic cloves, peeled and minced

2 TB. tomato paste

1½ cups dry red wine

1 (14.5-oz.) can beef stock

2 TB. fresh thyme or 2 tsp. dried

2 TB. chopped fresh rosemary or 2 tsp. dried

1 bay leaf

4 large boiling potatoes, scrubbed and cut into 1½-inch cubes

1 (10-oz.) pkg. frozen peas, thawed

3 TB. chopped fresh parsley

Ellen on Edibles

Shanks are anatomically the lowest part of the front leg of sheep, cattle, and pigs. They are incredibly flavorful cuts, but they also contain the most connective tissue, so they must be cooked slowly with moist heat to render them "fork-tender." Lamb and pork shanks are sold whole, while beef and veal shanks are cut into horizontal sections. Many stores market sections of veal shank under the name "osso buco." This refers to a specific Milanese dish, but it's also become synonymous for all veal shank recipes.

1. Preheat the oven to 350°F. Sprinkle lamb with salt and pepper and dust lamb with flour, shaking off any excess. Heat oil in a skillet over medium-high heat. Add lamb shanks to the skillet in a single layer and cook, turning pieces with tongs, until browned on all sides. Transfer lamb shanks to a large stovetop-safe roasting pan as they are browned.

2. Add onions, celery, carrots, and garlic to the skillet and cook, stirring frequently, for 3 minutes or until onion is translucent. Scrape the mixture into the roasting pan and stir in tomato paste, red wine, beef stock, thyme, rosemary, and bay leaf.

3. Place the roasting pan on the stovetop and bring to a boil. Cover, place in the oven, and bake for 1 hour. Add potatoes and bake for an additional 1 to 1½ hours or until lamb shanks are tender. Remove shanks and potatoes to a warm platter. Tilt the pan and spoon off grease from surface of sauce.

4. Place the roasting pan on the stovetop and cook sauce over medium heat until reduced in volume by half; then pour sauce over shanks. (You can do this up to 2 days in advance and refrigerate, tightly covered. Reheat, covered, in a 350°F oven for 25 to 35 minutes or until hot.) Add peas and cook 5 minutes. Remove and discard bay leaf, sprinkle shanks with parsley, and serve immediately.

Braised Lamb Shanks with Winter Root Vegetables in Jack Daniel's Barbecue Sauce

6 to 8 lamb shanks

Salt and freshly ground black pepper to taste

½ cup all-purpose flour

3 TB. olive oil

1 medium onion, peeled and diced

4 garlic cloves, peeled and minced

3 TB. chopped fresh rosemary or 1 TB. dried

1 cup barbecue sauce

2 cups Jack Daniel's

⅓ cup firmly packed light brown sugar

2 TB. dry mustard

1 (12-oz.) bottle or can beer

1 (14.5-oz.) can beef stock

½ to 1 tsp. hot red pepper sauce, or to taste

3 large boiling potatoes, scrubbed and cut into 1-inch cubes

3 large carrots, peeled and cut into 1-inch chunks

2 parsnips, peeled and cut into 1-inch chunks

1 *rutabaga*, peeled and cut into 1-inch cubes

Serves: 6 to 8
Prep time: 20 minutes
Cook time: 2½ hours

1. Preheat the oven to 350°F. Sprinkle lamb shanks with salt and pepper and dust lamb with flour, shaking off any excess. Heat olive oil in a large skillet over medium-high heat. Add lamb shanks to the skillet in a single layer and cook, turning pieces gently with tongs, until browned on all sides. Transfer lamb shanks to a deep roasting pan as they are browned. Add onion and garlic to the skillet and cook, stirring frequently, for 3 minutes or until onion is translucent. Scrape mixture into the roasting pan.

2. Combine rosemary, barbecue sauce, Jack Daniel's, brown sugar, mustard, beer, beef stock, and hot red pepper sauce in a mixing bowl and stir well. Pour mixture over lamb shanks and cover the roasting pan.

3. Bake for 1½ hours. Add potatoes, carrots, parsnips, and rutabaga and bake for 1 hour more or until lamb shanks are very tender.

 Ellen on Edibles

Rutabagas, like the turnips they resemble, are a root vegetable that is really a botanical cross between turnips and cabbage. The name is Swedish, which is why they are sometimes called Swedish turnips. Rutabagas have a pale yellow skin and a firm flesh of the same color. However, they are much sweeter than turnips.

Lamb Stew with Apples and Yams in Curried Coconut Sauce

Serves: 6 to 8
Prep time: 30 minutes
Cook time: 2 hours

1 cup shredded unsweetened coconut

2 lb. lean lamb, cut into 1-inch cubes, rinsed, and patted dry with paper towels

Salt and freshly ground black pepper to taste

¼ cup vegetable oil

6 scallions, trimmed and thinly sliced

4 garlic cloves, peeled and minced

2 TB. grated fresh ginger

2 TB. curry powder

2 (14-oz.) cans light coconut milk

¼ cup dry sherry

2 tsp. Chinese chili sauce

½ cup golden raisins

2 large yams, peeled and cut into ½-inch dice

3 Granny Smith apples, peeled, cored, and cut into ½-inch dice

2 carrots, peeled and cut into ½-inch dice

¼ lb. snow peas, stemmed and rinsed

1 TB. cornstarch

2 TB. cold water

1. Place coconut into a large, dry skillet over medium-high heat. Cook for 2 minutes, stirring constantly, or until lightly browned. Set aside. Sprinkle lamb cubes with salt and pepper. Heat oil in a Dutch oven over medium-high heat. Add lamb cubes to the Dutch oven and cook until browned on all sides. Remove lamb cubes with a slotted spoon and set aside.

2. Add scallions, garlic, ginger, and curry powder to the Dutch oven and cook, stirring constantly, for 1 minute. Add lamb cubes, coconut, coconut milk, sherry, chili sauce, and raisins. Bring to a boil, cover, and cook over low heat for 1 hour, stirring occasionally.

3. Add yams, apples, and carrots and simmer for 1 additional hour or until lamb and vegetables are tender. (You can do this up to 2 days in advance and refrigerate, tightly covered. Before continuing, reheat over low heat.)

4. Add snow peas, cover, and cook for 2 minutes or until snow peas are crisp-tender. Mix cornstarch with water and stir into Dutch oven. Cook for 2 minutes or until sauce is bubbly and lightly thickened. Serve immediately.

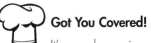 **Got You Covered!**

It's now becoming easier to find unsweetened coconut in health food stores, if not on the baking aisle of your supermarket. However, if you can't find it, don't despair. If you add a few tablespoons mild rice wine vinegar to the sauce, it will counteract the sweetness of the coconut.

Creole Osso Buco with Andouille Sausage, Vegetables, and Fusilli

6 to 8 veal shanks, rinsed, patted dry with paper towels, and tied into a circular shape with kitchen string

Salt and freshly ground black pepper to taste

½ cup all-purpose flour

¼ cup olive oil

2 TB. (¼ stick) butter

1¼ lb. andouille or other spicy sausage, thinly sliced

1 large onion, peeled and diced

4 garlic cloves, peeled and minced

1 jalapeño chili, seeds and ribs removed, finely chopped

½ lb. white mushrooms, trimmed, wiped with a damp paper towel, and halved

1 (14.5-oz.) can chicken stock

1 cup dry white wine

1 TB. Worcestershire sauce

2 TB. fresh thyme or 2 tsp. dried

¼ cup chopped fresh oregano or 1 TB. dried

2 carrots, peeled and cut into ½-inch slices

2 celery stalks, trimmed and cut into ½-inch slices

1 lb. fusilli or other similar-size pasta, cooked according to pkg. directions

Serves: 6 to 8
Prep time: 25 minutes
Cook time: 1½ hours

1. Preheat the oven to 350°F. Sprinkle veal shanks with salt and pepper. Dust veal shanks with flour, shaking off any excess. Heat oil in a large skillet over medium-high heat. Add veal shanks and cook until browned on all sides. Remove veal shanks and place in a large stovetop-safe roasting pan.

2. Add butter to the skillet and then add andouille, onion, garlic, jalapeño chili, and white mushrooms. Cook, stirring frequently, for 3 minutes or until onion is translucent. Add chicken stock, white wine, Worcestershire sauce, thyme, and oregano. Bring to a boil and pour mixture over veal shanks.

3. Cover the roasting pan and bake for 45 minutes. Add carrots and celery and bake for an additional 45 minutes or until veal shanks are very tender.

4. Remove veal shanks and vegetables from the roasting pan with a slotted spoon and keep warm. Place the pan on the stovetop over high heat and cook until liquid is reduced in volume by ¼. Stir fusilli into sauce. Cook until pasta is hot and then serve immediately with veal and vegetables on top of fusilli.

 **Got You Covered!**

Lamb and beef shanks can hold their own while being cooked, but delicate cross-cut veal shanks need a bit of help to keep their round shape. Cut a piece of kitchen twine about two times the diameter of the veal shank, and tie it around the center of the sides to keep the shanks circular. Otherwise, you will have pieces of tender veal floating in your sauce.

Gratin of Veal with Wild Mushrooms and Onions

Serves: 6 to 8

Prep time: 20 minutes

Cook time: 1¼ hours

---

2 lb. veal scallops

Salt and freshly ground black pepper to taste

4 TB. (½ stick) butter

5 large onions, peeled and diced

¾ lb. fresh shiitake mushrooms, stems removed, wiped with a damp paper towel, and sliced

2 cups plain breadcrumbs

2 cups grated Gruyère cheese

1 (14.5-oz.) can chicken stock

1½ cups dry white wine

Ellen on Edibles

Gratin (pronounced *grah-TAN*) is the French term for any dish topped with cheese and/or breadcrumbs and heated until it's brown and crispy. Gratin dishes are always cooked in a low, shallow dish to maximize their surface area. In fact, the pans known as gratin pans are typically shallow baking dishes with handles.

1. Preheat the oven to 350°F. Pound veal scallops between 2 sheets of wax paper or plastic wrap to an even thickness of ¼ inch. Season veal scallops with salt and pepper and set aside.

2. Melt 2 tablespoons butter in a large skillet over medium heat. Add onions and stir to coat them well. Cover and cook onions over low heat, stirring occasionally, for 10 minutes. Uncover, increase heat to medium-high, and sprinkle onions lightly with salt. Cook, stirring frequently, for about 5 minutes or until onions are soft but not brown.

3. Scrape onions into a 9×13-inch *gratin* pan or baking dish. Melt remaining butter in the skillet over medium-high heat. Add shiitake mushrooms, sprinkle lightly with salt and pepper, and cook, stirring frequently, for about 5 minutes or until mushrooms are soft and browned. Set aside.

4. Mix breadcrumbs with 1½ cups grated Gruyère cheese. Sprinkle ½ cup of the mixture on top of the onions. Place overlapping veal slices on top of onions and breadcrumbs. Firmly press remaining 1 cup of breadcrumb mixture into veal with a spatula and then scatter shiitake mushrooms over veal. Sprinkle remaining ½ cup Gruyère cheese on top and pour chicken stock and white wine over all. (You can do this a day in advance and refrigerate, tightly covered. Add 10 minutes to initial bake time.)

5. Cover the gratin pan with aluminum foil and bake for 30 minutes. Remove foil and bake for an additional 45 minutes or until top is browned and veal is fork-tender. Serve immediately.

Braised Veal Shanks with Baby Carrots and Scallions in Asian Mushroom Sauce

18 large dried shiitake mushrooms

1 cup very hot water

10 scallions, trimmed

6 to 8 veal shanks, rinsed, patted dry with paper towels, and
tied into a circular shape with
kitchen string

Salt and freshly ground black
pepper to taste

3 TB. sesame oil

3 TB. grated fresh ginger

6 garlic cloves, peeled and
minced

1 cup dry sherry

1 cup chicken stock

¼ cup *oyster sauce*

3 TB. soy sauce

½ lb. baby carrots

1 TB. cornstarch mixed with
2 TB. cold water

3 cups cooked jasmine rice, hot

Serves: 6 to 8	
Prep time: 25 minutes	
Cook time: 1½ hours	

1. Place dried shiitake mushrooms in a small bowl and soak in hot water 15 minutes; then drain, reserving liquid. Remove and discard mushroom stems and cut mushrooms into halves or quarters if they're large. Reserve mushrooms and liquid.

2. Cut off all but 1 inch of green tops from 4 scallions. Thinly slice those scallions, reserving tops. Cut reserved tops and remaining 6 scallions into 1½-inch pieces and set aside.

3. Sprinkle veal shanks with salt and pepper. Heat sesame oil in a large skillet over medium-high heat. Add veal shanks and cook, browning on all sides. Remove veal shanks and set aside.

4. Add sliced scallions, ginger, and garlic to the skillet. Cook, stirring constantly, for 30 seconds. Combine sherry, chicken stock, oyster sauce, and soy sauce in a mixing bowl. Add veal shanks and shiitake mushrooms and pour stock mixture over them. If liquid does not come halfway up side of shanks in the skillet, add some reserved mushroom soaking water. Bring to a boil, reduce heat to low, and cook for 1 hour, turning veal shanks after 30 minutes.

5. Add carrots and cook for 15 minutes. Add remaining scallions and cook for 5 minutes. Stir in cornstarch mixture. Cook for 2 minutes or until bubbly and sauce is lightly thickened. Serve immediately over jasmine rice.

Ellen on Edibles

Oyster sauce is a traditional Chinese condiment and cooking sauce, and although it does contain oysters, it's not "fishy" in flavor. The oysters and their liquor are cooked with soy sauce and some subtle seasonings until thick, which gives dishes a richness. It's now available in the Asian section of almost all supermarkets.

Caribbean Veal Stew in Rum Sauce with Yams and Plantains

Serves: 6 to 8
Prep time: 25 minutes plus 4 hours to marinate
Cook time: 1½ hours

1 cup dark rum

1 TB. cider vinegar

1½ tsp. dried oregano

½ tsp. ground cloves

Salt and freshly ground black pepper to taste

⅓ cup olive oil

2 lb. lean veal stew meat, cut into 1-inch pieces, rinsed, and patted dry with paper towels

½ cup all-purpose flour

¾ cup firmly packed dark brown sugar

2 (12-oz.) bottles or cans beer

½ cup diced ham

¼ cup chopped pimiento-stuffed green olives

18 pitted prunes, diced

3 carrots, peeled and cut into ½-inch slices

3 large yams, peeled and cut into ½-inch dice

2 TB. (¼ stick) butter

2 ripe *plantains*, peeled and cut into ½-inch slices on the diagonal

2 TB. granulated sugar

1. Combine rum, vinegar, oregano, cloves, salt, and pepper in a heavy resealable plastic bag. Seal and shake to dissolve seasonings, add 1 tablespoon olive oil, seal, and shake well again. Add veal pieces, seal, and refrigerate meat for at least 4 hours and up to 12 hours. Turn the bag from time to time to marinate veal evenly.

2. Remove veal pieces from bag, drain, and reserve marinade. Pat veal pieces dry with paper towels. Coat veal with flour and shake off any excess. Heat remaining oil in a Dutch oven over medium-high heat. Add veal pieces to Dutch oven in a single layer and cook, turning pieces with tongs, until browned on all sides.

3. Pour reserved marinade into the Dutch oven, add brown sugar, beer, ham, olives, and prunes. Bring to a boil, reduce heat to low, and simmer stew, covered, for 1 hour. Add carrots and yams and simmer for an additional 30 minutes or until yams and veal are tender.

4. While stew is simmering, melt butter in a large skillet over medium heat. Add plantain slices and sprinkle with sugar. Cook gently for 2 minutes per side or until plantains are soft. Serve stew in bowls with plantain slices on top.

Ellen on Edibles

Plantains are a subset of the banana family, are picked green, and ripen after they're harvested. They are not eaten raw; their starchy texture is better when cooked. Plantains have a delicate flavor similar to that of a butternut squash and hold their shape when cooked.

Part 6

Vegetable Patch Panache

An old-fashioned term for any two-for-one commodity is a "twofer," and all the recipes in Part 6 fulfill that definition. They can be vegetarian entrées or can serve as side dishes when the center of the plate is occupied by a simple piece of grilled or broiled food. Only one aspect of a meal should claim starring status, and that's why these dishes add such versatility to your repertoire.

Part 6 begins with a chapter on vegetarian pastas from around the world, and there's also a chapter on other carbohydrates, such as rice and grains. Carbohydrates also play a supporting role in Chapter 15, full of recipes for beans and other healthful legumes, because these little wonders create a complete protein when combined with rice or pasta.

Chapter 16's recipes are for easy and hearty vegetarian entrées. These dishes are vibrantly colored as well as vibrantly flavored, and they encompass seasonings from many cuisines.

Pasta Power: Vegetarian Noodle and Pasta Dishes from Around the World

In This Chapter

- ◆ Pastas of all shapes and sizes
- ◆ Quick and healthful vegetarian one-dish meals from every continent
- ◆ Versatile recipes that double as side dishes

If you're a vegetarian or one of the increasing number of people who limit your meat intake, you're not alone. A growing percentage of Americans eat at least one dinner a week exclusively from the vegetable patch.

The recipes in this chapter are intended to expand your pasta options with double-duty dishes. You can serve them either as a one-dish dinner or as a side dish to glamorize a simple grilled or broiled entrée.

Positives of Pasta

Good-quality dried pasta is made with a high percentage of high-gluten semolina, the inner part of the grain of hard durum wheat. The gluten gives the pasta resilience and allows it to cook while remaining somewhat firm, thus reaching the state of al dente, or just slightly firm against the teeth.

Pasta is merely flour and water, so it is high in carbohydrate. The higher the semolina content of pasta, the more protein it contains. The protein in pasta is an incomplete protein, like that of rice, which can be completed by eating it with foods such as beans.

Eggless pasta contains no fat and other nutrients are added if spinach or tomato flour is used. Each ounce of pasta is approximately 100 calories.

The Dried Dilemma

As a general rule, pasta imported from Italy is superior to American factory-made products due to its higher semolina content. Try to purchase pasta you can see through a cellophane window in the box. The pasta should be smooth and shiny, not crumbly.

Store pasta in sealed plastic bags after you open the boxes, and it will stay fresh for at least 6 months. You can still use pasta if it's stale; just add a few minutes to the cooking time.

Traditional dried Italian pastas are named according to their shape. For example, fusilli are twists, and fiochetti are bows. You could fill an entire kitchen with boxes of different-shaped pasta if you wanted a complete selection. Not many people have such a pantry luxury, so instead, look at the cooking times and sizes in the following table to determine alternatives you might have on hand to make a recipe.

Pasta Name	Cooking Time
Farfalle, fiochetti, fusilli, orecchiette, penne, rigatoni, ziti	10 to 12 minutes
Anelli, cavatappi, macaroni, manicotti, mostaccioli, orzo, rotelle	8 to 10 minutes
Fettuccine, linguine, spaghetti, tagliatelli	6 to 9 minutes

Cook pasta according to package directions if it's going to be sauced and served, and undercook it by a few minutes if it's going to be baked in a sauce. During the 20-plus minutes a pasta bakes, it absorbs moisture from the sauce and softens further.

New Age Lasagna

One of the great pasta advances of the past decade has been the invention of precooked pasta strips to short-cut making any form of lasagna. These "no-boil" or "oven-ready" pastas are precooked and then dehydrated at the factory. They soften in the oven and regain their supple texture.

You can use these strips in place of any pastas to save time and washing another pot, but use with one caution: they require much more liquid in a dish because they must rehydrate as they bake. If you're substituting the precooked, no-boil strips for cooked pasta, adjust the amount of liquid in the recipe to reflect the total listed on the box.

Noodling Around

Although noodles are a form of pasta, pasta is not a noodle. The main difference between noodles and pasta is that noodles contain eggs or egg yolks. This makes noodle dough softer, so it will not retain its shape if molded like pasta.

Noodles are cut into strips of different widths or left freeform like German spaetzle. Most commercial noodles today have also been enriched with vitamins and minerals, which, when added to the protein of the eggs, produces a more nutritious product than most pastas.

Asian Alternatives

Some Asian-style noodles are wheat based, while many others are made from ingredients such as rice flour, potato flour, buckwheat flour, cornstarch, and bean, yam, or soybean starch. Among the more popular are Chinese cellophane noodles (which are made from mung bean starch), egg noodles (usually wheat based), and rice flour noodles. Noodles of Japanese origin found in American markets are ramen, which are wheat based, and soba, which contain buckwheat flour as well. I created all the recipes in this chapter with common types of noodles that you can find in supermarkets—without a trek to Chinatown.

Chinese Hot and Sour Noodles with Vegetables

Serves: 6 as an entrée or 10 to 12 as a side dish
Prep time: 20 minutes
Cook time: 15 minutes

1 lb. dried Chinese egg noodles, cooked according to pkg. directions

2 TB. sesame oil

12 dried shiitake mushrooms

1 cup very hot tap water

2 TB. sesame seeds

8 scallions, trimmed

¼ cup soy sauce

1 TB. Chinese chili oil

2 TB. rice vinegar

1 TB. granulated sugar

2 TB. vegetable oil

2 carrots, peeled and cut into *julienne* pieces

2 celery stalks, peeled and cut into julienne pieces

1 red bell pepper, seeds and ribs removed, cut into julienne pieces

1 cup mung bean sprouts, rinsed

1. Toss noodles with sesame oil and set aside. Soak dried shiitake mushrooms in hot water for 10 minutes. Drain, reserving liquid. Discard mushroom stems and slice mushrooms. Reserve mushrooms and liquid.

3. Meanwhile, toast sesame seeds in a small dry skillet over medium-high heat for 2 minutes or until lightly browned. Remove from the skillet and set aside.

4. Trim off all but 2 inches of the green tops from 3 scallions, reserve tops, and thinly slice scallions. Cut remaining 5 scallions and reserved tops into 1-inch lengths and set aside.

5. Combine sliced scallions with soy sauce, chili oil, rice vinegar, and sugar. Set aside.

6. Heat vegetable oil in a wok or deep skillet over medium-high heat. Add carrots, celery, and red bell pepper. Cook, stirring constantly, for 2 minutes or until vegetables are crisp-tender. Add shiitake mushrooms, remaining scallions, and bean sprouts and cook 1 for minute, stirring constantly.

7. Add noodles and soy sauce mixture and cook until heated through. Add some mushroom soaking liquid if mixture seems dry and serve immediately, sprinkled with sesame seeds.

Ellen on Edibles

Julienne is the French word for very thin sticks of vegetables that can cook very quickly. To cut a vegetable julienne style, first cut into long, thin slices, about ⅛-inch thick or smaller. Stack these layers, and cut into thin strips. Then cut the strips into any length, as determined by the recipe.

Korean Noodles with Vegetables

6 oz. cellophane noodles

½ cup *tamari*

3 TB. sesame oil

3 TB. granulated sugar

3 scallions, trimmed and cut into 1-inch pieces

2 garlic cloves, peeled

2 TB. vegetable oil

1 medium red onion, peeled, halved, and thinly sliced

3 medium carrots, peeled and cut into julienne pieces

1 red bell pepper, peeled and cut into julienne pieces

¼ lb. white mushrooms, trimmed, wiped with damp paper towel, and thinly sliced

3 cups baby spinach, rinsed and stemmed

Serves: 6 as an entrée or 10 to 12 as a side dish
Prep time: 15 minutes
Cook time: 20 minutes

1. Soak noodles in a bowl of warm water to cover for about 10 minutes or until softened; then drain in a colander. Bring a large pot of water to a boil and cook noodles for 2 minutes or until tender. Drain noodles in a colander and rinse under cold water until cool.

2. Combine tamari, sesame oil, sugar, scallions, and garlic in a food processor fitted with a steel blade or in a blender. Blend until smooth.

3. Heat vegetable oil in a wok or deep skillet over medium-high heat. Add red onion, carrots, and red bell pepper and cook, stirring constantly, for 2 minutes. Add white mushrooms and cook, stirring constantly, for 3 minutes. Add spinach and cook for 30 seconds. Add noodles and tamari mixture and toss to coat. Reduce heat to low and simmer, stirring occasionally, for 3 to 5 minutes or until most of liquid is absorbed. Serve immediately.

Ellen on Edibles

Similar to soy sauce, **tamari** is a dark sauce made from soy beans. But it has a distinctive and mellow flavor rather than being overwhelmingly salty like soy sauce. You can substitute a light Japanese-style soy sauce in a pinch.

Minted Couscous with Mushroom Mélange

Serves: 6 as an entrée or 10 to 12 as a side dish

Prep time: 15 minutes
Cook time: 20 minutes

¼ cup pine nuts

¼ cup olive oil

6 scallions, trimmed with all but 2 inches of green tops discarded, thinly sliced

1 yellow bell pepper, seeds and ribs removed, finely diced

½ tsp. saffron threads, crushed

1 tsp. ground cinnamon

5 TB. butter

½ lb. white mushrooms, stems removed, wiped with a damp paper towel, and sliced

½ lb. fresh shiitake mushrooms, stems removed, wiped with a damp paper towel, and sliced

2½ cups vegetable stock

12 oz. (2 cups) couscous

½ cup fresh mint leaves, coarsely chopped

Salt and freshly ground pepper to taste

1. Toast pine nuts in a small dry skillet over medium heat for 2 minutes or until lightly browned. Remove from the skillet and set aside.

2. Heat olive oil in a large skillet over medium-high heat. Add scallions and yellow bell pepper and cook, stirring frequently, for 3 minutes or until vegetables are softened. Stir in saffron and cinnamon and cook 30 seconds more. Add 2 tablespoons butter. Add white mushrooms and shiitake mushrooms and cook, stirring frequently, for 8 to 10 minutes or until all mushroom liquid has evaporated. Set aside.

3. In a medium saucepan, bring vegetable stock to a boil over high heat. Add remaining butter and stir until melted. Stir in couscous. Cover and remove from heat and allow to sit for 5 minutes. Fluff couscous with a fork and stir in vegetables and mint. Season to taste with salt and pepper and garnish with pine nuts. Serve immediately.

Got You Covered!

These recipes are written to be strictly vegetarian and can also be served to people who keep a kosher diet. However, if you're not concerned about keeping the dish vegetarian, you can substitute chicken stock for the vegetable stock.

Couscous with Vegetables, Chickpeas, and Dried Currants

2½ cups couscous

3 (14.5-oz.) cans vegetable stock

2 TB. olive oil

6 large, fresh cilantro sprigs, rinsed and patted dry

6 garlic cloves, peeled

3 (2-in.) cinnamon sticks

2 tsp. ground cumin

2 tsp. curry powder

4 leeks, white part only, trimmed, halved lengthwise, well rinsed and cut into 1-inch lengths

4 medium carrots, peeled, halved lengthwise, and cut into 1-inch chunks

2 Idaho potatoes, peeled and cut into eighths

½ lb. small white turnips, peeled and quartered

3 small onions, peeled and halved

2 medium zucchini, ends trimmed, halved lengthwise, and cut into 1-inch chunks

3 ripe large tomatoes, cored, seeded, and cut into six pieces

1 (15-oz.) can chickpeas, drained and rinsed

1 cup pitted prunes, halved

½ cup dried currants

4 TB. chopped fresh cilantro

Salt and freshly ground black pepper to taste

Serves: 6 to 8
Prep time: 20 minutes
Cook time: 1½ hours

1. Bring a saucepan of water to a boil over high heat. Prepare couscous according to package directions, set aside, and keep warm.

2. Combine vegetable stock, oil, cilantro sprigs, garlic, cinnamon sticks, cumin, and curry powder in a Dutch oven. Bring to a boil, reduce heat to medium, and simmer, uncovered, for 30 minutes. Strain stock through a fine-mesh strainer, discard solids, and return stock to the Dutch oven.

3. Add leeks, carrots, potatoes, turnips, and onions to stock. Bring to a boil, reduce heat to medium, and simmer, uncovered, for 30 minutes.

4. Add zucchini, tomatoes, chickpeas, prunes, and dried currants. Simmer, uncovered, for an additional 30 minutes. Stir in chopped cilantro and season to taste with salt and pepper. Fluff couscous with a fork, spoon it into shallow bowls, and top with vegetables and broth.

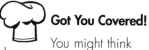 **Got You Covered!**

You might think it's a waste to discard the ingredients that simmer with the broth, but it's not. Their purpose is to create a more intensely flavored stock. In classic French cooking, the resulting product is called a *court bouillon,* and it's used to poach foods such as chicken and fish.

Linguine with Scallions and Bean Sprouts in Asian Pasta Sauce

Serves: 6 as an entrée or 10 to 12 as a side dish
Prep time: 20 minutes
Cook time: 20 minutes

1 (14.5-oz.) can vegetable stock

1 oz. dried porcini mushrooms

⅓ cup dry sherry

⅓ cup tamari

2 TB. sesame oil

1 TB. cornstarch

1 tsp. granulated sugar

6 TB. (¾ stick) butter

6 scallions, trimmed and thinly sliced

4 garlic cloves, peeled and minced

½ lb. fresh shiitake mushrooms, stems removed, wiped with a damp paper towel, and thinly sliced

½ lb. fresh portobello mushrooms, stems removed, peeled with gills scraped out, and thinly sliced

½ lb. fresh white mushrooms, stems removed, wiped with a damp paper towel, and sliced

1 lb. linguine, broken into 2-inch lengths and cooked according to pkg. directions

2 cups mung bean sprouts, rinsed

Salt and freshly ground black pepper to taste

3 TB. chopped fresh cilantro

Grated Parmesan cheese to taste

1. Bring vegetable stock to a boil in a small saucepan over high heat. Add dried porcini mushrooms, remove the saucepan from heat, and allow to sit for 10 minutes. Remove mushrooms and chop finely. Stir in sherry, tamari, sesame oil, cornstarch, and sugar. Set aside.

2. Melt butter in a large skillet over medium-high heat. Add scallions and garlic and cook, stirring constantly, for 1 minute. Add shiitake mushrooms, portobello mushrooms, white mushrooms, and chopped porcini mushrooms. Cook, stirring frequently, for 8 to 10 minutes or until all mushroom liquid has evaporated.

3. Stir stock mixture into mushroom mixture and bring to a boil, stirring occasionally. Simmer for 1 minute; then stir in linguine and bean sprouts. Heat for 2 minutes or until linguine is hot. Season with salt and pepper to taste. Sprinkle with cilantro and serve immediately, passing grated Parmesan cheese on the side.

Pasta with Oven-Roasted Tomato Sauce, Kalamata Olives, and Feta

3 lb. ripe plum tomatoes, cored, seeded, and diced

⅓ cup olive oil

5 garlic cloves, peeled and minced

1 TB. balsamic vinegar

½ tsp. crushed red pepper flakes

Salt and freshly ground black pepper to taste

3 TB. chopped fresh oregano or 1 TB. dried

3 TB. chopped fresh basil or 2 tsp. dried

1 lb. linguine

½ cup pine nuts

½ cup pitted kalamata olives, halved

½ lb. feta cheese, crumbled

Serves: 6 as an entrée or 10 to 12 as a side dish	
Prep time: 15 minutes	
Cook time: 48 minutes	

1. Preheat the oven to 375°F. Combine tomatoes, oil, garlic, vinegar, and crushed red pepper flakes in a 9×13-inch baking pan. Season to taste with salt and pepper. Roast, stirring occasionally, for 45 minutes or until tomatoes are tender and juicy. Stir in oregano and basil. (You can do this a day in advance and refrigerate, tightly covered. Before continuing, reheat in a saucepan over low heat until simmering.)

2. Bring a large pot of salted water to a boil over high heat. Cook linguine according to package directions until al dente. Return pasta to the pot and keep warm.

3. While tomatoes and pasta are cooking, toast pine nuts in a small dry skillet over medium heat for 2 minutes or until lightly browned. Remove from the skillet and set aside.

4. Add roasted tomato mixture to linguine; then add olives and feta. Stir over medium heat for about 3 minutes or until heated through and feta is melted and creamy. Divide pasta among dinner plates, sprinkle with pine nuts, and serve.

 **Got You Covered!**

Oven-roasting tomatoes caramelizes their natural sugars and intensifies the flavor. Some of the liquid evaporates, and the tomatoes are rendered tender, too.

Radicchio, Mushroom, Asparagus, and Smoked Mozzarella Lasagna

Serves: 6 as an entrée or 10 to 12 as a side dish
Prep time: 30 minutes
Cook time: 40 minutes

4 TB. olive oil

1½ lb. *radicchio*, rinsed, cored, and chopped

1 lb. white mushrooms, trimmed, wiped with a damp paper towel, and finely chopped

Salt and freshly ground black pepper to taste

4 TB. (½ stick) butter

4 TB. all-purpose flour

2½ cups milk

2 garlic cloves, peeled and minced

2 TB. chopped fresh parsley

½ lb. thin asparagus, woody stems discarded, cut into 1-inch lengths

1 lb. smoked mozzarella, grated

¼ lb. plain mozzarella, grated

9 (7×3½-inch) sheets dry no-boil lasagna

1. Heat 2 tablespoons oil in a large skillet over medium-high heat. Add radicchio and cook, stirring frequently, for 3 minutes or until radicchio is wilted and golden. Add white mushrooms and season to taste with salt and pepper. Cook, stirring frequently, for 5 to 7 minutes or until mushroom liquid is evaporated. Set aside.

2. Melt butter in a saucepan over low heat. Add flour and cook, stirring constantly, for 2 minutes. Whisk in milk, bring to a boil, and simmer, whisking occasionally, for 5 minutes or until thickened. Stir sauce into mushroom mixture. (You can do this up to 2 days in advance and refrigerate, tightly covered. Before continuing, reheat over low heat.)

3. Heat remaining 2 tablespoons oil over moderately low heat. Add garlic and cook for 1 minute, stirring constantly. Add parsley and asparagus, increase heat to medium-high, and cook for 2 minutes. Reserve ½ cup smoked mozzarella for topping. In a bowl, combine remaining smoked mozzarella with plain mozzarella.

4. Preheat the oven to 375°F. Grease a 9×13-inch baking dish. Pour 1 cup mushroom sauce into the prepared baking dish and cover with 3 lasagna sheets, being sure they don't touch each other. Spread about 1 cup mushroom sauce over lasagna. Top with ⅓ asparagus mixture and ½ cheese mixture. Make 1 more layer in same manner, beginning and ending with pasta. Spread remaining sauce evenly over lasagna, being sure lasagna is completely covered. Spread remaining ⅓ asparagus mixture evenly over sauce and sprinkle with reserved smoked mozzarella.

5. Cover tightly with foil, tenting the foil slightly to prevent it from touching surface of lasagna, and bake for 30 minutes. Remove foil and bake lasagna for 10 minutes more or until top is bubbling and golden. Let lasagna stand 5 minutes before serving.

Ellen on Edibles

Radicchio (pronounced *rah-DEE-key-oh*) is a bright burgundy-colored lettuce with strong white ribs related to the chicory family. Native to Italy, radicchio comes in two types. Radicchio di Verona is what we find in American markets and grows in small, round heads. Radicchio di Treviso has tapered heads and grows in looser bunches.

Baked Fusilli with Three Cheese Sauce

Serves: 6 as an entrée or 10 to 12 as a side dish

Prep time: 15 minutes
Cook time: 50 minutes

1 lb. spinach fusilli

1 cup light cream

½ cup dry white wine

2 cups grated cheddar cheese

1½ cups grated gorgonzola cheese

1 cup diced brie cheese, rinds removed

2 TB. chopped fresh sage or 2 TB. dried

1 TB. fresh thyme or 1 tsp. dried

Salt and freshly ground black pepper to taste

4 ripe plum tomatoes, cored, seeded, and thinly sliced

½ cup Italian breadcrumbs

2 TB. chopped fresh parsley

1. Preheat the oven to 350°F. Grease a 9×13-inch baking pan. Bring a large pot of salted water to a boil and cook fusilli according to package directions for 2 minutes less than suggested. Drain and return pasta to pot.

2. Place cream and white wine in a saucepan over medium heat and bring to a boil, stirring occasionally. Stir in 1 cup cheddar cheese along with gorgonzola, brie, sage, and thyme. Stir until cheeses are melted; then reduce heat to low and simmer, uncovered, for 3 minutes. Season with salt and pepper to taste.

3. Place ½ fusilli in the prepared baking pan and top with ½ cheese sauce. Sprinkle with remaining 1 cup cheddar cheese and top with remaining pasta and sauce. (You can do this a day in advance and refrigerate, tightly covered. Add 10 minutes to initial baking time.)

4. Cover the baking pan with aluminum foil and bake for 15 minutes. Remove foil and bake for 20 additional minutes. Arrange tomato slices on top and sprinkle with breadcrumbs and parsley. Bake for an additional 15 minutes. Serve immediately.

 **Got You Covered!**

You can change this dish simply by changing the type of pasta you use. Use a tomato pasta and add ¼ cup chopped sun-dried tomatoes packed in olive oil to the cheese sauce, or try a tri-colored pasta for a bright buffet supper dish.

Baked Penne Pasta with Wild Mushroom Ragout

1 (14.5-oz.) can vegetable stock

½ oz. dried porcini mushrooms

6 TB. (¾ stick) butter

2 large onions, peeled and finely chopped

½ lb. white mushrooms, trimmed, wiped with a damp paper towel, and sliced

½ lb. fresh shiitake mushrooms, stems removed, wiped with a damp paper towel, and sliced

3 TB. all-purpose flour

2½ cups whole milk

¾ cup grated Parmesan cheese

½ cup finely chopped fresh chives

Salt and freshly ground black pepper to taste

1 lb. penne pasta, cooked for 2 minutes less than pkg. directions

½ cup Italian breadcrumbs

Serves: 6 as an entrée or 10 to 12 as a side dish
Prep time: 20 minutes
Cook time: 25 minutes

1. Bring vegetable stock to a boil in a small saucepan over high heat. Add dried porcini mushrooms; remove the saucepan from heat and allow to sit for 10 minutes. Remove mushrooms and chop finely.

2. Melt 3 tablespoons butter in a large, heavy skillet over medium-high heat. Add onions and cook, stirring frequently, for 3 minutes or until onion is translucent. Add white mushrooms and shiitake mushrooms and cook, stirring frequently, for 5 minutes. Add chopped porcini and reserved soaking liquid and simmer over medium-high heat for 10 minutes.

3. Melt remaining 3 tablespoons butter in a saucepan over low heat. Add flour and cook, stirring constantly, for 2 minutes. Gradually whisk in milk, increase heat to medium, and cook, whisking constantly, until sauce thickens and boils. Stir sauce into mushroom mixture. Simmer, stirring occasionally, for 2 minutes. Stir in ½ cup Parmesan cheese and chives. Season to taste with salt and pepper and set aside.

4. Preheat oven to 425°F. Grease a 9×13-inch baking pan. Combine mushroom sauce and pasta, toss well to coat, and transfer to the prepared baking dish. Sprinkle with breadcrumbs and remaining ¼ cup Parmesan. Bake for about 25 minutes or until heated through and light golden.

Half Baked

Don't try to reheat pasta in a saucepan or it will become tough. Cooked pasta is best reheated in a microwave oven, covered, on full power for 1 minute. Check the temperature, and if necessary, continue to reheat at 30-second intervals.

Baked Rigatoni with Broccoli Rabe

Serves: 6 as an entrée or 10 to 12 as a side dish

Prep time: 40 minutes

Cook time: 30 minutes

2 TB. olive oil

1 onion, peeled and diced

2 garlic cloves, peeled and minced

¼ cup vodka

1 (8-oz.) can tomato sauce

1 (14.5-oz.) can diced tomatoes, undrained

1 cup heavy cream

2 TB. chopped fresh oregano or 2 tsp. dried

2 TB. fresh thyme or 2 tsp. dried

1 lb. broccoli rabe, tough stems discarded and cut into 1-inch lengths

1 lb. rigatoni

⅓ lb. fontina cheese, cut into ½-inch cubes

1. Heat olive oil in a saucepan over medium heat. Add onion and garlic and cook, stirring frequently, for 3 minutes or until onion is translucent. Add vodka and cook for about 3 minutes or until liquid has almost evaporated. Stir in tomato sauce, canned tomatoes and their juice, cream, oregano, and thyme. Cook at a gentle simmer, stirring occasionally, for about 30 minutes. (You can do this 2 days in advance and refrigerate, tightly covered. Before continuing, reheat over low heat.)

2. Preheat the oven to 375°F. Grease a 9×13-inch baking pan. While the sauce is simmering, bring a large pot of salted water to a boil, and have a bowl of ice water handy. Submerge broccoli rabe and *blanch* for 1 minute. Remove broccoli rabe with a slotted spoon and plunge into ice water for about 1 minute. After broccoli is chilled, drain and set aside.

3. Return water to a boil, add pasta, and cook according to package directions for 2 minutes less than suggested. Drain, return pasta to pot, and stir in vodka sauce and broccoli rabe.

4. Pour pasta mixture into the prepared baking dish and cover with aluminum foil. Bake for 10 minutes. Remove foil and sprinkle with fontina cheese. Bake for an additional 20 minutes or until bubbling and top is lightly browned. Serve immediately.

Baked Southwestern Egg Noodles with Black Beans

1 lb. medium egg noodles

¼ cup olive oil

1 large onion, peeled and chopped

3 garlic cloves, peeled and minced

1 small serrano chili, seeds and ribs removed, finely chopped

1 (15-oz.) can black beans, drained and rinsed

1 (10-oz.) can mild enchilada sauce

1 cup grated Monterey Jack cheese

½ cup sour cream

1 cup crushed tortilla chips

3 scallions, trimmed with all but 2 inches of green tops discarded, thinly sliced

1 large tomato, cored, seeded, and chopped

Serves: 6 as an entrée or 10 to 12 as a side dish
Prep time: 20 minutes
Cook time: 30 minutes

1. Bring a large pot of salted water to a boil. Add noodles and cook according to package directions until al dente. Drain and return to pot.

2. Preheat the oven to 375°F. Grease a 9×13-inch baking pan. While pasta is cooking, heat olive oil in a saucepan over medium-high heat. Add onion, garlic, and serrano chili and cook, stirring frequently, for 3 minutes or until onion is translucent.

3. Add beans and enchilada sauce to the saucepan and simmer, stirring occasionally, for 5 minutes or until lightly thickened. Add Monterey Jack cheese and stir until cheese is melted. Stir sauce into pasta and spread mixture into the prepared baking pan.

4. Cover with foil and bake for 15 minutes. Remove foil and spread sour cream over top. Scatter tortilla chips, scallions, and tomato on top of sour cream. Bake an additional 15 minutes or until browned. Serve immediately.

 Half Baked

Don't substitute salsa for the enchilada sauce. Salsa does not have the flavor intensity and will separate when cooked.

Angel Hair in Chipotle Sauce with Monterey Jack Cheese

> *Serves: 6 as an entrée or 10 to 12 as a side dish*
>
> **Prep time:** 15 minutes
>
> **Cook time:** 20 minutes

Got You Covered!

Toasting pasta, as in this recipe, is a technique used in much of Mexico and Latin America. The toasting keeps the strands much more separate as they cook; however, they take longer to cook because the starch on the surface has hardened.

¼ cup olive oil

2 onions, peeled and finely chopped

4 garlic cloves, peeled and minced

1 lb. angel hair or vermicelli pasta, broken into 2-inch lengths

1 TB. dried oregano, preferably Mexican

1 tsp. ground cumin

1 (14-oz.) can diced tomatoes, drained

1 (8-oz.) can tomato sauce

2 canned chipotle chilies in adobo sauce, drained and finely chopped

1 (14.5-oz.) can vegetable stock

Salt and freshly ground black pepper to taste

2 cups grated Monterey Jack cheese

¼ cup chopped fresh cilantro

1. Heat oil in a large covered skillet over medium-high heat. Add onions and garlic and cook, stirring frequently, for 3 minutes or until onion is translucent. Add angel hair, oregano, and cumin. Cook, stirring constantly, for 2 to 3 minutes or until angel hair is lightly browned.

2. Add tomatoes, tomato sauce, chipotle chilies, and vegetable stock and bring to a boil over high heat, stirring occasionally. Reduce heat to medium and simmer for 8 to 10 minutes or until pasta is soft and liquid has almost evaporated. Season to taste with salt and pepper and stir in Monterey Jack cheese. Sprinkle with cilantro and serve immediately.

Chapter 15

Where Have You Bean All My Life?: Vegetarian Recipes with Beans and Other Legumes

In This Chapter

◆ Nutritious, bean-y vegetarian recipes

◆ Seasoning: the sky's the limit!

◆ Exotic dishes made with quick-cooking lentils

The world has changed its attitude toward the formerly lowly regarded legume. We now praise beans for their nutritional value as well as their availability and economic value.

Dried beans play a role in almost all the world's cuisines, as you'll see in these recipes. Although beans have some inherent flavor on their own, they are like magnets that absorb the seasonings around them.

You'll find recipes for both dried and canned beans in this chapter, because some days you have time to monitor simmering and other days you want dinner on the table in minutes.

Completing Proteins

What generations before us knew instinctively, and we now know scientifically, is that the protein in beans is "incomplete." To deliver the best nutritional content, beans need to be paired with carbohydrate-rich grains such as rice.

When beans and grains are eaten together, they supply a quality of protein that's as good as that from eggs or beef. If you're serving any of these dishes as a vegetarian entrée rather than as a side dish, serve some rice alongside.

Up-Front Action

Before using beans, rinse them in a colander or sieve under cold running water and pick through them to discard any broken beans or pebbles that might have found their way into the bag.

Then, after you cover the beans with water, discard any that float to the top. These beans are broken and can contain bacteria.

"You're (Pre)Soaking in It!"

Presoaking dried beans is necessary (this is not the case for small beans such as black-eyed peas and their cousins in the legume family, split peas and lentils). If you don't presoak, the beans might eventually become tender, but it might also take a whole day of cooking!

The easiest way to soak beans is to cover them with cold water and let them sit on the counter overnight. Let them soak for a minimum of 6 hours; 8 to 12 hours is preferable.

Another way is to cover the beans with water and bring them to a boil on the stove. After they've boiled for 1 minute, turn off the heat, cover the pan, and let the beans soak for 1 hour.

Whichever method you use, after they have soaked, drain the beans and start cooking with them as soon as possible. After beans have been soaked, bacteria can begin to grow and cause the beans to ferment.

Cooking Beans

Cook dried beans until they're no longer crunchy but still have texture. If the beans are going to be cooked and then cooked again in a dish, such as in cassoulet, stop the initial cooking when the beans are still slightly crunchy. They'll finish cooking in the dish.

One caveat of bean cookery: be sure to cook the beans to the proper consistency before adding any acidic ingredient, such as tomatoes or lemon, because the acid prevents the beans from becoming tender.

Cajun Red Beans and Rice

3 TB. olive oil

2 medium onions, peeled and chopped

4 garlic cloves, peeled and minced

1 green bell pepper, seeds and ribs removed, finely diced

2 tsp. paprika

1 (14.5-oz.) can diced tomatoes, undrained

1 (8-oz.) can tomato sauce

1 chipotle chili in adobo sauce, drained and finely chopped

3 (15-oz.) cans kidney beans, drained and rinsed

Salt and freshly ground black pepper to taste

5 cups cooked long-grain rice, hot

Serves: 6 as an entrée or 10 to 12 as a side dish
Prep time: 10 minutes
Cook time: 20 minutes

1. Heat oil in a large skillet over medium heat. Add onions, garlic, and green bell pepper and cook, stirring frequently, for 8 to 10 minutes or until pepper is tender. Add paprika and cook for 30 seconds.

2. Stir in tomatoes, tomato sauce, chipotle, and kidney beans. Bring to a boil and simmer, stirring frequently for about 10 minutes or until mixture is slightly thickened. Season with salt and pepper to taste and serve immediately over rice.

 **Got You Covered!**

Although chipotle chilies are not part of the Cajun tradition, they give dishes a slightly smoky flavor. In this case, chipotles add the nuances to this vegetarian dish that a ham bone would traditionally provide.

Cuban-Style Red Beans and Rice

Serves: 6 as an entrée or 10 to 12 as a side dish

Prep time: 15 minutes plus a minimum of 1 hour for soaking beans

Cook time: 1½ hours

1½ cups dried small red kidney beans, rinsed and picked over to remove broken beans or pebbles

2 qt. water

2 large onions and ½ small onion, peeled

4 garlic cloves, peeled

2 fresh cilantro sprigs

1 tsp. ground cumin

Salt and freshly ground black pepper to taste

1½ cups long-grain white rice, rinsed well

3 TB. olive oil

½ red bell pepper, seeds and ribs removed, chopped

½ tsp. dried oregano

 Half Baked

The water the beans have cooked in contains some of the starch the beans released during the cooking process. If that starch is cooked over too-high heat, it can scorch. That's why you cook the rice in this recipe over very low heat.

1. Place red kidney beans in a Dutch oven and fill the pot with cold water. Soak kidney beans for 8 to 12 hours; then drain and continue. Or bring kidney beans to a boil, cover, allow to sit for 1 hour, and then drain. Whichever soaking method you use, begin cooking with beans as soon as possible after soaking.

2. Combine kidney beans, water, ½ small onion, 2 garlic cloves, cilantro sprigs, and ½ teaspoon cumin in a Dutch oven. Bring to a boil over medium-high heat. Reduce heat to medium-low, cover, and simmer, stirring occasionally, for 1 hour or until kidney beans are tender. Season to taste with salt and pepper. Drain, reserving kidney beans and cooking liquid separately. Discard vegetables and cilantro sprigs. (You can do this a day in advance and refrigerate, tightly covered. There's no need to reheat before continuing.)

3. Bring 3 cups bean cooking liquid to a boil in a saucepan over medium-high heat. Add rice, reduce heat to very low, cover, and simmer for 15 to 20 minutes or until almost all liquid is absorbed. Remove from heat, fluff rice with a fork, and keep warm.

4. While rice is cooking, chop remaining 2 large onions and mince remaining 2 garlic cloves. Set aside. Heat oil in a large, heavy skillet over medium-high heat. Add chopped onions, red bell pepper, and garlic. Cook, stirring frequently, for 3 minutes or until onion is translucent. Add remaining ½ teaspoon cumin and oregano and cook, stirring constantly, for 1 minute. Stir in kidney beans and rice, reduce heat to low, and cook for 3 to 5 minutes or until heated through. Season to taste with salt and pepper and serve immediately.

Hoppin' John with Greens

1½ cups dried black-eyed peas, rinsed and picked over to remove broken peas or pebbles

6 to 7 cups vegetable stock

1 lb. collard greens, stemmed, rinsed well, and thinly sliced

1 canned chipotle chili in adobo sauce, drained and finely chopped

1 large onion, peeled and chopped

1½ cups long-grain rice

Salt and freshly ground black pepper to taste

Serves: 6 as an entrée or 10 to 12 as a side dish	
Prep time: 15 minutes	
Cook time: 2 hours	

1. Place black-eyed peas, vegetable stock, collard greens, chipotle chili, and onion in a Dutch oven. Bring to a boil over high heat, reduce heat to low, and simmer for 1½ hours or until black-eyed peas are tender but not mushy. Drain black-eyed peas and greens, reserving cooking liquid.

2. Return 3 cups cooking liquid to the Dutch oven, stir in rice, and bring to a boil over high heat. Reduce heat to low, cover, and simmer for about 20 minutes or until rice is tender and liquid is absorbed.

3. Uncover, fluff rice with a fork, and stir in black-eyed peas and greens. Reheat over low heat until hot, stir with a fork, and season to taste with salt and pepper. Serve immediately.

 Bake Lore

Hoppin' John dates to the Colonial era Carolinas, and folks still eat it on New Year's Day to bring good luck. The black-eyed peas, called "pigeon peas" in Africa, were brought over with the slaves in the seventeenth century, and the first printed recipe for Hoppin' John comes from *The Carolina Housewife*, published in 1847.

Red Lentils with Pineapple, Mango, and Bananas

Serves: 6 as an entrée or 10 to 12 as a side dish

Prep time: 15 minutes

Cook time: 40 minutes

½ lb. red *lentils*, rinsed and picked over to remove broken lentils or pebbles

3 (14.5-oz.) cans vegetable stock

2 celery ribs with leaves, halved

1 medium carrot, scrubbed, trimmed, and halved

8 fresh parsley sprigs

2 TB. olive oil

1 small onion, peeled and diced

2 garlic cloves, peeled and minced

2 tsp. ground coriander

½ tsp. ground cinnamon

1 (28-oz.) can diced tomatoes, drained, ¼ cup juice reserved

½ cup golden raisins

Salt and freshly ground black pepper to taste

1 (20-oz.) can pineapple chunks packed in pineapple juice, drained

2 bananas, peeled and cut into ½-inch dice

1 mango, peeled and cut into ½-inch dice

3 cups cooked basmati rice, hot

Ellen on Edibles

Lentils, high in iron and vitamins A and B, have long been used as a meat substitute in the Middle East and India (in the latter they are called *dal*). These tiny, lens-shaped pulses (the dried seed of a legume) come in various colors, ranging from grayish-brown to fiery red and bright yellow. Due to their size, they are one of the few dried legumes that do not require any presoaking before cooking. They are also one of the few legumes that are not sold canned.

1. Place lentils in a Dutch oven with vegetable stock, celery, carrot, and parsley sprigs. Bring to a boil, reduce heat to medium-low, and simmer, uncovered, for 20 minutes or until lentils are tender but not mushy. Some liquid will remain in the pot. Remove and discard celery, carrot, and parsley sprigs and drain lentils. Return lentils to the Dutch oven.

2. While lentils are cooking, heat oil in a large, heavy saucepan over low heat. Add onion and garlic and cook, stirring frequently, for 3 minutes or until onion is translucent. Stir in coriander and cinnamon and cook, stirring constantly, for 1 minute.

3. Add tomatoes with reserved juice and raisins to onion mixture. Simmer, uncovered, over medium heat, stirring occasionally, for 10 minutes. Season to taste with salt and pepper. Stir in pineapple, bananas, and mango and cook for an additional 5 minutes.

4. Add tomato mixture to cooked lentils in the Dutch oven and gently fold ingredients together. Serve immediately over hot rice.

Curried Spicy Lentils with Toasted Cashew Nuts

¼ cup vegetable oil

2 onions, peeled and chopped

3 garlic cloves, peeled and minced

1 fresh jalapeño chili, seeds and ribs removed, finely chopped

1 TB. curry powder

1 tsp. ground cumin

1 tsp. ground coriander

½ tsp. turmeric

2 medium tomatoes, cored, seeded, and chopped

1½ cups brown lentils, rinsed well and picked over to re-move broken lentils or pebbles

4 cups vegetable stock (or more as needed)

2 (3-in.) cinnamon sticks

2 *cardamom* pods

Salt and freshly ground black pepper to taste

½ cup cashews

3 medium zucchini, trimmed and cut into ½-inch dice

¼ cup chopped fresh cilantro

3 cups cooked basmati rice, hot

Serves: 6 as an entrée or 10 to 12 as a side dish
Prep time: 20 minutes
Cook time: 55 minutes

1. Heat vegetable oil in a Dutch oven over medium-high heat. Add onions, garlic, and jalapeño chili and cook, stirring fre-quently, for 3 minutes or until onion is translucent. Stir in curry powder, cumin, coriander, and turmeric. Cook, stirring constantly, for 1 minute.

2. Add tomatoes, lentils, vegetable stock, cinnamon sticks, and cardamom pods. Season to taste with salt and pepper and bring to a boil over medium-high heat. Simmer mixture, uncovered, for 40 minutes or until lentils are very soft, adding more stock, if necessary, to keep ingredients just covered with liquid.

3. While lentils are cooking, heat the oven to 350°F. Place cashews on a baking sheet and toast in the oven for 5 to 7 minutes or until lightly browned. Remove nuts from the oven and set aside.

4. Discard cinnamon sticks and cardamom pods and add zucchini to the Dutch oven. Cover and cook for 10 minutes, until zuc-chini is tender. Stir in cilantro and season again with salt and pepper if necessary. Serve immediately over rice, sprinkled with toasted cashew nuts.

Ellen on Edibles

Cardamom, an aromatic spice native to tropical countries, is a member of the ginger family. Each pod contains about 20 cranberry-size seeds. The pod shells can be lightly crushed and will disin-tegrate while the dish cooks. (If they don't disintegrate, they are easy to remove.)

Black Bean Tamale Casserole

*Serves: 6 as an entrée or
10 to 12 as a side dish*

Prep time: 15 minutes
Cook time: 35 minutes

2 TB. olive oil

1 onion, peeled and chopped

3 garlic cloves, peeled and minced

1 TB. chili powder

2 tsp. ground cumin

½ cup chopped fresh cilantro

2 (4-oz.) cans diced mild green chilies, drained

½ cup bottled salsa verde (tomatillo salsa)

Salt and freshly ground black pepper to taste

1 (18-oz.) roll prepared polenta, cut into 18 rounds

½ cup whipping cream

2 (15-oz.) cans black beans, drained and rinsed

3 cups grated Monterey Jack cheese

 Bake Lore

In Mexico, tamales date back to the time of the Mayas. The word comes from the Nahuatl Indians, and the salient feature of a tamale is that various fillings are wrapped in a cornmeal dough, called *masa*. Traditional tamales are formed and steamed in corn husks, but a pie such as this one replicates the flavor with far less work.

1. Preheat the oven to 450°F. Grease a 9×13-inch baking pan. Heat oil in a skillet over medium-high heat. Add onion and garlic and cook, stirring frequently, for 3 minutes or until onion is translucent. Add chili powder and cumin and cook, stirring constantly, for 1 minute.

2. Mix ¼ cup cilantro, green chilies, and salsa verde into the skillet. Season mixture to taste with salt and pepper. Evenly space 9 polenta rounds in the prepared baking pan and drizzle with ¼ cup whipping cream. Top with ½ black beans and ½ green chili mixture. Sprinkle with 1½ cups Monterey Jack cheese. Repeat layering.

3. Cover with aluminum foil and bake for 20 minutes. Increase the oven temperature to 475°F. Remove foil and bake for 15 minutes or until top is golden brown. Let stand 5 minutes, sprinkle with remaining ¼ cup cilantro, and serve.

Asian Chili with Cilantro and Rice

1½ cups dried kidney beans, rinsed and picked over to remove broken beans or pebbles

2 TB. sesame oil

8 scallions, trimmed and sliced into ½-inch pieces

3 garlic cloves, peeled and minced

2 TB. grated fresh ginger

3 (14.5-oz.) cans vegetable stock

½ cup dry sherry

¼ cup hoisin sauce

¼ cup tamari

2 TB. Chinese black bean sauce

2 TB. white wine vinegar

2 tsp. Asian chili sauce

½ tsp. granulated sugar

Salt and freshly ground black pepper to taste

½ cup chopped fresh cilantro

3 cups cooked jasmine rice, hot

Serves: 6 as an entrée, or 10 to 12 as a side dish

Prep time: 15 minutes plus a minimum of 1 hour for soaking beans

Cook time: 1½ hours

1. Place kidney beans in a Dutch oven and fill the pot with cold water. Soak kidney beans for 8 to 12 hours; then drain and continue. Or bring kidney beans to a boil, cover, allow to sit for 1 hour, and then drain. Whichever soaking method you use, begin cooking with kidney beans as soon as possible after soaking.

2. Heat sesame oil in a Dutch oven over medium-high heat. Add scallions, garlic, and ginger and cook for 30 seconds, stirring constantly. Add drained kidney beans, vegetable stock, sherry, hoisin sauce, tamari, black bean sauce, vinegar, chili sauce, and sugar. Bring to a boil, reduce heat to low, and simmer, uncovered, for 1½ hours or until kidney beans are tender, stirring occasionally and adding water if mixture seems dry.

3. Season kidney bean mixture to taste with salt and pepper and stir in cilantro. Serve kidney beans over rice.

Bake Lore

In traditional Hawaiian cooking, fresh ginger—not ground or crystallized—is added to all recipes containing beans as a way to counteract the gas produced by eating fiber-rich legumes.

Hearty Vegetarian Chili

<table>
<tr><td>

Serves: 6 as an entrée or 10 to 12 as a side dish

Prep time: 15 minutes

Cook time: 30 minutes

</td></tr>
</table>

Ellen on Edibles

Bulgur is frequently called cracked wheat, and this ancient cereal grain consists of wheat kernels that have been steamed, dried, and crushed. It has a nutty flavor and chewy texture when cooked, which is why this vegetarian chili tastes "meaty."

2 TB. olive oil

1 onion, peeled and chopped

5 garlic cloves, peeled and minced

2 carrots, peeled and chopped

1 red bell pepper, seeds and ribs removed, chopped

2 jalapeño chilies, seeds and ribs removed, finely chopped

2 TB. chili powder

1½ tsp. ground cumin

1½ tsp. ground coriander

1 (28-oz.) can crushed tomatoes in tomato purée

2 cups water

4 (15-oz.) cans kidney beans, drained and rinsed

½ cup *bulgur*

Salt and freshly ground black pepper to taste

2 (5-oz.) pkg. cooked yellow rice, hot

¼ cup chopped fresh cilantro

6 scallions, trimmed and thinly sliced

1 cup sour cream

1 cup grated cheddar cheese

1. Heat olive oil in a Dutch oven over medium-high heat. Add onion and garlic and cook, stirring frequently, for 3 minutes or until onion is translucent. Add carrots, red bell pepper, and jalapeño chili and cook for 2 minutes. Add chili powder, cumin, and coriander and cook for 1 minute, stirring constantly.

2. Add tomatoes, water, kidney beans, and bulgur. Bring to a boil, reduce heat to medium, and cook, uncovered, stirring occasionally, for 20 minutes or until bulgur is tender. Season to taste with salt and pepper and serve immediately over rice, sprinkled with cilantro. Pass scallions, sour cream, and cheese in bowls separately.

Spicy Chickpea and Kale Stew

1½ cups dried chickpeas, rinsed and picked over to remove broken beans or pebbles

10 cups water

¼ cup olive oil

2 large onions, peeled and diced

3 garlic cloves, peeled and minced

2 green bell peppers, seeds and ribs removed, chopped

3 TB. chili powder

1 tsp. dried thyme

1 tsp. dried oregano

½ to 1 tsp. crushed hot red pepper flakes

1 tsp. ground cumin

1 tsp. granulated sugar

1 bay leaf

1½ lb. kale, coarse stems discarded and leaves washed well and chopped

2 (28-oz.) cans diced plum tomatoes, undrained

1 (6-oz.) can tomato paste

Salt to taste

3 to 4 cups cooked rice, hot

Serves: 6 as an entrée or 10 to 12 as a side dish
Prep time: 15 minutes plus a minimum of 1 hour for soaking beans
Cook time: 2½ hours

1. Place chickpeas in a Dutch oven and fill the pot with cold water. Soak chickpeas for 8 to 12 hours; then drain and continue. Or bring chickpeas to a boil, cover, allow to sit for 1 hour, and then drain. Whichever soaking method you use, begin cooking chickpeas as soon as possible after soaking.

2. Return chickpeas to Dutch oven, add 10 cups water, and bring to a boil over high heat. Reduce heat to medium and cook, uncovered, for 1½ hours or until tender. Drain chickpeas, reserving cooking liquid.

3. While chickpeas are simmering, heat oil in a Dutch oven over medium-high heat. Add onions and garlic and cook, stirring frequently, for 3 minutes or until onion is translucent. Add green bell peppers and cook for an additional 2 minutes. Add chili powder, thyme, oregano, red pepper flakes, cumin, sugar, and bay leaf. Cook, stirring constantly, for 1 minute.

4. Add 2 cups reserved cooking liquid, chickpeas, kale, tomatoes with their juice, and tomato paste to the Dutch oven. Stir well and bring to a boil over medium heat. Reduce heat to low and simmer, uncovered, for 1 hour. Add more cooking liquid if the mixture seems to be drying out.

5. Discard bay leaf and season stew with salt. Serve over rice.

 **Got You Covered!**

If you don't have time to simmer the beans, here's a shortcut: use 3 (15-ounce) cans chickpeas drained and rinsed. Then substitute 2 cups vegetable stock for the cooking liquid for the final simmering.

Tuscan-Style White Beans with Tomatoes and Rosemary

Serves: 6 as an entrée or 10 to 12 as a side dish

Prep time: 15 minutes

Cook time: 45 minutes

---

4 TB. olive oil

1 medium onion, peeled and chopped

2 celery stalks, trimmed and thinly sliced

6 garlic cloves, peeled and minced

3 medium zucchini, trimmed, quartered lengthwise, and thinly sliced

3 (14.5-oz.) cans diced tomatoes, drained

3 (15-oz.) cans small white navy beans, drained and rinsed

⅓ cup oil-cured black olives, pitted and halved

3 TB. chopped fresh rosemary or 3 tsp. dried

Salt and freshly ground black pepper to taste

1 cup Italian breadcrumbs

½ cup grated Parmesan cheese

¼ cup chopped fresh parsley

1. Preheat the oven to 350°F. Grease a 9×13-inch baking pan. Heat 2 tablespoons oil in a skillet over medium-high heat. Add onion, celery, and 5 garlic cloves and cook, stirring frequently, for 3 minutes or until onion is translucent. Add zucchini and cook, stirring frequently, for an additional 3 minutes or until zucchini has started to soften.

2. Remove the skillet from heat and stir in tomatoes and navy beans. Mash about ¼ beans with the back of a large spoon and mix into whole navy beans. Stir in olives and rosemary and season to taste with salt and pepper.

3. Scrape navy bean mixture into the prepared baking pan and cover with aluminum foil. Bake for 15 minutes. While navy beans are baking, combine remaining 2 tablespoons oil, remaining 1 garlic clove, breadcrumbs, Parmesan cheese, and parsley in a mixing bowl. Mix well.

4. Remove the pan from the oven, remove foil, and sprinkle topping over navy beans. Bake for an additional 30 minutes or until bubbling and the top is golden brown. Cool 5 minutes before serving.

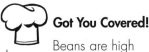 **Got You Covered!**

Beans are high in carbohydrates, which makes them a natural thickener for dishes. That's why you mash some of the beans in this dish. You can use the same procedure when cooking any bean dish.

Creamy Southwestern Bean Bake

2 TB. olive oil

1 large onion, peeled and chopped

3 garlic cloves, peeled and minced

1 TB. chili powder

1 tsp. dried oregano, preferably Mexican

¾ tsp. ground cumin

2 large eggs, lightly beaten

1½ cups plain yogurt

¾ cup sour cream

1 (4-oz.) can whole mild green chilies, drained and chopped

3 TB. all-purpose flour

4 (15-oz.) cans pink beans or pinto beans, drained and rinsed

¾ cup grated sharp cheddar cheese

¾ cup (2 oz.) grated Monterey Jack cheese

Salt and freshly ground black pepper to taste

Serves: 6 as an entrée or 10 to 12 as a side dish
Prep time: 15 minutes
Cook time: 35 minutes

1. Preheat the oven to 325°F. Grease a 9×13-inch baking pan. Heat oil in a large skillet over medium-high heat. Add onion and garlic and cook, stirring frequently, for 3 minutes or until onion is translucent. Add chili powder, oregano, and cumin. Cook, stirring constantly, for 1 minute. Scrape onto a plate to cool.

2. Combine eggs, yogurt, sour cream, chilies, and flour in a mixing bowl. Stir well; then stir in sautéed vegetables, pink beans, ½ cheddar cheese, and ½ Monterey Jack cheese. Season to taste with salt and pepper and spread mixture into the prepared baking pan.

3. Cover with aluminum foil and bake for 15 minutes. Remove the foil, sprinkle with remaining cheddar and Monterey Jack cheese, and bake for an additional 20 minutes or until bubbly and top is browned. Allow to sit for 5 minutes; then serve.

 Half Baked

It's important to cool cooked ingredients before stirring them into a mixture that contains raw eggs because the residual heat from foods can scramble the eggs.

Chapter 16

Reds, Whites, and Greens: Vegetarian Casseroles for All Seasons

In This Chapter

- ◆ International vegetable medleys
- ◆ Spruced-up hearty root vegetables
- ◆ Getting the most from delicate summer crops

More than 2,000 vegetables are being cultivated around the world today, and they come in a rainbow of colors, flavors, and textures. And with advances in modern transportation, we can now enjoy vegetables from every climatic zone on a year-round basis, thus opening previously closed options.

The recipes in this chapter reflect these advances and draw from many of the world's cuisines. You can serve them as well-balanced vegetarian main courses or as side dishes.

The Root of the Matter

Beets, carrots, parsnips, salsify, rutabaga, and turnips are all root vegetables, or what we call "white vegetables"—although they come in many colors. Add into this cornucopia such popular vegetables as potatoes, sweet potatoes, and yams. We might think of them more as carbohydrates than vegetables, but they are botanically classified the same. All these species grow underground and have a very long storage time. Before refrigeration was invented, root vegetables were kept at home in cool root cellars and were the only vegetables available in most parts of America during the winter months.

You can substitute most root vegetables for one another, and they are also delicious when used in combination for a purée or gratin because the cooking times are all almost the same. Cut root vegetables into square pieces not larger than 2 inches, or the outside will become mushy before the inside is cooked. Depending on the vegetable, they may or may not need peeling.

Most root vegetables, including sweet potatoes and yams, can be assembled in advance of baking. An exception to this rule is any type of potato. They will turn brown if not cooked immediately.

Odiferous Onions

Onions are relatives of leeks and garlic, which are all bulbs grown underground. Usually, the milder the climate in which an onion is grown, the sweeter the flavor will be. Onions are always more pungent raw because when they are cooked, the heat converts the sulfurous flavor and aroma to sugars. Onions take well to many cooking techniques.

Here are some common types of onions:

◆ **Common onions.** When a recipe calls for an onion, a common onion is what's needed. Common onions are fully mature; have either white, yellow, or brown skins; and have a strong, assertive flavor.

◆ **Leeks.** Leeks resemble large scallions, and although they are not technically onions, their flavor is related and they are cooked in the same ways. They add a delicate onion flavor to foods; however, because the green tops can be bitter, you should usually trim them off.

◆ **Red onions.** The beautiful red-violet color of these onions will bleed into dishes when they're cooked, so consider that before substituting them for yellow onions. The flavor is not constant and can range from sweet to sharp.

- **Scallions (or green onions).** These have long cylindrical green stems and small bulbs. They are cultivated in many sizes and have a mild, almost grassy flavor. Scallions are actually seedlings, and if their bulbs are allowed to develop, they're called spring onions and the green stems are detached before they are sold.

- **Shallots.** A shallot's flavor is milder than an onion's and less pungent than garlic. Shallots are usually about 1 to 1½ inches long, are oval in shape, and may come as one bulb or a pair. They are excellent in sauces, in salad dressings, and roasted whole.

- **Sweet onions.** These include Bermuda, Maui, Vidalia, and Walla Walla. They come from different warm locations, but they all can be used interchangeably. They are usually much larger in diameter than common onions and caramelize better, because they contain more natural plant sugars.

The Fresh vs. Frozen Dilemma

On one hand you're looking at a huge produce department with brightly colored vegetables piled high. On the other, you're looking at small boxes of solidly frozen food. Your choice? That should depend on the vegetable.

Some vegetables, such as corn, spinach, lima beans, broccoli, peas, and cut green beans, are fine to use frozen, as long as their individual cooking times are respected. Because green vegetables such as green beans or peas are blanched before freezing, they just require thawing and a short time in the pot to warm them through. Others, such as lima beans, require a few minutes of additional cooking.

Always drain thawed vegetables well, especially those such as spinach that give off a large quantity of green water that can color dishes.

Other vegetables, such as zucchini, summer squash, carrots, celery, and mushrooms, suffer badly from being frozen and should be used fresh.

The Layered Look

Many of the recipes in this chapter specify layering the ingredients rather than tossing them together. This is a matter of aesthetics, because the vegetables all end up in the same place—your mouth and stomach. If you think spending the time to layer a casserole is too great, then toss the ingredients in a bowl to combine them evenly. It will taste just as great.

Southwest Spinach Loaf

Serves: 6 as an entrée or 10 to 12 as a side dish
Prep time: 10 minutes
Cook time: 1 hour

4 large eggs

2 (10-oz.) pkg. frozen chopped spinach, thawed

1½ cups corn tortilla chips

1 cup grated jalapeño Jack cheese

½ cup grated Parmesan cheese

½ cup cottage cheese

3 scallions, trimmed with all but 2 inches of green tops discarded, thinly sliced

1 (2-oz.) jar sliced pimientos, drained and chopped

½ cup Italian breadcrumbs

3 TB. heavy cream

Pinch granulated sugar

Salt and freshly ground black pepper to taste

⅛ tsp. grated nutmeg

Ellen on Edibles

Bain marie is the French term for a water bath that cooks food gently by surrounding it with simmering water. The water temperature is actually lower than the oven temperature because water only reaches 212°F, so delicate custards set without getting rubbery.

1. Preheat the oven to 350°F. Grease a 2-quart loaf pan or soufflé dish. Bring a kettle of water to a boil over high heat.

2. Whisk eggs in a large mixing bowl. Place spinach in a colander and press with the back of a spoon to extract as much liquid as possible. Add spinach to the mixing bowl. Place corn tortilla chips in a heavy plastic bag and pound with the flat side of a meat mallet or the bottom of a small skillet until coarse crumbs are formed. Add ½ crumbs to the mixing bowl.

3. Add jalapeño Jack cheese, Parmesan cheese, cottage cheese, scallions, pimientos, breadcrumbs, cream, sugar, salt, pepper, and nutmeg to the mixing bowl. Stir well.

4. Scrape mixture into the prepared loaf pan and smooth with a rubber spatula. Sprinkle on remaining corn chip crumbs and cover lightly with aluminum foil.

5. Place loaf pan in a large roasting pan and pour enough boiling water into the pan to come halfway up the sides to form a *bain marie*. Bake for 20 minutes. Remove the foil and bake for an additional 40 minutes or until a skewer inserted in the center comes out clean. Remove the loaf pan from the roasting pan and serve immediately.

Caribbean Stuffed Eggplant

3 medium eggplants

4 TB. olive oil

6 scallions, trimmed with all but 2 inches of green tops discarded, thinly sliced

2 garlic cloves, peeled and minced

½ cup breadcrumbs

¼ cup milk

3 large eggs, lightly beaten

2 TB. chopped fresh cilantro

1 TB. chopped fresh basil or 1 tsp. dried

1 dash hot red pepper sauce such as Tabasco

1 tsp. grated lemon zest

Salt and freshly ground black pepper to taste

> *Serves: 6 as an entrée or 10 to 12 as a side dish*
>
> **Prep time:** 20 minutes
> **Cook time:** 30 minutes

1. Preheat the oven to 375°F. Grease a 10×14-inch baking pan.

2. Cut eggplants in half lengthwise and trim off caps. Heat 2 tablespoons olive oil in a large skillet over medium heat. Slash cut eggplants' sides several times, being careful not to cut through the skin. Place eggplants cut side down in oil, cover, and cook for 10 minutes, working in batches if necessary.

3. Scoop out eggplant pulp using a grapefruit knife or a sharp spoon, leaving shells about ¼-inch thick. Set shells aside. Coarsely chop eggplant pulp. Heat remaining 2 tablespoons oil in the skillet over medium heat and add eggplant pulp, scallions, and garlic. Cook for 5 minutes and cool for at least 10 minutes.

4. In a large bowl, moisten breadcrumbs with milk and mix thoroughly with eggs. Stir in cooked pulp mixture, cilantro, basil, hot red pepper sauce, and lemon zest. Season to taste with salt and pepper.

5. Stuff eggplant shells with mixture and place stuffed shells in the prepared baking pan. (You can do this a day in advance and refrigerate, tightly covered. Add 15 minutes to initial baking time.)

6. Cover with aluminum foil and bake for 20 minutes. Remove foil and bake for an additional 15 minutes or until a toothpick inserted in the center comes out clean. Serve immediately.

 **Got You Covered!**

If you're making this recipe as a side dish, use small Italian eggplants rather than the larger European ones. The same proportions will work for 5 or 6 Italian eggplants, and then you'll have individual servings.

Eastern European Root Vegetable and Sweet Potato Casserole (*Tsimmis*)

> *Serves: 6 as an entrée or 10 to 12 as a side dish*
>
> **Prep time:** 20 minutes
> **Cook time:** 1½ hours

1½ lb. carrots, peeled and cut into ½-inch slices

1 lb. sweet potatoes, peeled and cut into ½-inch cubes

½ lb. rutabaga, peeled and cut into ½-inch cubes

1 large onion, peeled and diced

1 cup dried apricots, diced

1 cup pitted prunes, diced

1 cup apple cider

1 cup vegetable stock

½ tsp. grated nutmeg

½ tsp. ground cinnamon

Salt and freshly ground black pepper to taste

1. Preheat the oven to 400°F. Grease a 10×14-inch baking pan.

2. Place carrots, sweet potatoes, rutabaga, onion, apricots, and prunes in a mixing bowl and toss to combine. Transfer mixture to the prepared baking pan. Combine apple cider, vegetable stock, nutmeg, cinnamon, salt, and pepper in the same bowl and stir well.

3. Pour apple cider mixture into the baking pan and cover with aluminum foil. Bake for 1 hour or until vegetables are almost tender. Remove foil and bake for an additional 30 minutes or until lightly browned and liquid has almost evaporated. (You can do this up to 2 days in advance and refrigerate, tightly covered. Reheat in a 350°F oven for 20 to 30 minutes or until hot.) Serve immediately.

 Bake Lore

Tsimmis is a traditional dish served by Eastern European Jews. Its name has slang meaning in Yiddish: "What's the big tsimmis?" means "What's the big deal?"

Hot and Sweet Asian Ratatouille

2 TB. vegetable oil

2 TB. sesame oil

1 onion, peeled and diced

6 garlic cloves, peeled and minced

3 TB. grated fresh ginger

2 small zucchini, trimmed and cut into ½-inch slices

2 small yellow squash, trimmed and cut into ½-inch slices

1 lb. white mushrooms, stems removed, wiped with damp paper towel, and halved if small or quartered if large

3 Japanese eggplants, trimmed and cut into ½-inch slices or 1 small Italian eggplant, trimmed and cut into ½-inch cubes

¾ cup vegetable stock

½ cup tomato sauce

¼ cup dry sherry

2 TB. black bean sauce

2 TB. hoisin sauce

2 TB. tamari

2 TB. red wine vinegar

½ tsp. Chinese chili sauce

Salt and freshly ground black pepper to taste

3 to 4 cups cooked jasmine rice, hot

Serves: 6 as an entrée or 10 to 12 as a side dish
Prep time: 20 minutes
Cook time: 30 minutes

1. Heat vegetable oil and sesame oil in a Dutch oven over medium-high heat. Add onion, garlic, and ginger and cook, stirring frequently, for 3 minutes or until onion is translucent. Add zucchini, yellow squash, mushrooms, and eggplants. Cook, stirring frequently, for 3 minutes or until squash begins to soften.

2. Add vegetable stock, tomato sauce, sherry, black bean sauce, hoisin sauce, tamari, red wine vinegar, and chili sauce. Bring to a boil, stirring occasionally. Cover, reduce heat to low, and cook for 10 minutes. Uncover, increase heat to medium, and simmer for 20 minutes, stirring frequently, or until vegetables are tender and sauce has thickened slightly. Season to taste with salt and pepper. Serve immediately over rice if an entrée (the rice is optional if served as a side dish).

 **Got You Covered!**

Zucchini is Italian in origin, and its native name was retained when it was integrated into American cooking. Choose small zucchini because they tend to have a sweeter flavor and the seeds are tender and less pronounced.

Spaghetti Squash with Mexican Chili Sauce and Monterey Jack Cheese

Serves: 6 as an entrée or 10 to 12 as a side dish
Prep time: 15 minutes
Cook time: 1½ hours

1 medium *spaghetti squash*

2 TB. olive oil

1 medium red onion, peeled and chopped

2 garlic cloves, peeled and minced

1 jalapeño chili, seeds and ribs removed, finely chopped

2 tsp. dried oregano, preferably Mexican

1 tsp. ground cumin

1 (14.5-oz.) can diced tomatoes, undrained

1 (8-oz.) can tomato sauce

1 (4-oz.) can diced mild green chilies, drained

1 tsp. granulated sugar

1 tsp. cider vinegar

Salt and freshly ground black pepper to taste

1 cup grated Monterey Jack cheese

¼ cup chopped fresh cilantro

1. Preheat the oven to 350°F. Grease a 9×13-inch baking pan. Pierce squash with a sharp fork in several places and place on a baking sheet. Bake for 45 minutes to 1 hour, turning once during baking, or until skin yields to pressure when pressed. Remove from the oven.

2. While squash is baking, heat olive oil in a saucepan over medium-high heat. Add red onion, garlic, and jalapeño chili and cook, stirring frequently, for 3 minutes or until onion is translucent. Add oregano and cumin and cook, stirring constantly, for 1 minute.

3. Add tomatoes, tomato sauce, chilies, sugar, vinegar, salt, and pepper and bring to a boil. Reduce heat to low and simmer for 20 minutes. Remove from heat and set aside.

4. When squash is cool enough to handle, slice in half lengthwise and discard seeds and membranes. Remove squash from shell by combing halves lengthwise with the tines of a fork.

5. Place squash in the prepared baking pan and stir in chili sauce. Cover with aluminum foil and bake for 15 minutes. Remove foil, sprinkle with Monterey Jack cheese and cilantro, and bake for an additional 15 minutes or until cheese is melted and top is lightly browned. Serve immediately.

Ellen on Edibles

Spaghetti squash is a relative newcomer in the vegetable patch whose popularity has been growing because those on low-carbohydrate diets can use the squash like spaghetti. Shaped like a small watermelon, spaghetti squash weigh about 3 to 5 pounds, and after the cooked flesh is forked vertically, it separates into distinct spaghettilike strands.

Chard, Tomato, and Cheese Casserole

2 TB. olive oil

2 bunches *Swiss chard*, washed, center ribs cut away, and coarsely chopped (about 8 cups)

3 red bell peppers, seeds and ribs removed, chopped

1 large onion, peeled and chopped

Salt and freshly ground black pepper to taste

2 cups grated Monterey Jack cheese

½ cup grated Parmesan cheese

2 large tomatoes, cored, seeded, and thinly sliced

Serves: 6 as an entrée or 10 to 12 as a side dish
Prep time: 15 minutes
Cook time: 50 minutes

1. Preheat the oven to 350°F. Grease a 9×13-inch baking pan. Heat 1 tablespoon oil in a Dutch oven over high heat. Add Swiss chard and cook, stirring frequently, for 3 minutes or until Swiss chard is wilted. Transfer Swiss chard to a colander and drain well, pressing with the back of a spoon to extract as much liquid as possible.

2. Heat remaining 1 tablespoon oil in a large, heavy saucepan over medium heat. Add red bell peppers and onion and cook, stirring frequently, for 5 minutes or until vegetables are tender. Mix in Swiss chard, toss to combine, and season to taste with salt and pepper. Mix in ½ Monterey Jack cheese and ½ Parmesan cheese and spread in the prepared baking pan.

3. Overlap tomato slices atop vegetable mixture, covering vegetables completely. Season tomatoes with salt and pepper and sprinkle with remaining Monterey Jack cheese and Parmesan cheese. Cover with aluminum foil and bake for 40 minutes. Remove the foil and bake for an additional 10 minutes or until top begins to brown. Serve immediately.

Ellen on Edibles

Swiss chard, available year-round but best in the summer, is a member of the beet family, grown for its crinkly green leaves and silvery, celerylike stalks. The variety with dark green leaves and reddish stalks has a stronger flavor than those bunches with lighter leaves and stalks. You can substitute the greens for spinach and can steam or stir-fry the stalks like asparagus.

Herbed Potato, Onion, and Celery Root Casserole

Serves: *6 as an entrée or 10 to 12 as a side dish*

Prep time: 20 minutes
Cook time: 1 hour plus 10 minutes sitting time

Ellen on Edibles

Celery root, also called *celeriac*, is a knobby brown root vegetable that won't win any beauty prizes. It tastes like celery, but with a more pronounced flavor, and has the texture of a turnip when it's cooked. Celery root can range in size from as small as an apple to as large as a cantaloupe, and the smaller ones are better and less fibrous.

1 lb. *celery root*, peeled, quartered, and thinly sliced

1½ lb. russet potatoes, peeled and thinly sliced

Salt and freshly ground black pepper to taste

½ tsp. grated nutmeg

1 large onion, peeled and thinly sliced

3 garlic cloves, peeled and minced

2 cups grated Gruyère cheese

1 (14.5-oz.) can vegetable stock

1 cup heavy cream

1 TB. fresh thyme or 1 tsp. dried

1 TB. chopped fresh rosemary or 1 tsp. dried

1 TB. chopped fresh tarragon or 1 tsp. dried

1. Preheat the oven to 400°F. Grease a 9×13-inch baking pan. Arrange ⅓ celery root slices in the baking pan. Top with ⅓ potato slices. Season to taste with salt and pepper, then top with ¼ teaspoon nutmeg. Top with ½ onion slices, ½ garlic, and ½ Gruyère cheese. Repeat, layering once more. Cover with remaining ⅓ celery root and then add potatoes.

2. Bring vegetable stock and cream to a simmer in a saucepan over medium heat, stirring occasionally. Add thyme, rosemary, and tarragon and simmer for 2 minutes. Season to taste with salt and pepper and pour over vegetables.

3. Cover with aluminum foil and bake for 20 minutes. Remove foil and bake for an additional 40 minutes or until vegetables are very tender and liquid bubbles thickly. Remove from the oven. Let stand 10 minutes, then serve. (You can do this up to 2 days in advance and refrigerate, tightly covered. Reheat in a 350°F oven, covered with foil, for 20 to 30 minutes or until hot.)

Southwestern Corn Pudding

3 TB. butter

1 red bell pepper, seeds and ribs removed and chopped

4 scallions, trimmed with all but 2 inches of green tops discarded, thinly sliced

2 garlic cloves, peeled and minced

2 (10-oz.) pkg. frozen corn, thawed and well drained

1½ cups cornbread stuffing crumbs

2 cups grated jalapeño Jack cheese

1 (4-oz.) can diced mild green chilies, drained

1¾ cups buttermilk

1 cup canned enchilada sauce

4 large eggs

Salt and freshly ground black pepper to taste

Serves: 6 as an entrée or 10 to 12 as a side dish
Prep time: 15 minutes plus 1 hour chilling
Cook time: 1 hour

1. Grease a 13×9-inch glass baking dish. Melt butter in a skillet over medium-high heat. Add red bell pepper, scallions, and garlic. Cook, stirring often, for 5 minutes or until softened. Stir in corn and cook for 1 minute. Remove from heat and stir in cornbread stuffing crumbs, jalapeño Jack cheese, and green chilies.

2. Whisk buttermilk, enchilada sauce, eggs, salt, and pepper together in a medium bowl. Add to cornbread mixture and toss gently to combine. Transfer mixture to the prepared baking dish. Cover and refrigerate for at least 1 hour. (You can do this up to 2 days in advance and refrigerate, tightly covered.)

3. Preheat the oven to 350°F. Cover the baking dish with aluminum foil. Bake for 15 minutes. Remove the foil and bake for an additional 45 minutes or until slightly crisp and golden on top. Let stand 5 minutes before serving.

Got You Covered!

This is a great way to use up leftover corn-on-the-cob during corn season. There's usually about ½ cup corn per ear, so each box of frozen corn represents 4 ears. If you're using uncooked fresh corn, add about 5 minutes to the time the corn kernels are sautéed to cook them properly.

Herbed Summer Squash and Potato Torte with Parmesan Cheese

Serves: 6 as an entrée or 10 to 12 as a side dish
Prep time: 25 minutes
Cook time: 65 minutes

8 scallions, trimmed with all but 2 inches of green tops discarded, thinly sliced

⅔ cup grated Gruyère cheese

½ cup grated Parmesan cheese

2 TB. all-purpose flour

2 TB. chopped fresh rosemary or 2 tsp. dried

1 TB. chopped fresh thyme or 1 tsp. dried

Salt and freshly ground black pepper to taste

1½ lb. russet potatoes, peeled and thinly sliced

1 lb. yellow crookneck squash, cut into ⅛-inch-thick rounds

2 TB. olive oil

1. Preheat the oven to 375°F. Grease two 8-inch-round cake pans. Set aside ¼ cup sliced scallions. Combine remaining scallions, Gruyère, Parmesan cheese, flour, rosemary, thyme, salt, and pepper in a medium bowl. Stir well to blend.

2. Layer ⅙ potatoes in concentric circles in the bottom of one prepared cake pan, overlapping them slightly. Layer ¼ squash in concentric circles on top of potatoes. Drizzle with 1 teaspoon oil. Sprinkle with ⅙ cheese mixture. Repeat with ⅙ potatoes, then ¼ squash and 1 teaspoon oil. Sprinkle with ⅙ cheese mixture. Top with ⅙ potatoes. Drizzle with 1 teaspoon oil. Sprinkle with ⅙ cheese mixture and press gently to flatten. Repeat procedure with the second cake pan and remaining potatoes, squash, oil, and cheese mixture.

3. Cover the cake pans with foil. Bake for about 40 minutes or until potatoes are almost tender. Remove foil and bake for an additional 25 minutes or until tortes begin to brown and potatoes are tender. (You can do this up to a day in advance and refrigerate, tightly covered. Reheat, covered with foil, in a 350°F oven for 25 minutes or until heated through.)

4. Cut each torte into wedges. Sprinkle wedges with remaining scallions and serve immediately.

 **Got You Covered!**

Sturdy potatoes take much longer to bake than delicate summer squash, so be sure to slice the potatoes much more thinly. Thickness is a way to equalize uneven cooking times when combining different foods.

Vegetable Enchiladas with Cheese Sauce

4 TB. (½ stick) butter

3 cups coarsely chopped zucchini and/or yellow crookneck squash (or some combination of the two)

1 onion, peeled and chopped

2 garlic cloves, peeled and minced

1 (10-oz.) pkg. frozen corn, thawed

1 (4-oz.) can diced mild green chilies, drained

½ cup chopped fresh cilantro

Salt and freshly ground black pepper to taste

3 TB. chili powder

2 TB. all-purpose flour

1½ tsp. ground cumin

2½ cups whole milk

2 cups grated Monterey Jack cheese

6 to 8 (8-in.) flour tortillas or 10 to 12 (6-in.) flour tortillas

> *Serves: 6 to 8 as an entrée or 10 to 12 as a side dish*
>
> **Prep time:** 20 minutes
>
> **Cook time:** 45 minutes

1. Preheat the oven to 350°F. Grease a 9×13-inch baking pan. Melt 2 tablespoons butter in a large, heavy skillet over medium-high heat. Add zucchini, onion, and garlic and cook, stirring frequently, for 5 to 7 minutes or until vegetables are soft. Mix in 1 cup corn, green chilies, and ¼ cup cilantro. Season to taste with salt and pepper.

2. Melt remaining 2 tablespoons butter in a saucepan over low heat. Whisk in chili powder, flour, and cumin and cook, stirring constantly, for 1 minute. Gradually whisk in milk. Cook, whisking occasionally, for about 5 minutes or until sauce is thick and bubbling. Add 1½ cups Monterey Jack cheese and whisk until smooth. Season to taste with salt and pepper.

3. Spread ¼ cup sauce in bottom of the prepared baking pan. Mix ¾ cup sauce into filling. Wrap tortillas in plastic wrap and microwave on high (100 percent) for 3 seconds or until warm and pliable.

4. Place generous ⅓ cup filling in center of each tortilla and roll up to enclose filling. Place enchiladas in baking dish seam side down. Cover enchiladas with remaining sauce; then sprinkle with remaining 1 cup corn and ½ cup Monterey Jack cheese. (You can do this a day in advance and refrigerate, tightly covered. Add 10 minutes to initial baking time.)

5. Cover with aluminum foil and bake for 20 minutes. Remove the foil and bake for an additional 25 minutes. Sprinkle with remaining ¼ cup cilantro and serve immediately.

Half Baked

It's important to wrap flour tortillas in plastic before softening them in the microwave because the plastic seals in the inherent moisture. If they're not covered, the tortillas will instantly turn brittle and break when they are rolled.

Chapter 17

Going With the Grains: Vibrant, Vegetarian Rice and Other Grain Recipes

In This Chapter

◆ Exotic rice dishes from around the world
◆ Ways to add excitement to leftover cooked rice
◆ Recipes for nutty, nutritious grains

Many of the world's culinary divisions are based on the grain that serves as the foundation for the diet. Americans and most Europeans have wheat filling that bill, but for the majority of the world's population, the grain is rice.

In this chapter, you'll find diverse, exciting, and delicious rice dishes from all over Asia and Latin America that you can make in a matter of minutes. As with other chapters in Part 6, you can serve these dishes both as a side dish and as an entrée.

But rice isn't the only grain on today's hit parade. And so some recipes later in this chapter use nutty wild rice and other nutritious grains.

From the Paddy to the Pan

All grains, including rice, are the fruit produced by grasses. Many of the nonrice varieties, with their interesting textures, innately sweet and nutty flavors, and high nutrient and fiber content, are now vying in popularity with rice. When I talk about grains, however, I usually think of categories like barley and buckwheat; rice is rice.

The 7,000-plus varieties of rice are grown in one of two ways. Aquatic rice (or paddy grown) is cultivated in flooded fields. The lower-yielding, lower-quality hill-grown rice can be grown on almost any tropical or subtropical terrain.

For all grains, the most nutritious part is the endosperm, where we find the carbohydrates, vitamins, minerals, and oils. The endosperm is always present when we cook grains, regardless of the other milling it has undergone. This nugget of nutrition is the tissue that surrounds the embryo of each grain of rice.

As rice and grains are processed, certain nutrients such as the fiber content are scraped away. That's why brown rice, which has only the inedible husk removed, is considered more nutritious than white rice. The other side of the equation is convenience. Whole grains take much longer to cook than grains that have been processed.

Store grains in a cool, dry place, or their oils may turn rancid. During warm weather, it is best to store them refrigerated or frozen; they will last for months.

Size Specifics

Rice is classified by the length of individual grains. Perhaps the most popular is *long-grain* rice. The length of the grain is four or five times the size of the width. When cooked, it produces light, dry grains that separate easily.

Along with basic white rice, other species are popular:

♦ *Basmati and jasmine rice* are long-grain varieties that are both from Asia and produce a nutlike fragrance when cooked. The aroma is created by a high concentration of acetyl pyroline, a compound naturally found in all rice.

♦ *Brown rice* is the entire grain with only the inedible outer husk removed. The nutritious, high-fiber bran coating gives it a light tan color, nutlike flavor, and chewy texture. The presence of the bran means that brown rice is subject to rancidity, which limits its shelf life to only about 6 months. It also takes slightly longer to cook (about 30 minutes total) than regular white long-grain rice.

♦ *Arborio rice*, almost all of which is imported from Italy, is a medium-grain rice (a softer rice that is two to three times as long as it is wide). Arborio rice has a high starch content. This natural carbohydrate is released as the rice is stirred to create a creamy texture in risotto dishes.

Creative Cooking

You can cook all rice in water, and most people add salt to the water for a bit of flavor. But you can also use stock or any other boiling liquid, including fruit juice, as a cooking medium. Rice absorbs the flavor of seasonings very well as it simmers, so any herbs and spices go a long way to deliver flavor.

After it's cooked, allow rice to sit for a few minutes, covered. This allows the grains to settle down after absorbing the cooking liquid.

 Bake Lore

Short-grain rice (sometimes called sushi rice and eaten in many Asian countries) is intended to be sticky so that it's easy to eat with chopsticks. But long-grain rice should be fluffed with a fork after cooking. The grains will separate easily and look more attractive.

A Walk on the Wild Side

Wild rice is a grain that is native to North America, specifically, the Chippewa Indian lands in the lake country of Minnesota. Not a rice at all, but an aquatic grass, *Zizania aquatica*, it was named "wild rice" because, growing, it looked so much like the rice fields familiar to European settlers.

Wild rice contains more protein than most rice and is processed by first fermenting it to develop the characteristic nutty flavor and then roasting it, which accounts for the brown color.

Look for unbroken grains at least ⅓ inch long that have been grown in Canada or the northern United States. Avoid broken grains because they will cook unevenly. Store wild rice in an airtight plastic bag or container for up to a year. The older the rice, the longer it will take to become soft.

Before cooking, place the wild rice in a strainer and rinse under cold running water about 2 minutes, until the water runs clear. Wild rice is best braised in stock, but salted boiling water will also work. Start 1 cup wild rice with 3½ cups liquid, and check after 45 minutes to see if additional liquid is needed.

Species of true rice cook relatively quickly, but wild rice is best when it is allowed to cook for up to 1½ hours, either in the oven or on top of the stove. This long, slow process renders the grains light and fluffy.

Persian Pilaf with Dried Fruit

Serves: 6 as an entrée or 10 to 12 as a side dish
Prep time: 15 minutes
Cook time: 20 minutes

1 TB. butter

1 TB. olive oil

1 small onion, peeled and coarsely chopped

3 garlic cloves, peeled and minced

4 medium carrots, peeled and cut into ¼-inch dice

½ tsp. ground cumin

½ tsp. ground cardamom

½ tsp. crumbled saffron threads

¼ tsp. ground allspice

1½ cups long-grain rice

3½ cups vegetable stock

¼ cup dried cherries

¼ cup dried currants

Salt and freshly ground black pepper to taste

1. Heat butter and oil in a Dutch oven over medium-low heat until butter is melted. Add onion, garlic, and carrots and cook, stirring frequently, for 5 to 7 minutes or until carrots have begun to soften. Stir in cumin, cardamom, saffron, and allspice and cook, stirring constantly, for 1 minute. Add rice and cook, stirring constantly, for 1 minute. Stir in vegetable stock, cherries, and currants and season to taste with salt and pepper.

2. Increase heat to medium-high and bring rice to a boil. Reduce heat to low, stir well, cover, and cook for 15 to 20 minutes or until liquid is absorbed and rice is tender. Serve immediately.

Ellen on Edibles

Pilaf is the method of cooking rice or grains by browning them first in butter and/or oil before adding liquid to keep the grains separated. Pilafs can be cooked both on top of the stove and in the oven. This method originated in the Near East and is used now all over the Middle East and Central and South Asia. A pilaf always contains some seasonings and can also contain vegetables or meats.

Spiced Basmati Rice with Lentils and Caramelized Onions

2 TB. (¼ stick) butter

2 TB. olive oil

6 medium onions, peeled and sliced

1 TB. granulated sugar

Salt and freshly ground black pepper to taste

¾ cup dried lentils, picked over and rinsed well

3¾ cups water

4 whole cardamom pods

3 whole allspice

1 bay leaf

1½ cups basmati rice

Serves: 6 as an entrée or 10 to 12 as a side dish
Prep time: 45 minutes
Cook time: 35 minutes

1. Heat butter and oil in a large skillet over medium-low heat until butter is melted. Add onions and toss to coat. Cover and cook, stirring occasionally, for 10 minutes or until onions are tender. Uncover the pan and sprinkle onions with sugar, salt, and pepper. Increase heat to medium-high and cook, stirring frequently, for 10 to 20 minutes or until well browned. Scrape onions into the prepared baking pan and level with a rubber spatula.

2. Preheat the oven to 400°F. Grease a 9×13-inch baking pan.

3. While onions are cooking, cook lentils in a pot of boiling water for about 20 minutes or until almost tender but still firm to bite. Drain.

4. Combine water, cardamom pods, allspice, and bay leaf in a saucepan and bring to boil. Add rice and lentils and stir well. Return to a boil, reduce heat to low, cover, and simmer for 15 minutes or until rice is tender and water is absorbed. Remove and discard cardamom pods, allspice, and bay leaf. Season mixture to taste with salt and pepper.

5. Spoon rice mixture on top of onions, pressing with the back of a spoon to compact rice. Smooth top with a rubber spatula. (You can do this up to 2 days in advance and refrigerate, tightly covered. To continue, bake at a lower oven temperature of 350°F and increase baking time to 55 minutes.)

6. Cover the baking pan with aluminum foil and bake for 35 minutes or until heated through. Remove foil and let stand for 5 minutes. Place a platter over the baking pan and invert the pan to release rice and onions. Scrape any remaining onions onto rice and serve immediately.

 **Got You Covered!**

The most time-consuming part of this dish is caramelizing the onions, and there's no reason you couldn't do a double or triple batch and freeze what's not needed for this recipe. With the leftovers, future onion soup or any number of dishes are just moments away from completion.

Spicy Louisiana Vegetable Pilaf with Toasted Peanuts

Serves: 6 as an entrée or 10 to 12 as a side dish

Prep time: 15 minutes

Cook time: 18 minutes

½ cup bottled mango chutney

2½ cups canned vegetable stock

2 TB. olive oil

1 medium onion, peeled and diced

1 red bell pepper, seeds and ribs removed, chopped

4 garlic cloves, peeled and minced

1 cup long-grain white rice

1 TB. curry powder

½ tsp. dried thyme

1 (15-oz.) can kidney beans, drained and rinsed

1 small sweet potato, peeled and cut into ½-inch pieces

1 (10-oz.) pkg. frozen chopped *collard greens,* thawed and squeezed dry

Salt and freshly ground black pepper to taste

½ cup salted peanuts, coarsely chopped

1. Place chutney in a blender. Add vegetable stock and purée until smooth. Set aside. Heat oil in a saucepan over medium-high heat. Add onion, red bell pepper, and garlic and cook, stirring frequently, for 3 minutes or until onion is translucent. Add white rice, curry powder, and thyme and stir for 1 minute.

2. Add kidney beans, sweet potato, collard greens, and stock mixture and bring to a boil. Season to taste with salt and pepper. Reduce heat to low, cover, and simmer for 18 to 25 minutes or until rice and vegetables are tender and liquid is absorbed. Turn off heat and let stand for 5 minutes. Fluff rice with a fork and serve immediately, sprinkled with chopped peanuts.

 Ellen on Edibles _____

Collard greens have long been a staple of traditional Southern fare, where they fit the definition of "soul food" by providing satisfying flavors. A member of the cabbage family, collards do not form a head, but grow on tall stems with floppy leaves. They are extremely high in both calcium and iron, two nutrients missing from many of the other vegetables that were the mainstay of the African American diet.

Curried Rice with Cauliflower, Scallions, and Peas

2 TB. (¼ stick) butter

1 TB. olive oil

½ red bell pepper, seeds and ribs removed, finely chopped

6 scallions, trimmed and thinly sliced

3 garlic cloves, peeled and minced

2 TB. grated fresh ginger

1 TB. curry powder

1 tsp. grated lemon zest

1½ cups long-grain white rice

2 cups small cauliflower florets

3 cups vegetable stock

Salt and freshly ground black pepper to taste

1 cup frozen peas, thawed

Serves: 6 as an entrée or 10 to 12 as a side dish
Prep time: 10 minutes **Cook time:** 15 minutes

1. Heat butter and oil in a large saucepan over medium-high heat until butter is melted. Add red bell pepper, scallions, and garlic and cook, stirring frequently, for 3 minutes or until scallions are translucent. Add ginger, curry powder, and lemon zest and cook, stirring constantly, for 30 seconds. Add rice and cook, stirring constantly, for 1 minute.

2. Add cauliflower and vegetable stock and season to taste with salt and pepper. Bring to a boil, stirring occasionally. Reduce heat to low, cover, and simmer for 15 to 20 minutes or until water is absorbed and rice is tender. Remove from heat and mix in peas. Cover and let stand for 5 minutes. Fluff rice with a fork and serve immediately.

 Half Baked

It's important to use both butter and oil when sautéing vegetables because the combination raises the relative smoke point of the mixture. The butter imparts its characteristic flavor and gives foods a nice golden color, but the dairy solids in it cause it to burn at a fairly low temperature; the oil ensures that the vegetables can cook without burning.

Coconut and Cilantro Jasmine Rice with Vegetables

Serves: 6 as an entrée or 10 to 12 as a side dish
Prep time: 15 minutes
Cook time: 20 minutes

½ cup unsweetened shredded coconut

2¾ cups water

Salt and freshly ground black pepper to taste

1½ cups jasmine rice

1 cup chopped fresh cilantro

¾ cup light coconut milk

4 tsp. minced fresh ginger

1 TB. lime juice

2 garlic cloves, peeled and minced

1 TB. sesame oil

1 TB. vegetable oil

6 scallions, trimmed and thinly sliced

1 tsp. ground cumin

¼ tsp. crushed red pepper flakes, or to taste

¼ lb. snow peas, stemmed and rinsed

1 cup small cherry tomatoes

½ cup salted peanuts, coarsely chopped

1. Stir shredded coconut in a small nonstick skillet over medium heat for 5 minutes or until light golden. Set aside.

2. Bring water, salt, and pepper to a boil in a saucepan. Stir in rice and bring to a boil. Reduce heat to low, cover the saucepan, and simmer for about 18 minutes or until water is absorbed and rice is tender.

3. While rice is cooking, combine cilantro, ½ cup coconut milk, 1 teaspoon ginger, lime juice, and ½ garlic in a blender. Purée until smooth and stir purée and coconut into rice. Set aside.

4. Heat sesame oil and vegetable oil in a large nonstick skillet over medium-high heat. Add remaining ½ garlic, remaining 3 teaspoons ginger, scallions, cumin, and red pepper flakes and cook, stirring constantly, for 1 minute. Stir in snow peas, tomatoes, and remaining coconut milk. Cover and cook for 1 minute or until snow peas are bright green. Season to taste with salt and pepper.

5. To serve, place rice on a platter and top with vegetables. Sprinkle with peanuts.

Bake Lore

Rice is an ancient and venerable grain that has been cultivated since at least 5000 B.C.E., and archaeological explorations in China have uncovered sealed pots of rice that are almost 8,000 years old. Today, rice is a staple for almost half the world's population—particularly in parts of China, India, Japan, and Southeast Asia.

Mexican Red Rice (*Arroz Rojo*)

1 (14.5-oz.) can peeled whole tomatoes, drained

½ small onion, peeled and diced

2 garlic cloves, peeled

3 TB. olive oil

1½ cups long-grain white rice

2 tsp. dried oregano, preferably Mexican

1 tsp. ground cumin

2 cups vegetable stock

1 medium carrot, peeled and thinly sliced

¼ cup chopped fresh cilantro

2 or 3 small serrano chilies, halved lengthwise

Salt and freshly ground black pepper to taste

1 cup frozen peas, thawed

1 cup frozen corn kernels, thawed

Serves: 6 as an entrée or 10 to 12 as a side dish	
Prep time: 15 minutes	
Cook time: 30 minutes	

1. Combine tomatoes, onion, and garlic in a blender and purée until smooth. Set aside.

2. Heat oil in a heavy saucepan over medium-high heat. Add rice, oregano, and cumin and cook, stirring constantly, for 1 minute. Stir in purée and cook, stirring constantly, for 1 minute. Add vegetable stock, carrot, cilantro, and serrano chilies. Season to taste with salt and pepper and bring to a boil.

3. Reduce heat to low, cover, and cook for about 15 minutes or until almost all liquid is absorbed. Stir in peas and corn and uncover the pan. Cook for about 10 minutes or until rice is tender and all liquid is absorbed. Remove from heat, cover, and let stand for 5 minutes. Remove and discard chilies and fluff rice with a fork and serve immediately.

Got You Covered!

This preparation method of "frying" the sauce before adding other ingredients is traditional in Mexican cooking. This short time of cooking without additional liquid intensifies the flavors.

Baked Rice, Cheese, and Vegetable Casserole

Serves: 6 as an entrée or 10 to 12 as a side dish
Prep time: 15 minutes
Cook time: 25 minutes

 **Got You Covered!**

This dish is a master recipe for using up leftover cooked rice, and you can change it in many ways as long as you keep the proportions the same. Use any mild flavored vegetable or vegetable mix, and substitute cheddar cheese for the Swiss.

3 TB. butter

1 onion, peeled and chopped

1 green bell pepper, seeds and ribs removed, chopped

1 (10-oz.) pkg. frozen mixed vegetables, thawed

1 large tomato, cored, seeded, and chopped

3 cups cooked rice

2 cups grated Swiss cheese

3 TB. heavy cream

1 TB. chopped fresh thyme or 1 tsp. dried

Salt and freshly ground black pepper to taste

1. Preheat the oven to 350°F. Grease a 9×13-inch baking pan. Melt butter in a large, heavy skillet over medium-low heat. Add onion and green bell pepper and cook, stirring frequently, for 5 to 7 minutes or until pepper is tender.

2. Add mixed vegetables, tomato, rice, 1 cup Swiss cheese, cream, and thyme. Season to taste with salt and pepper and scrape mixture into the prepared baking pan.

3. Cover with aluminum foil and bake for 10 minutes. Remove foil, sprinkle with remaining 1 cup Swiss cheese, and bake for an additional 15 minutes or until bubbly. Serve immediately.

Oven-Baked Risotto with Beans and Greens

3 TB. butter

1 onion, peeled and chopped

1 large leek, white part only, trimmed, chopped, and well rinsed

2 garlic cloves, peeled and minced

1½ cups Arborio rice

½ cup dry white wine

2 (14.5-oz.) cans vegetable stock

1 (15-oz.) can kidney beans, drained and rinsed

1 large head radicchio, cored and chopped

2 bunches arugula, rinsed, stemmed, and thinly sliced

Salt and freshly ground black pepper to taste

½ cup grated Parmesan cheese

Serves: 6 as an entrée or 10 to 12 as a side dish
Prep time: 20 minutes
Cook time: 35 minutes

1. Preheat the oven to 400°F. Grease a 9×13-inch baking pan.

2. Melt butter in a saucepan over medium heat. Add onion, leek, and garlic and cook, stirring frequently, for 3 minutes or until onion is translucent. Add rice and cook, stirring constantly, for 2 minutes.

3. Add wine, increase heat to high, and cook, stirring constantly, for 3 minutes or until wine is almost evaporated. Add vegetable stock and bring to a boil.

4. Scrape mixture into the prepared baking pan, cover with aluminum foil, and bake for 15 minutes. Remove foil; stir in kidney beans, radicchio, and arugula; season to taste with salt and pepper. Bake for an additional 15 to 20 minutes or until rice is soft and has absorbed liquid. Stir in Parmesan cheese and serve immediately.

Got You Covered!

This is not the traditional way to make risotto, but it's a lot easier. If you want to get some exercise by trying the Italian method, heat the stock to a simmer, and add it ½ cup at a time, stirring continuously with a wooden spoon. Wait until the stock has been absorbed before adding the next ½ cup. It's the stirring that produces the creamy texture.

Spicy Asian Brown Rice and Vegetable Stir-Fry

Serves: 6 as an entrée or 10 to 12 as a side dish

Prep time: 15 minutes

Cook time: 10 minutes

3 TB. sesame oil

3 garlic cloves, peeled and minced

4 TB. grated fresh ginger

1 small leek, white part only, trimmed, cut lengthwise into julienne strips and well rinsed

2 carrots, peeled and cut into 2-inch julienne strips

2 zucchini, trimmed and cut into 2-inch julienne strips

¼ lb. fresh shiitake mushrooms, stems removed, wiped with a damp paper towel, and cut into thin strips

¼ lb. snow peas, stemmed, rinsed, and halved lengthwise

⅓ cup tamari

¼ cup water

2 TB. hoisin sauce

1 tsp. Chinese chili paste or to taste

6 cups cold cooked brown rice

Freshly ground black pepper to taste

3 scallions, trimmed and thinly sliced

 **Got You Covered!**

Brown rice now comes in instant and quick-cooking varieties that are partially cooked before packaging. If you want to save time in creating dishes that specify cooked brown rice, start with one of these convenience foods.

1. Heat oil in a large skillet over high heat. Add garlic and ginger and stir-fry 1 minute. Add leek, carrot, zucchini, shiitake mushrooms, and snow peas and cook, stirring frequently, for 3 minutes or until vegetables are crisp-tender.

2. Add tamari, water, hoisin sauce, and chili paste and cook for 1 minute. Stir in rice and cook, stirring frequently, for 2 minutes or until rice is hot. Season to taste with pepper and serve immediately, sprinkled with scallions.

Wild Rice Casserole

½ cup slivered almonds

3 TB. butter

1 large onion, peeled and diced

2 garlic cloves, peeled and minced

2 celery stalks, trimmed and thinly sliced

½ red bell pepper, seeds and ribs removed, chopped

2 tsp. dried thyme

2 TB. chopped fresh parsley

5 cups cooked wild rice

1½ cups grated cheddar cheese

¾ cup whole milk

Salt and freshly ground black pepper to taste

Serves: 6 as an entrée or 10 to 12 as a side dish	
Prep time: 20 minutes	
Cook time: 40 minutes	

1. Preheat the oven to 325°F. Grease a 9×13-inch baking pan. Toast almonds in a small dry skillet over medium heat for 3 minutes or until lightly browned. Remove from the skillet and set aside.

2. Melt butter in a skillet over medium heat. Add onion, garlic, celery, and red bell pepper and cook, stirring frequently, for 5 to 8 minutes or until vegetables are tender. Stir in thyme and parsley and cook for 1 minute.

3. Stir wild rice, almonds, cheddar cheese, and whole milk into the skillet. Season to taste with salt and pepper and scrape mixture into the prepared baking pan. Cover with aluminum foil and bake for 40 to 45 minutes or until heated through. Serve immediately.

 Half Baked

It's important to clean wild rice thoroughly before cooking it. The best method is to place the rice in a medium bowl and fill it with cold water. Give it a couple stirs, and set it aside for a few minutes. Any debris will float to the surface, and you can scoop off the debris with a strainer, and then drain the rice. Depending on the method you use, wild rice can take up to an hour to cook.

Bulgur, Chickpea, and Tomato Pilaf

*Serves: 6 as an entrée or
10 to 12 as a side dish*

Prep time: 10 minutes
plus 30 minutes for bulgur
to soak

Cook time: 6 minutes

1½ cups vegetable stock

1 TB. fresh thyme or 1 tsp. dried

2 TB. chopped fresh parsley

½ tsp. crushed red pepper flakes

1½ cups bulgur or cracked wheat, rinsed

3 TB. olive oil

6 scallions, trimmed with all but 2 inches of green tops discarded, cut into ¼-inch pieces

3 garlic cloves, peeled and minced

4 ripe plum tomatoes, cored, seeded, and diced

3 TB. lemon juice

1 (15-oz.) can chickpeas, drained and rinsed

Salt and freshly ground black pepper to taste

1. Bring vegetable stock, thyme, parsley, and red pepper flakes to a boil in a medium saucepan over high heat. Place bulgur in a mixing bowl and pour stock over. Cover the bowl and allow bulgur to sit for 30 minutes.

2. While bulgur is soaking, heat olive oil in a skillet over medium-high heat. Add scallions and garlic and cook, stirring frequently, for 3 minutes. Add tomatoes and cook for 2 minutes. Stir in lemon juice and chickpeas and cook for 1 minute or until beans are hot. Season to taste with salt and pepper and stir mixture into hot bulgur. Serve immediately.

Got You Covered!

If you have any leftovers from this dish, chill them to serve as a salad. Even when freshly made, the dish can be served hot or at room temperature.

Risotto-Style Barley with Spring Greens

3 TB. olive oil

2 leeks, white part only, trimmed, chopped, and well rinsed

1 fennel bulb, trimmed and finely chopped

1 tsp. dried thyme

2 cups pearl barley, rinsed well

6½ cups vegetable stock

½ tsp. saffron threads

1 (10-oz.) pkg. frozen peas, thawed

1 (6-oz.) pkg. fresh baby spinach, rinsed, stemmed, and thinly sliced

½ cup grated Parmesan cheese

2 TB. chopped fresh basil

Salt and freshly ground black pepper to taste

Fresh basil sprigs

Serves: 6 as an entrée or 10 to 12 as a side dish	
Prep time: 15 minutes	
Cook time: 45 minutes	

1. Heat oil in a Dutch oven over medium-high heat. Add ½ leeks and ½ fennel and cook, stirring frequently, for 5 minutes or until vegetables begin to soften.

2. Stir in thyme, barley, 2½ cups vegetable stock, and saffron. Simmer, stirring frequently, for about 10 minutes or until liquid is almost absorbed. Add remaining leeks, fennel, and remaining 4 cups vegetable stock and bring to a simmer. Reduce heat to medium-low and cook until barley is tender and mixture is creamy, stirring often, about 30 minutes.

3. Add peas, spinach, Parmesan cheese, and chopped basil and stir to blend. Season to taste with salt and pepper. Serve immediately, garnished with basil sprigs.

Got You Covered!

This recipe is slightly unusual in that the vegetables are added at two different times. Those added initially flavor the dish, while those added later lend texture as well as flavor. Use the same method in creating risotto.

Part 7

Just Desserts

Although you might want to make a meal from desserts, these sweet goodies are the treat at the end and not the main event. So why are they in a book on cover and bake one-dish meals? Because they partially fit the definition—the whole dessert is right there in the one dish. There's no need for further augmentation or assembly. Sweet *and* easy!

Chocolate is a favorite at all times of year. Chapter 18 contains recipes that all deliver an intense chocolate taste. The chocolate fix is followed by two chapters divided by their appropriateness to cold and warm months, and the fruits that are plentiful and economical in the market. Chapter 19 highlights the glories of homey apple desserts along with other winter fruits, and recipes for summer's luscious berries and other delicate fruits comprise Chapter 20.

Chapter 18

Chocolate Cravings: Divine and Decadent for Any Time of Year

In This Chapter

- ◆ Homey dessert casseroles with chocolate, breads, and rice
- ◆ Simple chocolate puddings and baked custards
- ◆ Delicate white chocolate recipes

In the way that true oenophiles maintain that the first responsibility of a fine wine is to be red, many people believe that the *only* responsibility of a dessert is to be chocolate.

In this chapter, you see how versatile chocolate can be. All these recipes are assembled in one pan, perhaps with the addition of a sauce. There is no "assembly" involved, as there is with a chocolate cake or torte.

Chocolate 101

The key to success for all chocolate desserts is to use a high-quality product. It's also important (with the following exceptions) to use the type of chocolate specified in the recipe because the amount of additional sugar and other ingredients are calculated according to the sweetness level of the chocolate. If you use a different chocolate, things could taste off.

Now on to the sweet stuff. Here's a quick guide to chocolate:

- **Unsweetened.** Also referred to as baking or bitter chocolate, this is the purest of all cooking chocolate. It is hardened chocolate liquor (the essence of the cocoa bean, not an alcohol) that contains no sugar. It is usually packaged in a bar of 8 (1-ounce) blocks. According to the U.S. standard of identity, unsweetened chocolate must contain 50 to 58 percent cocoa butter.

- **Bittersweet.** This chocolate is slightly sweetened with sugar, and the amount varies depending on the manufacturer. This chocolate must contain 35 percent chocolate liquor and should be used when intense chocolate flavor is desired. Also use it interchangeably with semisweet chocolate in cooking and baking.

- **Semisweet.** This chocolate is sweetened with sugar, but unlike bittersweet, it also can have added flavorings such as vanilla. It is available in bar form as well as chips and pieces.

Bake Lore

Scientists named the bean of the tropical cocoa tree *Theobroma cacoa*, meaning "food of the gods."

- **Sweet cooking.** This chocolate must contain 15 percent chocolate liquor, and it almost always has a higher sugar content than semisweet chocolate. It is usually found in 4-ounce bars.

- **Milk.** This is a mild-flavored chocolate used primarily for candy bars but rarely (except for milk chocolate chips) in cooking. It can have as little as 10 percent chocolate liquor but must contain 12 percent milk solids.

- **Unsweetened cocoa powder.** This is powdered chocolate that has had a portion of the cocoa butter removed. Cocoa keeps indefinitely in a cool place.

- **Dutch process cocoa powder.** This type of cocoa powder is formulated with reduced acidity and gives foods a more mellow flavor. However, it also burns at a lower temperature than more common cocoa.

- **White.** Actually ivory in color, white chocolate is technically not chocolate at all; it is made from cocoa butter, sugar, and flavoring. It is difficult to work with and should be used in recipes that are specifically designed for it. Do not substitute it for other types of chocolate in a recipe.

Subbing with Success

Bittersweet, semisweet, and sweet chocolate can be used interchangeably in recipes, depending on personal taste. Most chocolate desserts tend to be sweet, so it's better to go from a semisweet to a bittersweet rather than the other direction.

Do not substitute chocolate chips and bits of broken chocolate for one another. Chocolate chips are formulated to retain their shape at high heat and react differently when baked than chopped chocolate does. Chocolate chips can form gritty granules in a cooled dessert.

Sweet Savvy

Always wrap chocolate tightly after it's opened because it can absorb aromas and flavors from other foods. Store chocolate in a cool, dry place, but do not refrigerate or freeze it. If chocolate is stored at a high temperature, the fat will rise to the surface and become a whitish powder called a bloom. This will disappear, however, as soon as the chocolate is melted.

Like red wine, chocolate ages and becomes more deeply flavored after 6 months and can be kept for years if stored properly. However, because of the milk solids in both milk chocolate and white chocolate, these shouldn't be stored for longer than 9 months.

Proper Chocolate Handling

Except when you're eating chocolate out of your hand or folding chips into a cookie dough, chocolate needs a bit of special handling. Use these tips when dealing with the common tasks associated with chocolate:

Chopping chocolate: Chopping it into fine pieces makes melting easier. You can do this in a food processor fitted with a steel blade. Begin by breaking it with a heavy knife rather than breaking it with your hands. Body heat is sufficiently high enough to soften the chocolate so it will not chop evenly.

Melting chocolate: Most chocolate needs careful melting because it scorches easily. You can melt it in a number of ways:

- Melt chunks in the top of a double boiler placed over barely simmering water.
- Put chopped chocolate in a microwave-safe bowl and microwave on 100 percent (high) for 20 seconds. Stir and repeat as necessary.
- Preheat the oven to 250°F. Place chopped chocolate in the oven and then turn off the heat immediately. Stir after 3 minutes and return to the warm oven if necessary.

With all these methods, melt the chocolate until it is just about smooth; the heat in the chocolate will complete the process.

Fancy Flourishes

Decorating with melted chocolate is easy:

- ◆ For random lines or drizzles, dip the tip of a knife or spatula in the melted chocolate and swing it back and forth. For a more controlled look, place the melted chocolate in a small, heavy plastic bag and snip off the tip; the amount you snip off will determine the thickness of your line.

- ◆ For an elegant chocolate garnish, brush a thick layer of melted chocolate on the underside of well-washed heavy leaves, such as lemon or holly. Chill, pull away the leaf, and the chocolate will have molded into a veined pattern.

- ◆ To make chocolate "shells" as edible bowls, cover the back of scallop shells (available in kitchen specialty stores) or glass custard cups with foil, smoothing it with your hand. Brush a layer of melted chocolate on the outside, to within ¼ inch of the edge, being careful not to get any on the edge. Chill for 5 minutes; then repeat this procedure 2 more times and chill the shells for at least 1 hour. Remove the form and gently pull away the foil.

Chocolate Bread Pudding with Easy Bourbon Caramel Sauce

1 cup chopped pecans

1¼ cups whole milk

1¼ cups light cream

½ cup granulated sugar

½ lb. semisweet chocolate, chopped

8 large eggs

¾ tsp. pure vanilla extract

Pinch salt

½ lb. unsliced egg bread, such as challah, crusts trimmed, cut into 1-inch cubes

1 cup bottled caramel sauce

¼ cup bourbon

Serves: 6 to 8
Prep time: 20 minutes plus 30 minutes standing time
Cook time: 45 minutes

1. Preheat the oven to 350°F. Grease a 9×13-inch baking pan. Place pecans on a baking sheet and toast in the oven for 5 to 7 minutes or until browned. Remove nuts from the oven and set aside.

2. Combine whole milk, light cream, and sugar in a large, heavy saucepan over medium-high heat. Stir until sugar dissolves and mixture comes to a boil. Remove from heat. Add semisweet chocolate and stir until smooth. Beat eggs, vanilla, and salt in a large bowl to blend. Gradually whisk in chocolate mixture. Add bread cubes. Let stand, stirring occasionally, for about 30 minutes or until bread absorbs some of custard.

3. Transfer mixture to the prepared baking pan and cover with aluminum foil. Bake for 35 minutes, remove foil, and bake for an additional 10 minutes or until a knife inserted in the center comes out clean. Cool for 5 minutes before serving. (You can do this a day in advance and refrigerate, tightly covered. Heat in a 350°F oven, covered with aluminum foil, for 30 minutes or until hot.)

4. While pudding is baking, combine caramel sauce, pecans, and bourbon in a small saucepan. Heat, stirring occasionally, until hot. To serve, spoon sauce on top of warm bread pudding.

Half Baked

To meet Food and Drug Administration standards, pure vanilla extract must contain about 1 pound vanilla beans per gallon. It's about twice as expensive, but it's clearly worth the money when compared to the artificial taste of imitation vanilla extract, which is made from chemicals and can leave a bitter aftertaste. Look at the labels carefully before you buy.

Mexican Chocolate Rice Pudding

Serves: 6 to 8
Prep time: 15 minutes plus at least 4 hours chilling
Cook time: 48 minutes

4½ cups whole milk

⅔ cup long-grain white rice

3 TB. granulated sugar

2 (2-in.) cinnamon sticks, broken in half

½ cup slivered blanched almonds

4 large egg yolks

3 oz. bittersweet chocolate, finely chopped

1½ tsp. pure vanilla extract

1. Mix 4 cups whole milk, rice, sugar, and cinnamon sticks in a large, heavy saucepan. Cook over medium-low heat, stirring often for about 45 minutes or until rice is tender and mixture is very thick. Remove from heat. Remove and discard cinnamon sticks.

2. While rice is cooking, toast almonds in a small dry skillet over medium heat for 2 to 3 minutes or until lightly browned. Remove from the skillet and set aside.

3. Whisk egg yolks with remaining ½ cup milk in a medium bowl. Whisk in some hot rice mixture. Pour egg mixture into remaining rice mixture in saucepan. Stir over low heat for about 3 minutes or until an instant-read thermometer registers 160°F. Do not allow mixture to boil.

4. Remove from heat. Add bittersweet chocolate and stir until melted and smooth. Stir in vanilla and almonds. Transfer pudding to a large bowl. Cover and refrigerate until well chilled, at least 4 hours or overnight. (You can do this a day in advance. Keep refrigerated.) Serve cold.

 Bake Lore

This dish is called "Mexican chocolate" because of the vanilla, cinnamon, and almonds. In Mexican markets, chocolate is sold in blocks with those ingredients added.

White Chocolate Rice Pudding with Cranberry Framboise Sauce

4½ cups whole milk

⅔ cup long-grain white rice

⅔ cup granulated sugar

2 tsp. pure vanilla extract

¼ tsp. salt

1½ cups dried cranberries, coarsely chopped

¾ cup cranberry juice cocktail

¼ cup framboise, Chambord, or another raspberry-flavored liqueur

2 large egg yolks

¼ lb. good-quality white chocolate, chopped

1 TB. grated orange zest

Serves: 6 to 8
Prep time: 15 minutes plus at least 4 hours chilling time
Cook time: 48 minutes

1. Combine 4 cups whole milk, rice, sugar, vanilla extract, and salt in a large, heavy saucepan. Cook over medium-low heat, stirring occasionally, for about 45 minutes or until mixture thickens and rice is very tender.

2. While rice is simmering, prepare sauce. Combine dried cranberries, cranberry juice, and framboise in a small saucepan and bring to a boil. Cover and remove from heat. Let stand until cranberries have absorbed liquid but are still slightly chewy, about 1 hour. Refrigerate until cold. (You can do this up to 2 days in advance.)

3. To finish pudding, reduce heat to low. Whisk egg yolks with remaining ½ cup whole milk in a medium bowl. Whisk in some hot rice mixture. Pour egg mixture into remaining rice mixture in the saucepan. Stir over low heat for about 3 minutes or until an instant-read thermometer registers 160°F. Do not allow mixture to boil.

4. Remove from heat. Add white chocolate and stir until melted and smooth. Stir in orange zest. Transfer pudding to a large bowl. Cover and refrigerate until well chilled, at least 4 hours or overnight. (You can do this a day in advance. Keep refrigerated.) Serve cold, topped with cranberry sauce.

 Got You Covered!

Some recipes call for only egg yolks, or a combination of whole eggs and egg yolks, to produce a creamier and richer texture for the finished dish. The egg whites do not contain the same amount of protein.

White Chocolate Bread Pudding with Irish Whiskey Sauce

Serves: 6 to 8
Prep time: 25 minutes
Cook time: 45 minutes

½ cup whole milk

2 cups light cream

¾ cup granulated sugar

¾ lb. imported white chocolate, chopped

4 large eggs

1½ tsp. pure vanilla extract

¾ lb. French bread, cut into ¾-inch cubes

2 cups whipping cream

6 TB. Irish whiskey

2 tsp. cornstarch

2 tsp. cold water

Got You Covered!

If you're worried about children eating a sauce that contains alcohol, boil the liquor first with a few tablespoons water added in a small saucepan over medium heat. Within a few moments, the alcohol burns off, leaving just the flavor.

1. For bread pudding, preheat the oven to 350°F. Grease a 9×13-inch baking pan.

2. Combine whole milk, light cream, and ½ cup sugar in a large, heavy saucepan over medium-high heat. Stir until sugar dissolves and mixture comes to a boil. Remove from heat. Add white chocolate and stir until smooth. Beat eggs and 1 teaspoon vanilla in a large bowl until well blended. Gradually whisk in chocolate mixture. Add bread cubes. Let stand, stirring occasionally, for about 30 minutes or until bread absorbs some custard.

3. Transfer mixture to the prepared baking pan and cover with aluminum foil. Bake for 35 minutes, remove foil, and bake for an additional 10 minutes or until a knife inserted in the center comes out clean. Cool for 5 minutes before serving. (Do this up to a day in advance and refrigerate, tightly covered. Remove from refrigerator 30 minutes before serving. Heat in a 350°F oven, covered with aluminum foil, for 30 minutes or until hot.)

4. While pudding is baking, prepare sauce. Bring whipping cream, whiskey, ¼ cup sugar, and ½ teaspoon vanilla extract to a boil in a heavy saucepan over medium-high heat, stirring frequently. Mix cornstarch and water in a small bowl to blend; then whisk into cream mixture. Boil, stirring constantly, for about 3 minutes or until sauce thickens. Cool to room temperature. (You can make this up to 2 days in advance and refrigerate, tightly covered. Reheat over low heat until tepid before serving.)

5. To serve, drizzle warm bread pudding with warm sauce.

Chocolate Kahlúa Flan

1 (14-oz.) can sweetened condensed milk

1 (12-oz.) can evaporated milk

¼ lb. semisweet chocolate, chopped

2 TB. cream cheese, at room temperature

2 TB. Kahlúa or other coffee liqueur

½ tsp. ground cinnamon

Large pinch salt

3 large eggs, lightly beaten

Serves: 6
Prep time: 15 minutes
Cook time: 35 minutes plus 3 hours for chilling

1. Preheat the oven to 350°F. Arrange 6 (¾-cup) custard cups in 9×13-inch baking pan. Heat a kettle of water over high heat.

2. Combine condensed milk and evaporated milk in a medium saucepan and bring to a simmer, stirring frequently. Remove from heat and stir in semisweet chocolate, cream cheese, Kahlúa, cinnamon, and salt. Whisk until chocolate is melted and mixture is smooth. Whisk in eggs.

3. Divide mixture among the custard cups. Pour enough hot water into the baking pan to come halfway up the sides of the cups. Bake *flans* for about 35 minutes or until set in the center. Remove flans from the water bath and chill, uncovered, for at least 3 hours and up to 1 day or until very cold and firm. Serve cold.

Ellen on Edibles

Flan is a traditional Spanish custard made with a caramel coating that is baked in the pan. The term is now used for any slowly baked custard.

Mini-Molten Chocolate Cakes

Serves: 6
Prep time: 20 minutes
Cook time: 12 to 14 minutes

2 TB. plus ¾ cup butter

¼ cup granulated sugar

6 oz. semisweet chocolate, chopped

3 large eggs

3 large egg yolks

⅓ cup confectioners' sugar or more for garnish

1½ tsp. pure vanilla extract

¼ cup all-purpose flour

2 TB. unsweetened cocoa powder

Sweetened whipped cream (optional)

Fresh raspberries

1. Preheat the oven to 400°F. Grease 6 (6-ounce) custard cups with 2 tablespoons butter and sprinkle with granulated sugar. Place in a shallow baking pan and set aside. Heat a kettle of water over high heat.

2. Combine ¾ cup butter and chopped semisweet chocolate in a small saucepan and melt over low heat, stirring constantly. Remove from heat and cool. Beat eggs, egg yolks, ⅓ cup confectioners' sugar, and vanilla extract in a mixing bowl with an electric mixer set on high speed for about 5 minutes or until mixture is thick and pale yellow. Beat in chocolate mixture on medium speed. Sift flour and cocoa powder over chocolate mixture and beat on low speed just until blended. Spoon into the prepared custard cups. (You can do this up to 4 hours in advance.)

3. Bake for 12 to 14 minutes or until cakes rise slightly and feel firm at the edges and softer in the center when pressed gently. Cool in custard cups for 5 minutes. Invert with pot holders onto dessert plates. Cool for 5 minutes and serve, if desired, sprinkled with additional confectioners' sugar or sweetened whipped cream and top with fresh raspberries.

 **Got You Covered!**

If you want to make this a sinfully rich dessert, place a chocolate truffle in the center of each cup before baking. The short bake time will just melt the center.

Steamed Mocha Pudding

¾ cup (1½ sticks) plus 1 TB. butter, cut into 1-tablespoon pieces

6 oz. semisweet or bitter-sweet chocolate, chopped

¾ cup milk

1 TB. instant espresso powder

2 large eggs

¾ cup granulated sugar

1½ cups all-purpose flour, sifted before measuring

2 tsp. baking powder

2 TB. Kahlúa or other coffee liqueur

½ tsp. pure vanilla extract

Sweetened whipped cream or ice cream for serving

Serves: 8 to 10	
Prep time: 20 minutes	
Cook time: 2 hours	

1. Generously butter a 1½-quart pudding steamer or bundt pan. Bring a kettle of water to a boil over high heat. Combine bittersweet chocolate and ¾ cup butter in a small saucepan and set over low heat. Stir frequently until liquid and smooth. Scrape chocolate mixture into a mixing bowl and pour milk and espresso powder in the same saucepan. Heat over medium heat until coffee powder is dissolved and stir into chocolate.

2. Whisk eggs in a mixing bowl; then add sugar, flour, baking powder, Kahlúa, and vanilla extract. Combine egg mixture with chocolate mixture and scrape into the prepared pan. If you're using a pudding steamer which is air-tight, clamp on the lid. If you're using a bundt pan, stuff the hole in the center with aluminum foil to make it air-tight and top the mold with a double layer of heavy-duty foil, crimping it around the edges.

3. Set the mold on a wire rack in a pot or kettle large enough to accommodate it comfortably. Pour in enough boiling water to come halfway up the sides of the mold. Cover the pot and bring the water back to a boil over medium-high heat. Lower heat to a simmer and steam pudding for 2 hours. Add hot water to the pot as needed to maintain the water level.

4. With potholders, remove pudding mold from the outer pot and remove cover. Cool on a rack for 15 minutes or until pudding begins to shrink away from the sides of the mold. To serve, invert pudding onto a platter and pass sweetened whipped cream or ice cream separately. (You can make this up to 2 days in advance and refrigerate, wrapped tightly in heavy-duty aluminum foil. Bake in a 300°F oven for 30 to 40 minutes or until hot.)

 Bake Lore

Steamed puddings date back to Medieval England, and the most famous are the plum puddings or figgy puddings served with hard sauce at Christmas time. Traditionally, steamed puddings were made with beef suet, but most modern recipes use butter.

Baked Chocolate Mousse Cake

Serves: 8 to 10
Prep time: 20 minutes
Cook time: 35 minutes

1 TB. butter, softened

3 TB. unsweetened cocoa powder

1 lb. bittersweet chocolate, finely chopped

¼ cup Grand Marnier or other orange liqueur

¼ cup strong brewed espresso coffee

6 large eggs

½ cup granulated sugar

1 cup heavy cream

Confectioners' sugar for garnish, optional

1. Preheat the oven to 400°F and bring a kettle of water to a boil over high heat. Grease a 9-inch springform pan with butter, line the pan with a circle of parchment paper or wax paper, and then butter the paper. Dust the inside with cocoa powder and set aside.

2. Melt bittersweet chocolate with Grand Marnier and coffee in a small saucepan over low heat, stirring frequently. Set aside to cool.

3. Place eggs and sugar in a large bowl and beat with an electric mixer on high speed until eggs are thick and have tripled in volume. In another bowl, beat heavy cream with an electric mixer on medium speed until slightly thickened. Increase the speed to high, beat until stiff peaks form, and set aside. Beat cooled chocolate mixture into eggs until well blended. Fold in whipped cream and scrape into the prepared springform pan.

4. Place the springform pan in a larger baking pan and pour in enough boiling water to come ⅓ of the way up the sides of the springform pan. Bake for 25 to 35 minutes; then turn off the oven and let cake sit with the oven door ajar for 10 minutes. (You can do this up to 2 days in advance and refrigerate, tightly covered. Cover the springform pan with aluminum foil and reheat for 15 minutes at 325°F before unmolding.)

5. Remove from the oven and remove the springform pan from the baking pan. Run a knife around the sides of the springform pan. Remove the sides, cut cake into wedges, and dust with confectioners' sugar, if desired.

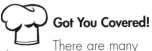 **Got You Covered!**

There are many ways of making a cake rise, and this recipe uses whipped cream and beaten eggs as the leavening agents. Both the eggs and the cream have had air incorporated during the beating, and this air heats and expands in the hot oven. This was the only way of leavening cakes before the invention of baking powder in the nineteenth century.

Chapter 19

Warm for Winter: Cozy Desserts for Cold Months

In This Chapter

- ◆ Apple treats from around the world
- ◆ Centuries-old hot, homey puddings
- ◆ Creative cobblers and other easy-to-assemble desserts

A bowl of chilled fresh berries topped with some sweetened whipped cream might hit the spot in July, but something sweet and warm is certainly more appealing in January. The recipes in this chapter are all homey, and a few could even add *haute* to their title.

Many of these recipes use apples because apples are one fruit universally available in the cold months. Others are based on pantry ingredients—from coconut milk to canned pumpkin—so you don't have to make a trek to the market on cold days.

All About Apples

With a selection of more than 300 varieties of apples grown in North America, Americans consume 18 pounds of apples per capita. But not all apples are created equal.

Some are better for munching raw, and others are better for cooking. Some, such as McIntosh, are good cooking apples for applesauce because they fall apart so well. But that wouldn't be an advantage in a pie or tart.

These apple varieties are good for cooking:

◆ **Cortland.** This medium to large all-purpose apple is crisp and juicy and has both sweet and tart flavors. It is a rich red color and is sometimes striped with green. The flesh is very white and resists browning.

◆ **Empire.** This is a beautiful, large, juicy red apple with a sweet, almost spicy flavor. It's wonderful baked, as well as eaten fresh.

◆ **Golden Delicious.** This round, rich yellow apple offers a spectrum of flavors from slightly tart to mellow and sweet. The skin color ranges from light green to pale or creamy yellow, depending upon maturity. The more yellow the skin, the sweeter the apple. Avoid goldens with "russeting," a bronze-colored, rough, and scablike condition principally on the stem end of the apple.

◆ **Granny Smith.** This tart, all-purpose apple is gaining popularity for its tart flavor, firm flesh that retains its texture when cooked, and its uniformity. The flavor tends to vary from mild to very tart, and on occasion the texture may be a bit on the dry side. Look for firm and bright-colored apples.

◆ **Jonathan.** This medium-size red apple with a yellow blush has firm, crisp, juicy flesh and is particularly well suited for pies and baking whole because it holds its shape very well.

◆ **McIntosh.** This medium-size, red-on-green apple has a crisp, sweet, aromatic flesh. It is excellent for eating and applesauce, but it does not hold its shape well for pies or baking whole.

◆ **Rome Beauty.** This large apple has a deep red color and is almost perfectly round. It is the best apple for baking because it retains its shape and the flavor develops best when cooked. Look for its brilliant, almost solid shade of red dotted with natural tiny white dots.

◆ **Winesap.** This bright, all-purpose apple with an old-fashioned tangy taste has crisp, crunchy, juicy flesh with a sweet-tart flavor. Look for apples with smooth, glossy bright red skin with hints of purple.

Choices for the Choosey

When picking apples, whether in an orchard or your grocery's produce section, look for large, firm apples with good color and no bruises. An apple's bruised cells release an enzyme called polyenoloxidase, which hastens the oxidation or decay of the flesh. Overripe apples feel soft, and the flesh will feel mushy. To check apples sold in a plastic bag, turn the bag upside down and examine the apples on the bottom.

Store apples in a perforated plastic bag in the refrigerator. The bag helps prevent moisture loss and protects the apples from absorbing other flavors in the refrigerator. If you store the apples in a plastic bag without holes, open the bag once a week to release accumulated gases and carbon dioxide.

Keep apples away from foods with strong odors such as cabbage or onions to prevent flavor transfer. As an alternative, store apples in a dark cabinet with lots of circulating air. However, do not store apples near potatoes. Apples give off ethylene gas, which causes potatoes to sprout.

French Upside-Down Caramel Apple Tart (*Tarte Tatin*)

Serves: 6
Prep time: 35 minutes
Cook time: 20 minutes

6 TB. (¾ stick) butter

1½ cups granulated sugar

6 Golden Delicious apples, peeled, cored, and quartered, with each quarter halved lengthwise

3 TB. lemon juice

3 TB. brandy

½ tsp. *apple pie spice*

1 sheet piecrust for single-crust pie

Ellen on Edibles

Apple pie spice is a pre-blended combination of fragrant spices. You can make your own by combining ½ teaspoon cinnamon, ¼ teaspoon nutmeg, ⅛ teaspoon allspice, ⅛ teaspoon ground cardamom, and ¼ teaspoon ground cloves. Or in a pinch, substitute cinnamon as the primary base, with a dash of any of the other spices you might have on hand.

1. Melt butter in a 12-inch cast-iron or other ovenproof skillet over medium-high heat. Stir in 1 cup sugar and cook, stirring frequently, for 6 to 8 minutes or until syrup is a deep walnut brown. Remove from heat and set aside.

2. Place Golden Delicious apple slices in a mixing bowl and toss with remaining ½ cup sugar, lemon juice, brandy, and apple pie spice. Allow to sit for 15 minutes.

3. Preheat the oven to 425°F. Drain apple slices and arrange them tightly packed in a decorative pattern on top of caramel in the skillet, making several layers if necessary. Place the skillet over medium-high heat and press down on the apples as they begin to soften.

4. Using a bulb baster, draw up juices from apples and pour juices over top layer of apples. Do not stir apples. After 5 minutes or when apples begin to soften, cover the skillet and cook for 10 to 15 minutes or until apples are soft and liquid is thick. Continue to baste apples during this time.

5. Remove from heat and roll piecrust dough into a circle 1 inch larger than the circumference of the skillet. Place crust on top of apples in the skillet and tuck edge of crust around apples on the sides of the skillet using the tip of a paring knife. Cut 6 (1-inch-long) vents in pastry to allow steam to escape.

6. Bake for 20 minutes or until pastry is golden and juice is thick. Remove from the oven and cool for 10 minutes.

7. Using a knife, loosen the edges of tart from the pan. Invert a serving plate over the pan and, holding the pan and plate together firmly, invert them. Lift off the pan. Place any apples that might have stuck to the bottom of the pan on top of tart.

8. Serve tart warm or at room temperature.

Apple Charlotte

11 TB. butter, softened

6 lb. McIntosh apples, cored and thinly sliced

¾ cup firmly packed light brown sugar

3 TB. crème de cassis or Chambord

2 TB. lemon juice

¼ tsp. pure vanilla extract

1 loaf thin-sliced white bread, crusts trimmed

Sweetened whipped cream, for serving (optional)

Serves: 6 to 8	
Prep time: 40 minutes	
Cook time: 30 minutes	

1. Melt 4 tablespoons butter in a large saucepan over medium heat. Add McIntosh apples, brown sugar, crème de cassis, lemon juice, and vanilla extract. Bring to a boil, stirring frequently, and cook for 20 minutes or until apples become a chunky applesauce. Reduce heat to low and cook for an additional 10 minutes or until sauce has reduced slightly and resists when pushed with the back of a spoon. Allow sauce to cool and refrigerate until cold. (You can do this up to 2 days in advance. Refrigerate, tightly covered.)

2. While apples are cooking, butter both sides of bread slices with softened butter. Preheat the oven to 400°F. Grease a charlotte mold or 2½-quart soufflé dish.

3. Place 4 bread slices together in a square and place the prepared charlotte mold or soufflé dish on top. Trace the shape of the mold onto bread with the tip of a knife and cut bread to fit into the bottom of the mold. Reserve at least 4 bread slices for the top; cut remaining slices in half lengthwise. They should be about the same height as the mold. Fit bread slices against the walls of the mold, overlapping them slightly. Fill the mold with apple mixture. Cut reserved bread to fit top of the mold and chill for 15 minutes.

4. Bake for 30 to 40 minutes or until bread is golden brown. Let cool in the mold for at least 30 minutes. Unmold and serve warm with sweetened whipped cream (if using).

 Bake Lore

Charlottes are named for the pan in which they are molded, which resembles a pail with small handles sticking off the top rim on both sides. Most charlottes are cold creations filled with a custard, but Apple Charlotte is always served warm.

Orange-Flavored Cranberry and Apple Cobbler

Serves: 6 to 8

Prep time: 25 minutes
Cook time: 35 minutes

3 cups fresh cranberries, picked over and rinsed

½ cup dried cranberries

1½ cups granulated sugar

1 cup cranberry juice cocktail

¼ cup Grand Marnier or Cointreau

1 TB. grated orange zest

3 Golden Delicious or Granny Smith apples, peeled, cored, and cut into ½-inch slices

1 cup all-purpose flour

2 tsp. baking powder

2 large eggs, beaten

1 cup milk

3 TB. melted butter

1 tsp. pure vanilla extract

1. Preheat the oven to 375°F. Grease a 9×13-inch baking pan.

2. Combine fresh cranberries, dried cranberries, ½ cup granulated sugar, cranberry juice, Grand Marnier, and orange zest in a large saucepan. Bring to a boil over medium-high heat, reduce heat to medium, and cook, stirring occasionally, for 10 minutes or until cranberries pop. Add Golden Delicious apples and cook, stirring occasionally, for an additional 10 minutes or until apples begin to soften. (You can do this up to 2 days in advance and refrigerate, tightly covered. Before continuing, reheat over low heat to a simmer.)

3. Sift flour and baking powder together in a large mixing bowl, then add remaining 1 cup sugar, eggs, milk, butter, and vanilla extract. Stir with a spoon until well blended.

4. Pour apple mixture into the prepared baking pan and scrape batter evenly over the top. Bake for 35 to 40 minutes or until golden. Serve hot or at room temperature with sweetened whipped cream or ice cream on top.

Biscuit-Topped Plum Cobbler

4 lb. plums (about 12 large), halved, pitted, and cut into ½-inch slices

1¼ cups granulated sugar

2½ TB. cornstarch

1 tsp. pure vanilla extract

2 cups all-purpose flour

1 TB. baking powder

½ tsp. salt

¼ tsp. ground cinnamon

8 TB. (1 stick) chilled butter, cut into ½-inch cubes

¾ cup heavy cream

1 large egg

Vanilla ice cream

Serves: 8	
Prep time: 15 minutes	
Cook time: 1 hour	

1. Preheat the oven to 400°F. Grease a 9×13-inch baking pan. Toss plums, 1 cup sugar, cornstarch, and vanilla extract in a large bowl to coat. Transfer plums to the prepared baking pan and bake for about 30 minutes or until thick and bubbling at the edges.

2. While plums are baking, prepare biscuits. Combine flour, remaining ¼ cup sugar, baking powder, salt, and cinnamon in a large bowl to blend. Cut in butter using a pastry blender, two knives, or your fingertips until mixture resembles coarse meal.

3. Whisk heavy cream and egg in a small bowl to blend. Stir cream mixture into flour mixture just until blended. Gently knead in the bowl until dough comes together, about 5 turns.

4. Remove plums from the oven and stir gently. Break off golf-ball-size pieces of dough and arrange over hot plums, spacing them 2 inches apart. Bake for 30 minutes or until fruit is bubbling and biscuits brown. Serve hot or warm with vanilla ice cream.

Half Baked

Baking powder does not live for-ever. This leavening agent tires out after long periods on the shelf, and your biscuits will be as hard and dense as rocks if you use old baking powder. To test if your powder is still viable, mix 1 teaspoon with ⅓ cup hot tap water. If it doesn't bubble furiously, buy a new can.

Pear Crisp with Ginger

Serves: 6 to 8
Prep time: 15 minutes
Cook time: 25 minutes

Got You Covered!

You can personalize this recipe in myriad ways with the topping. I suggest visiting the bulk food section of your market and selecting the granola flavor combination that appeals to you. You can also add nuts, more spices, or dried fruits.

6 medium pears, peeled, cored, and sliced

¾ cup firmly packed brown sugar

⅓ cup all-purpose flour

2 TB. finely chopped crystallized ginger

¾ tsp. ground cinnamon

½ tsp. ground ginger

1 tsp. pure vanilla extract

1½ cups granola cereal

5 TB. butter, melted

Vanilla ice cream or sweetened whipped cream

1. Preheat the oven to 375°F. Grease a 9×13-inch baking pan. Combine pears, ⅓ cup brown sugar, ¼ cup flour, crystallized ginger, ¼ teaspoon cinnamon, ground ginger, and vanilla extract. Spread mixture in the prepared baking pan.

2. Combine remaining brown sugar, remaining flour, remaining ½ teaspoon cinnamon, granola cereal, and melted butter. Mix well and sprinkle mixture over pears. Bake for 25 minutes or until pear mixture is bubbly and topping is golden brown.

3. Serve at room temperature with ice cream or sweetened whipped cream.

New England Indian Pudding

4 TB. (½ stick) butter, cut into small pieces

4 cups milk

½ cup yellow cornmeal

½ cup pure maple syrup

¼ cup firmly packed dark brown sugar

3 TB. finely chopped crystallized ginger

½ tsp. ground cinnamon

Pinch salt

½ cup golden raisins

2 large eggs, lightly beaten

Vanilla ice cream or sweetened whipped cream

Serves: 6 to 8	
Prep time: 20 minutes	
Cook time: 1 hour	

1. Preheat the oven to 325°F. Butter a 1½-quart casserole. Bring milk almost to a boil in a saucepan over medium-high heat; then add cornmeal in a steady stream, whisking constantly. Reduce heat to low and cook for 15 minutes or until mixture thickens. Stir in butter, maple syrup, brown sugar, crystallized ginger, cinnamon, and salt.

2. Remove from heat and stir constantly for 2 minutes. Stir in raisins and eggs. Scrape mixture into the prepared baking pan. Bake for 1 hour or until firm. (You can do this up to 2 days in advance and refrigerate, tightly covered. Reheat, covered with aluminum foil, in a 300°F oven for 20 minutes or until warm.)

3. Serve at room temperature with ice cream or sweetened whipped cream.

 **Bake Lore**

Because Native Americans introduced corn to the Pilgrims, anything made with corn had "Indian" as a prefix at one time or another. The other term for Indian Pudding is Hasty Pudding, and the Hasty Pudding Club at Harvard University was named for the dessert. Recipes for Indian or Hasty Pudding go back to the early eighteenth century.

Piña Colada Bread Pudding with Rum Sauce

Serves: 6 to 8

Prep time: 15 minutes, plus 30 minutes standing time

Cook time: 45 minutes

---

16 TB. (2 sticks) butter, softened

2 cups whole milk

1 (15-oz.) can *cream of coconut*

½ cup granulated sugar

3 eggs, lightly beaten

1 tsp. pure vanilla extract

1 (8-oz.) can crushed pineapple, undrained

1 (10-oz.) day-old French bread loaf, cut into 1-inch pieces

1 cup shredded coconut

1 lb. confectioners' sugar

⅓ cup rum

1. Preheat the oven to 350°F. Grease a 9×13-inch baking pan. Melt 1 stick butter in a microwave-safe dish on medium (50 percent) power for 45 seconds to 1 minute and set aside remaining butter.

2. Combine whole milk, cream of coconut, sugar, eggs, and vanilla extract in a large mixing bowl and whisk well. Stir in pineapple, bread, shredded coconut, and melted butter. Let stand, stirring occasionally, for about 30 minutes or until bread absorbs some custard.

3. Transfer mixture to the prepared baking pan and cover with aluminum foil. Bake for 35 minutes; remove foil and bake for an additional 10 minutes or until a knife inserted in the center comes out clean. Cool for 5 minutes before serving. (You can do this a day in advance and refrigerate, tightly covered. Remove from refrigerator 30 minutes before serving. Heat in a 350°F oven for 30 minutes, covered with aluminum foil, until hot.)

4. While pudding is baking, prepare sauce. Place remaining butter, confectioners' sugar, and rum in a mixing bowl and beat with an electric mixer on low speed to combine. Increase the speed to high and beat until mixture is light and fluffy.

5. To serve, spoon hot pudding onto plates and top with sauce.

Ellen on Edibles

Cream of coconut is not the same as coconut milk; do not substitute one for the other. Cream of coconut is a thick, highly sweetened mixture made basically from coconut and sugar. You might find it with the cocktail mixers rather than in the baking aisle.

Espresso-Coated Coconut Flan

1 TB. *instant espresso powder*

3 TB. very hot tap water

1¼ cups granulated sugar

1 (14-oz.) can light coconut milk, stirred well

1¼ cups whole milk

3 large eggs

2 large egg yolks

Pinch salt

½ cup sweetened shredded coconut

Serves: 6
Prep time: 15 minutes
Cook time: 1 hour plus at least 4 hours for chilling

1. Preheat the oven to 325°F. Grease 6 (6-ounce) ramekins or custard cups and place them on a cloth tea towel in the bottom of a roasting pan. Bring a kettle of water to a boil over high heat.

2. Stir together espresso powder and water in a small saucepan until powder dissolves. Stir in ½ cup sugar and place over high heat. Bring to a boil, swirling the handle of the pan but not stirring, and cook for 6 to 8 minutes or until mixture is thick and browned. Divide mixture among ramekins, tilting to coat bottoms, and let stand for about 10 minutes or until hardened.

3. Bring coconut milk and whole milk just to a simmer over moderate heat, stirring, and remove from heat. Whisk together eggs, egg yolks, salt, and remaining ¾ cup sugar in a large bowl; then add warm milk mixture in a steady stream, whisking as you pour. Stir in coconut and divide mixture among ramekins.

4. Arrange ramekins on the towel in the roasting pan and pour enough boiling water into the roasting pan to come halfway up the sides of the ramekins.

5. Bake for 1 hour or until set. Run a thin knife around the edge of each flan to loosen; then transfer ramekins to a rack and cool completely. Chill, covered, until cold, at least 4 hours. (You can do this up to 2 days in advance.) To unmold, invert small plates over the ramekins and invert flans onto plates.

Ellen on Edibles

Instant espresso powder, imported from Italy, is now becoming more common in America. It's made from real espresso coffee, which is then dehydrated and ground. Look for it in the supermarket along with other instant coffees.

Thanksgiving Pumpkin Custard

Serves: 6 to 8
Prep time: 10 minutes
Cook time: 50 minutes

1 (16-oz.) can solid-pack pumpkin

1 cup firmly packed light brown sugar

½ tsp. salt

1 tsp. ground cinnamon

½ tsp. ground nutmeg

¼ tsp. ground cloves

2 cups light cream

3 large eggs, lightly beaten

1½ cups chopped pecans

Vanilla ice cream or sweetened whipped cream

 Half Baked

There are two similar forms of canned pumpkin, and you want to be sure what you're buying is just pumpkin and not pumpkin pie filling. The filling is sweetened and already contains spices.

1. Preheat the oven to 350°F. Grease a 1½-quart casserole and set aside.

2. Scrape pumpkin into a large mixing bowl and stir in brown sugar, salt, cinnamon, nutmeg, and cloves. Stir until well blended and then whisk in cream and eggs.

3. Scrape mixture into the prepared casserole and sprinkle pecans on top. Bake for 50 to 55 minutes or until a knife inserted into the center comes out almost clean. Allow to cool for 10 minutes and then serve topped with vanilla ice cream or sweetened whipped cream.

Baked Lemon and Dried Blueberry Pudding

8 TB. (1 stick) butter, softened

¾ cup granulated sugar

2 large eggs

¼ cup lemon juice

1 TB. grated lemon zest

1½ cups all-purpose flour

2 tsp. baking powder

¾ cup milk

½ cup dried blueberries

Serves: 6 to 8	
Prep time: 10 minutes	
Cook time: 50 minutes	

1. Preheat the oven to 350°F. Butter a 1½-quart casserole and set aside. Bring a kettle of water to a boil over high heat.

2. *Cream* butter and sugar in a mixing bowl with an electric mixer on medium until light and fluffy. Add eggs, one at a time, beating well between each addition and scraping down the sides of the bowl as necessary. Add lemon juice and lemon zest and beat well. Sift flour and baking powder directly into mixture and stir it in. Gradually add milk, beating steadily as you add it. Stir in dried blueberries.

3. Scrape mixture into the prepared casserole. Place casserole in a large baking pan and pour enough boiling water into the baking pan to come up the sides of the casserole 1 inch. Bake for 50 to 55 minutes or until firm and slightly browned. Serve warm or at room temperature.

Ellen on Edibles

Cream, as a verb, means to beat ingredients together to form a homogeneous mixture. It's most often used as the first step in a dessert recipe because creaming together butter and sugar forms the basic structure for a dough or batter.

Meringue-Topped Sweet Potato Pudding

Serves: 6 to 8

Prep time: 20 minutes plus 1 hour to bake the potatoes

Cook time: 55 minutes

4 medium sweet potatoes (about 2 lb.)

¾ cup milk

½ cup heavy cream

⅓ cup firmly packed dark brown sugar

2 large eggs

¼ tsp. salt

¼ tsp. freshly grated nutmeg

Pinch ground cloves

¼ cup finely chopped crystallized ginger

5 large egg whites, at room temperature

Pinch cream of tartar

¾ cup superfine granulated sugar

2 tsp. ground cinnamon

1. Preheat the oven to 400°F. Line a baking sheet with foil. Grease a 1½-quart casserole.

2. Prick sweet potatoes in several places with a fork and bake on the prepared baking sheet for 60 to 75 minutes or until very soft. When cool enough to handle, halve and scoop out enough flesh to measure 2 cups. (You can do this up to 2 days in advance and refrigerate, tightly covered. Before continuing, bring to room temperature.)

3. Combine sweet potatoes, milk, cream, brown sugar, eggs, salt, nutmeg, and ground cloves in a mixing bowl. Mix with an electric mixer on medium speed until smooth, scraping the sides of the bowl as necessary. Stir in crystallized ginger.

4. Reduce the oven temperature to 375°F. Scrape sweet potato pudding into the prepared casserole and bake for 40 minutes.

5. Begin meringue after sweet potato pudding has been in the oven for 30 minutes. Place egg whites in a large mixing bowl and beat with an electric mixer on medium speed until frothy. Add cream of tartar and increase speed to high. After soft peaks form, gradually add superfine sugar, a few tablespoons at a time. Beat until glossy stiff peaks form and then beat in cinnamon.

6. Mound meringue in the center of hot sweet potato pudding and spread almost to the edge. Bake for an additional 15 minutes or until meringue is lightly browned. Serve pudding warm or at room temperature.

 **Got You Covered!**

When you use eggs in baking, they should always be at room temperature because the whites will not increase in volume properly if they are chilled. An easy way to do this is to place the eggs in a bowl of hot tap water for 5 minutes before separating them.

Summer Sweets: Homey Desserts with Summer Fruits

In This Chapter

◆ Recipes glorifying the bounty of summer's luscious fruits

◆ Easy to make old-fashioned American desserts

◆ Bake and serve cakes that don't need frosting or filling

Great fresh fruit picked at the peak of ripeness needs little augmentation to make it memorable. That's why the recipes for desserts in this chapter are so fast to assemble. And these succulent summer fruits also cook more quickly than heartier fruits such as apples, so these desserts also cook relatively quickly.

Many of these recipes, such as those for cobblers and slumps, have been around since Colonial times and are as delicious today as when they were first spooned out of casseroles. Both of these genre are deep-dish fruit pies with a topping, so they can be prepared in a matter of minutes.

A benefit we have over previous generations is that with freezers, we can create these sunny flavors at any time of year.

Tree-Ripened Treats

You'll encounter these tree fruits in this chapter:

◆ **Apricots.** A ripe apricot is soft when gently pressed, and the skin is thin enough that it does not have to be peeled. Just slice the apricot and discard the pit.

◆ **Cherries.** Discard the stems, rinse the cherries in a colander, cut them in half, discard the pits, and they're ready to go. Or you can easily freeze them for next winter's use. There is a specialized gadget called a cherry pitter that accomplishes the task without a mess, and it does double duty as an olive pitter, too.

◆ **Peaches.** Peaches are best used in their season because they don't ripen well off the tree. Peaches are ripe if they're soft when pressed gently. Whether or not you want to peel peaches is a personal decision. If you prefer peeled peaches, drop them into boiling water for 30 seconds, remove and drain lightly, and the skins will slip right off when you rub the fruit. You can also use already-peeled frozen peach slices.

◆ **Pears.** Pears do ripen well off the tree, and it might take up to a week for them to ripen if they're rock-hard when you buy them. You can substitute any variety of pear for another, but peel whichever pear you choose with a vegetable peeler before you use it. Toss pear slices with lemon juice to prevent discoloration. Certain species of pear are available in the fall, but the luscious juicy Comice are a summer treat.

◆ **Plums.** Plums are also best used in their season. Like peaches, they don't ripen well off the tree. You can tell a plum is ripe if it's soft when you gently press it with your finger. Plums have a crease on one side that runs parallel to the flat side of the pit. If you slice plums lengthwise along the crease, you should be able to see the pit. Discard it, and you're ready to slice or dice; peeling is not necessary.

It's the Berries!

One of the delights of summer is berries, with their bright color and intense flavor. We'll use these berries in this chapter:

◆ **Blackberries.** Blackberries, a rich purple-black in color, are actually a cluster of tiny fruits, each with its own seed. They're most common and affordable during the summer and can be successfully frozen after a quick rinse and gentle pat dry with paper towels.

◆ **Blueberries.** Look for berries that are plump, not shriveled, and have a slight grayish patina. Rinse the berries; discard any stems, twigs, or small green berries; and they're ready to go. You can use blueberries fresh or dry them on paper towels and freeze them in a plastic bag.

◆ **Raspberries.** Raspberries are now grown in a rainbow of colors, from classic red to golden amber. When choosing fresh raspberries, look at the bottom of the container and choose one that has the least amount of juice. That's a sign that the berries are not damaged or moldy. Place the berries in a bowl of water and stir them around to dislodge any lingering dirt. Then pat them dry gently on paper towels. You can also buy bags of frozen raspberries.

◆ **Strawberries.** Strawberries do not ripen after they've been picked, so what you buy is what you get. Because most manufacturers "top dress" the packages with the "hero berries" on the top, when you're buying fresh, check out the bottom of the package. Generally, the smaller the berry, the more intense the flavor. Tiny European *fraises du bois* are the sweetest of all. Rinse the berries and cut off the caps just prior to blending them. You can freeze them after a quick rinse and trimming the caps.

Fresh from the Freezer

There's nothing like the flavor and aroma of fresh fruit, but if your favorite fruit is out of season, it's better to use *dry-packed frozen fruit* rather than canned fruit or unripe fruit. Frozen fruits are picked and frozen at the peak of ripeness, and for any dessert that will be baked, it doesn't really matter that the fruits were frozen.

Modern air transportation has given us a new definition of "airline food," and we can now enjoy almost all fruits year-round thanks to air freight from other countries—but we do pay a price for this convenience. To avoid this pitfall, stock up on fruits when they are either in season locally or attractively priced, and freeze them yourself.

The best way to freeze fruit is to first prepare the fruit by cleaning, slicing, peeling, sectioning, etc., as appropriate. Then simply arrange ½- to 1-inch pieces on a baking sheet covered with plastic wrap, and put them into the freezer until they're frozen. After the berries are frozen, transfer them to a heavy, resealable plastic bag. Mark the date on the bag and use the fruit within 2 months.

Ellen on Edibles
Dry-packed frozen fruits are frozen in individual pieces without any syrup or additional sugar. You'll find the fruits in plastic bags in the freezer section of your supermarket.

Peach and Blackberry Cobbler

Serves: 6 to 8
Prep time: 15 minutes
Cook time: 25 minutes

1¼ cups granulated sugar

1 TB. *cornstarch*

¼ cup crème de cassis

2½ lb. ripe peaches, pitted and cut into ½-inch slices

2 (6-oz.) pkg. fresh or frozen blackberries, rinsed

2 cups all-purpose flour

2 tsp. baking powder

¾ tsp. salt

10 TB. (1¼ sticks) cold butter, cut into ½-inch pieces

¾ cup whole milk

Vanilla ice cream or sweetened whipped cream (optional)

1. Preheat the oven to 425°F. Grease a 9×13-inch baking pan.

2. Place sugar in a mixing bowl and stir cornstarch into crème de cassis. Add peaches and blackberries and toss to combine well. Transfer berry mixture to the prepared baking pan and bake for 10 minutes or until hot.

3. While fruit is baking, combine flour, baking powder, and salt in a large bowl. Cut in butter using a pastry blender, two knives, or your fingertips until mixture resembles coarse meal. Add whole milk and stir just until a dough forms.

4. Drop dough onto hot fruit mixture in 6 to 8 mounds. Bake in the center of the oven for 25 to 35 minutes or until top is golden. Cool for 10 minutes and serve topped with vanilla ice cream or sweetened whipped cream (if using).

Ellen on Edibles

Cornstarch is a powdery substance obtained from finely grinding the endosperm of corn kernels that is used as a thickening agent. Mix it with either a cold liquid or another granular powder such as granulated sugar to keep it from forming lumps in the finished dish.

Strawberry-Rhubarb Cobbler

1 cup granulated sugar

2 TB. Grand Marnier or Cointreau

1½ lb. rhubarb, rinsed and thinly sliced

1 TB. cornstarch

2 TB. cold water

1 cup all-purpose flour

1½ tsp. baking powder

4 TB. (½ stick) butter, cut into ½-inch pieces

1 large egg, lightly beaten

2 TB. milk

1 pt. fresh strawberries, rinsed, capped, and halved

Serves: 6 to 8	
Prep time: 15 minutes	
Cook time: 20 minutes	

1. Preheat the oven to 400°F. Grease a 9×13-inch baking pan.

2. Reserve 2 tablespoons sugar and set aside. Combine remaining sugar, Grand Marnier, and rhubarb in a saucepan. Bring to a boil over medium heat, stirring occasionally. Cook, stirring occasionally, for 12 minutes or until rhubarb is soft. Stir cornstarch into water and stir cornstarch mixture into rhubarb. Simmer for 2 minutes or until thick and bubbly. Remove from heat and keep warm.

3. Stir together flour, remaining 2 tablespoons sugar, and baking powder in a medium bowl. Cut in butter using a pastry blender, two knives, or your fingertips until mixture resembles coarse meal. Stir together egg and milk; then add to flour mixture, stirring just to moisten until a moist dough forms. Turn out dough onto lightly floured surface and knead five or six times. Roll dough to a rectangle 14 inches long. Cut lengthwise into ½-inch-wide strips.

4. Stir strawberries into rhubarb mixture. Transfer fruit to the prepared baking pan. Weave dough strips over fruit mixture to make a lattice top by placing alternate strips horizontally and vertically across the pan. Trim the strips to fit the baking pan. Place the baking pan on a foil-lined baking sheet. Bake for 20 to 25 minutes or until fruit is tender and lattice top is golden. Serve hot or at room temperature.

 Bake Lore

Rhubarb is Asian in origin, although it arrived in Europe in time to appear in the writings of both Pliny and Dioscorides. Its medicinal qualities were touted by European monks in the Middle Ages. The first recipes for rhubarb pie don't appear in cookbooks until the mid-nineteenth century. The plant—botanically a vegetable—was very popular with the Pennsylvania Dutch.

Peach Cobbler with Dried Cherries and Lemon Biscuit Topping

Serves: 6 to 8
Prep time: 15 minutes
Cook time: 55 minutes

2 lb. ripe peaches

½ cup dried cherries

1 cup granulated sugar

1½ TB. cornstarch

1 cup all-purpose flour

1 tsp. baking powder

Pinch salt

10 TB. (1¼ sticks) butter, softened and cut into ½-inch pieces

2 large egg yolks, lightly beaten

2 tsp. grated lemon zest

½ tsp. pure vanilla extract

Vanilla ice cream or sweetened whipped cream (optional)

1. Preheat the oven to 375°F. Grease a 9×13-inch baking pan. Bring a large pot of water to a boil. Add peaches and blanch for 1 minute. Remove peaches from water with a slotted spoon and slip off skins. Cut in half, discard pits, and cut peaches into ½-inch slices.

2. Combine peaches, dried cherries, ½ cup sugar, and cornstarch in a mixing bowl. Toss to combine and allow to sit for 5 minutes. Transfer mixture to the prepared baking pan.

3. Mix flour, baking powder, and salt in a small bowl. Place butter and remaining ½ cup sugar in a large mixing bowl. Beat with an electric mixer on medium speed until light and fluffy. Beat in egg yolks, lemon zest, and vanilla extract. Add flour mixture and mix just until moist dough forms. Spoon 6 to 8 mounds of dough on top of fruit.

4. Bake *cobbler* for 55 minutes or until juices bubble thickly and topping is golden. Cool for 5 minutes and serve with ice cream or sweetened whipped cream (if using).

Ellen on Edibles

Cobblers are deep-dish fruit pies that developed during the Colonial era, but what tops them varies. They are frequently topped with a rich dough similar to a biscuit, but they can also be topped with a rolled crust or some variation on a piecrust.

Apricot Upside-Down Cake

1 cup (2 sticks) butter, cut into pieces and softened

¾ cup firmly packed light brown sugar

1½ lb. ripe apricots, halved lengthwise and pitted

1¾ cups all-purpose flour

1½ tsp. baking powder

½ tsp. baking soda

½ tsp. salt

¾ cup granulated sugar

1½ tsp. pure vanilla extract

2 large eggs, at room temperature

¾ cup well-shaken buttermilk

Serves: 6 to 8
Prep time: 15 minutes
Cook time: 40 minutes

1. Preheat the oven to 375°F. Melt ½ cup (1 stick) butter in a 10-inch cast-iron or other ovenproof skillet over medium heat. Reduce heat to low and sprinkle brown sugar evenly over butter; then cook, without stirring, for 3 minutes. Not all of sugar will be dissolved. Remove the skillet from heat and arrange apricot halves, cut side down, close together on top of brown sugar.

2. Sift together flour, baking powder, baking soda, and salt into a small bowl. Combine remaining ½ cup (1 stick) butter, sugar, and vanilla extract in a mixing bowl. Beat with an electric mixer on medium speed for 3 to 4 minutes or until light and fluffy. Beat in eggs 1 at a time; then beat for 2 to 3 minutes or until mixture is creamy and doubled in volume.

3. Reduce mixer speed to low and add flour mixture in 3 batches, alternating with buttermilk, beginning and ending with flour mixture. Beat just until combined.

4. Gently spoon batter over apricots and spread evenly.

5. Bake for 40 to 45 minutes or until golden brown and a cake tester inserted in the center comes out clean. Run a thin knife around the edge of the skillet. Wearing oven mitts, immediately invert a serving plate over the skillet and, holding the skillet and plate together firmly, invert them. Carefully lift off the skillet. If necessary, place any fruit that might have stuck to the bottom of the skillet on top of the cake. Cool at least 15 minutes or to room temperature before serving.

Half Baked

When baking, it's important to use sticks of butter rather than whipped butter sold in tubs. The extra air incorporated into whipped butter will throw off your measurements.

Pear Gingerbread Upside-Down Cake

Serves: 6 to 8
Prep time: 15 minutes
Cook time: 40 minutes

3 ripe pears

¾ cup (1½ sticks) butter, softened

1¼ cups firmly packed light brown sugar

2½ cups all-purpose flour

1½ tsp. baking soda

1 tsp. ground cinnamon

1 tsp. ground ginger

¼ tsp. ground cloves

¼ tsp. salt

1 cup molasses

1 cup boiling water

1 large egg, lightly beaten

Vanilla ice cream (optional)

Got You Covered!

Use a melon baller to core fruits that will be arranged decoratively, such as these pears or apples for an apple tart. You'll get a very neat circular ball.

1. Preheat the oven to 350°F. Peel and core pears and cut each into 8 wedges. Melt ¼ cup (½ stick) butter in a 10-inch cast-iron or other ovenproof skillet over medium heat. Reduce heat to low and sprinkle ¾ cup brown sugar evenly over butter; then cook, without stirring, for 3 minutes. Not all of sugar will be dissolved. Remove the skillet from heat and arrange pear slices close together on top of brown sugar.

2. Whisk together flour, baking soda, cinnamon, ginger, cloves, and salt in a mixing bowl. Whisk together molasses and boiling water in a small bowl. Combine remaining ½ cup (1 stick) butter, remaining ½ cup brown sugar, and egg in a large bowl. Beat with an electric mixer on medium speed for 2 minutes or until light and fluffy.

3. Reduce mixer speed to low and add flour mixture in 3 batches, alternating with molasses mixture, beginning and ending with flour mixture. Beat until just combined. Gently spoon batter over pears and spread evenly.

4. Bake cake for 40 to 45 minutes or until golden brown and a cake tester inserted in the center comes out clean. Run a thin knife around the edge of the skillet. Wearing oven mitts, immediately invert a serving plate over the skillet and, holding the skillet and plate together firmly, invert them. Carefully lift off the skillet. If necessary, replace on top of the cake any fruit that might have stuck to the bottom of the skillet. Cool at least 15 minutes or to room temperature before serving and serve with vanilla ice cream (if using).

Plum Kuchen

1½ cups all-purpose flour

1½ tsp. baking powder

1 tsp. ground cinnamon

¼ tsp. salt

6 TB. (¾ stick) butter, softened

1 cup granulated sugar

2 large eggs

1½ tsp. pure vanilla extract

½ cup sour cream

6 large plums, halved, pitted, and cut into 8 wedges each

½ tsp. ground ginger

Serves: 6 to 8
Prep time: 15 minutes
Cook time: 40 minutes

1. Preheat the oven to 350°F. Grease a 9×13-inch baking pan. Sift flour, baking powder, cinnamon, and salt into a small bowl.

2. Combine butter and ⅔ cup sugar in a mixing bowl. Beat with an electric mixer on medium speed until well blended. Increase mixer speed to high and beat until light and fluffy. Add eggs, 1 at a time, beating well between each addition and scraping down the sides of the bowl. Beat in vanilla and sour cream. Reduce mixer speed to low and add flour mixture. Beat just long enough to blend. Scrape batter into the prepared baking pan.

3. Arrange plum wedges on their sides in 4 long rows atop batter. Mix ginger with remaining ⅓ cup sugar and sprinkle over plums.

4. Bake for 40 minutes or until a cake tester inserted into the center comes out clean. Transfer cake to a rack to cool for at least 10 minutes or until room temperature.

Got You Covered!

Flour is always added to a batter last and is only beaten briefly, to keep the cake tender. Flour contains a protein, gluten, that becomes tough if it's overworked. That's why bread dough is kneaded for a long time, so the gluten will allow the yeast to expand, but cakes are mixed for a short period of time.

Dumpling-Topped Skillet Berry Grunt

Serves: 6 to 8
Prep time: 15 minutes
Cook time: 22 minutes

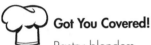 **Got You Covered!**

Pastry blenders were a part of every cook's kitchen until a generation ago, but they are becoming rare these days, as fewer people make pie crust from scratch without the aid of a food processor. Pastry blenders look like a half-moon, with three or four wire blades attached to a handle. Rocking them back and forth through a bowl with flour and butter breaks up the butter into tiny pieces similar to a coarse meal.

⅔ cup orange juice

1 cup fresh or frozen black-berries, rinsed

1 cup fresh or frozen blue-berries, rinsed

1 cup fresh or frozen straw-berries, rinsed, capped, and halved

2 tsp. grated orange zest

½ cup granulated sugar

1 TB. cornstarch

2 TB. cold water

¾ cup all-purpose flour

1 tsp. baking powder

¼ tsp. ground cinnamon

Pinch salt

3 TB. butter, cut into small pieces

⅓ cup milk

Vanilla ice cream (optional)

1. Combine orange juice, blackberries, blueberries, strawberries, orange zest, and ¼ cup sugar in a large skillet with a lid. Bring to a boil over medium-high heat, stirring occasionally. Cover, reduce heat to medium, and simmer for 5 minutes. Mix corn-starch into water and stir to dissolve. Uncover the skillet, stir cornstarch mixture into fruit, and simmer for 2 minutes or until lightly thickened.

2. Combine flour, remaining ¼ cup sugar, baking powder, cinna-mon, and salt. Cut in butter with a pastry blender, two knives, or your fingertips until the mixture resembles coarse meal. Add milk to flour mixture and mix just until moist dough forms. Spoon 6 to 8 mounds of dough on top of fruit.

3. Cover and simmer for 15 minutes or until a toothpick inserted in the topping comes out clean. Serve hot with vanilla ice cream (if using).

Blackberry Slump

4 cups (1½ lb.) fresh blackberries

1 cup granulated sugar

1 cup all-purpose flour

1½ tsp. baking powder

¼ tsp. salt

¾ cup whole milk

5 TB. butter, melted

Vanilla ice cream or sweetened whipped cream
(optional)

Serves: 4 to 6	
Prep time: 10 minutes	
Cook time: 40 minutes	

1. Preheat the oven to 375°F. Place berries in an ungreased 5- to
   6-cup gratin dish or deep-dish glass or ceramic pie plate and
   sprinkle evenly with ¾ cup sugar.

2. Sift together flour, baking powder, salt, and remaining ¼ cup
   sugar in a bowl. Add whole milk and butter and whisk until
   smooth; then pour over berries. It doesn't matter if berries are
   not completely covered.

3. Bake for 40 to 45 minutes or until top is golden. Transfer to a
   rack and cool for 15 minutes. Serve topped with vanilla ice
   cream or sweetened whipped cream (if using).

 Ellen on Edibles _____

A **slump** is a New England fruit dessert that dates back
to the mid-eighteenth century. It supposedly got its name
because it doesn't hold a shape, but slumps onto the plate.
Louisa May Alcott, author of _Little Women_, named her house in
Concord, Massachusetts, "Apple Slump."

Cherry Clafouti

Serves: 6 to 8
Prep time: 15 minutes
Cook time: 20 minutes

1 cup granulated sugar

6 TB. all-purpose flour

6 large eggs

2 cups whole milk

2 tsp. pure vanilla extract

2 tsp. grated orange zest

½ tsp. salt

3 cups dark sweet cherries, halved and pitted

2 TB. (¼ stick) butter, cut into bits

Vanilla ice cream (optional)

 Ellen on Edibles

Clafouti originated in the Limousin region of France. It is basically a dessert that combines fruit and a batter. Any fruit that holds its shape while baking, such as cherries, plums, or peaches, can be used.

1. Preheat the oven to 400°F. Grease a 9×13-inch baking pan.

2. Reserve 3 tablespoons sugar; combine remaining sugar, flour, eggs, whole milk, vanilla extract, orange zest, and salt in a food processor fitted with a steel blade or in a blender. Purée until smooth.

3. Arrange cherries in one layer in the prepared baking pan and pour custard over them. Bake for 20 to 25 minutes or until top is puffed and springy to the touch. Remove from the oven and increase the oven temperature to broil. Sprinkle with remaining 3 TB. sugar, dot with butter, and broil *clafouti* under the broiler about 3 inches from the heat for 1 minute or until it is browned. Serve immediately with ice cream (if using).

Pear and Almond Bake

6 Bartlett or other ripe pears, peeled, cored, and sliced

1 TB. lemon juice

¾ cup sliced almonds

6 TB. (¾ stick) butter

1½ TB. all-purpose flour

½ cup granulated sugar

¼ cup whipping cream

½ tsp. pure almond extract

Fresh raspberries or fresh sliced strawberries

Serves: 6 to 8	
Prep time: 20 minutes	
Cook time: 25 minutes	

1. Preheat the oven to 375°F. Grease a 9×13-inch baking pan. Place pears in the prepared pan and drizzle with lemon juice. Place almonds on a baking sheet and toast in the oven for 5 to 7 minutes or until lightly browned. Remove nuts from the oven and set aside.

2. Melt butter in a small saucepan over low heat. Stir in flour and sugar. Cook over medium heat, stirring, for 4 to 5 minutes or until thick and smooth. Remove from heat and stir in almonds, cream, and almond extract. Spread mixture over pears.

3. Bake for 25 minutes or until pears are tender. Top with raspberries or strawberries.

 Bake Lore

Bartlett pears, large bell-shaped fruit with yellow-green skin, were developed in the early eighteenth century in England. Enoch Bartlett, a resident of Dorchester, Massachusetts, introduced the species to America—thus the name. They are best from July through early October.

Rice Pudding with Mixed Berries

Serves: 6 to 8
Prep time: 10 minutes, plus 2 hours standing time
Cook time: 45 minutes

3 cups water

1 cup long-grain or medium-grain white rice

½ tsp. salt

⅓ cup plus 3 TB. granulated sugar

½ tsp. ground cinnamon

2 cups whole milk

1 tsp. pure vanilla extract

1 pt. fresh strawberries, rinsed, hulled, and sliced

1 (6-oz.) pkg. fresh raspberries, rinsed

1 (6-oz.) pkg. fresh blueberries or blackberries, rinsed

2 (4-oz.) containers (1 cup) vanilla pudding from the supermarket refrigerator aisle

1. Bring water to boil in a medium saucepan over high heat. Add rice and salt, reduce heat to medium-low, and simmer, uncovered, for 20 minutes or until rice is very tender and water is absorbed. Add ⅓ cup sugar and cinnamon and stir to blend. Reduce heat to low, add whole milk, and simmer, stirring frequently, for 25 minutes or until mixture is very thick. Remove from heat and stir in vanilla extract. Cool for about 2 hours or until pudding reaches room temperature.

2. Mix strawberries, raspberries, and blueberries with remaining 3 tablespoons sugar in a large bowl. Let stand for at least 30 minutes or until juices are released. (You can make rice pudding and strawberries 4 hours in advance. Cover and refrigerate separately. Before continuing, bring to room temperature.)

3. Stir vanilla pudding and 2 cups fruit mixture into rice pudding. Transfer to a large bowl. Top with remaining fruit and serve immediately.

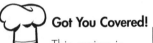 **Got You Covered!**

This recipe is open to many variations. Use chopped peaches, nectarines, or apricots, as well as any combination of berries. To trim fat, use 2 percent milk or nonfat vanilla yogurt in place of the creamier pudding.

Glossary

accoutrement   An accompaniment, trapping, or garnish.

al dente   Italian for "against the teeth." Refers to pasta (or other ingredient such as rice) that is neither soft nor hard, but just slightly firm against the teeth. This, according to many pasta aficionados, is the perfect way to cook pasta.

all-purpose flour   Flour that contains only the inner part of the wheat grain. Usable for all purposes from cakes to gravies.

allspice   Named for its flavor echoes of several spices (cinnamon, cloves, nutmeg), allspice is used in many desserts and in rich marinades and stews.

almonds   Mild, sweet, and crunchy nuts that combine nicely with creamy and sweet food items.

ancho chili   The sweetest of the dried chili peppers. They are the mild green poblano chilies in their fresh form, and they add a rich, almost fruity flavor to foods.

anchovies (also **sardines**)   Tiny, flavorful preserved fish that typically come in cans. The strong flavor from these salted fish is a critical element in many recipes. Anchovies are a traditional garnish for Caesar salad, the dressing of which contains anchovy paste.

andouille sausage   A sausage traditionally made with highly seasoned pork chitterlings and tripe, and a standard component of many Cajun dishes.

apple pie spice   A preblended mix of cinnamon, nutmeg, allspice, cardamom, and ground cloves.

arborio rice   A plump Italian rice used, among other purposes, for risotto.

artichoke hearts   The center part of the artichoke flower, often found canned in grocery stores and used as a stand-alone vegetable dish or as a flavorful base for appetizers or main courses.

arugula   A spicy-peppery garden plant with leaves that resemble a dandelion and have a distinctive—and very sharp—flavor.

au gratin   A topping of grated cheese and/or breadcrumbs made crusty and brown before serving.

bain marie   The French term for a water bath that cooks food gently by surrounding it with simmering water.

bake   To cook in a dry oven. Dry-heat cooking often results in a crisping of the exterior of the food being cooked. Moist-heat cooking, through methods such as steaming, poaching, etc., brings a much different, moist quality to the food.

balsamic vinegar   Vinegar produced primarily in Italy from a specific type of grape and aged in wood barrels. It is heavier, darker, and sweeter than most vinegars.

bamboo shoots   Crunchy, tasty white parts of the growing bamboo plant, often purchased canned.

basil   A flavorful, almost sweet, resinous herb delicious with tomatoes and used in all kinds of Italian or Mediterranean-style dishes.

baste   To keep foods moist during cooking by spooning, brushing, or drizzling with a liquid.

beat   To quickly mix substances.

Belgian endive   A plant that resembles a small, elongated, tightly packed head of Romaine lettuce. The thick, crunchy leaves can be broken off and used with dips and spreads.

black pepper   A biting and pungent seasoning, freshly ground pepper is a must for many dishes and adds an extra level of flavor and taste.

blanch   To place a food in boiling water for about 1 minute (or less) to partially cook the exterior and then submerge in or rinse with cool water to halt the cooking. Blanching sets the color of green vegetables and makes fruits such as peaches easier to peel.

blend   To completely mix something, usually with a blender or food processor, more slowly than beating.

blue cheese   A blue-veined cheese that crumbles easily and has a somewhat soft texture. Is usually sold in a block. The color is from a flavorful, edible mold that is often added or injected into the cheese.

boil   To heat a liquid to a point where water is forced to turn into steam, causing the liquid to bubble. To boil something is to insert it into boiling water. A rapid boil is when a lot of bubbles form on the surface of the liquid.

bok choy (also **Chinese cabbage**)   A member of the cabbage family with thick stems, crisp texture, and fresh flavor. It is perfect for stir-frying.

bouquet garni   A collection of French origin comprised of herbs including bay leaf, parsley, thyme, and others. Traditionally, these herbs are tied in a bunch or packaged in cheesecloth for cooking and subsequent removal. Bouquet garni is often found in the spice section of your grocery store and through specialty spice vendors.

braise   To cook with the introduction of some liquid, usually over an extended period of time.

breadcrumbs   Tiny pieces of crumbled dry bread. Breadcrumbs are an important component in many recipes and are also used as a coating; for example, with breaded chicken breasts.

brie   A creamy cow's milk cheese from France with a soft, edible rind and a mild flavor.

brioche   A French yeast bread made with both butter and eggs.

broil   To cook in a dry oven under the overhead high-heat element.

broth   *See* stock.

brown   To cook in a skillet, turning, until the food's surface is seared, brown in color, to lock in the juices.

brown rice   Whole-grain rice including the germ with a characteristic pale brown or tan color; more nutritious and flavorful than white rice.

bulgur   A wheat kernel that's been steamed, dried, and crushed and is sold in fine and coarse textures.

Cajun cooking   A style of cooking that combines French and Southern characteristics and includes many highly seasoned stews and meats.

capers   Usually sold preserved in jars, capers are the flavorful buds of a Mediterranean plant. The most common size is *nonpareil* (about the size of a small pea); others are larger, including the grape-size caper berries produced in Spain.

caramelize   To cook sugar over low heat until it develops a sweet caramel flavor. The term is increasingly gaining use to describe cooking vegetables (especially onions) or meat in butter or oil over low heat until they soften, sweeten, and develop a caramel color.

caraway   A distinctive spicy seed used for bread, pork, cheese, and cabbage dishes. It is known to reduce stomach upset, which is why it is often paired with, for example, sauerkraut.

carbohydrate   A nutritional component found in starches, sugars, fruits, and vegetables that causes a rise in blood glucose levels. Carbohydrates supply energy and many important nutrients, including vitamins, minerals, and antioxidants.

cardamom   An intense, sweet-smelling spice, common to Indian cooking, also used in baking and coffee.

carob   A tropical tree that produces long pods. The dried, baked, and powdered flesh (carob powder) is used in baking, and the fresh and dried pods are used for a variety of recipes. The flavor is sweet and reminiscent of chocolate.

cassoulet   A traditional dish from the Languedoc region of France made with beans and meats.

cayenne   A fiery spice made from (hot) chili peppers, especially the cayenne chili, a slender, red, and very hot pepper.

celery root   Also called *celeriac*, it's a knobby brown root that can be eaten either raw or cooked, and has a more pronounced flavor than stalks of celery.

challah   An egg-rich ceremonial Jewish bread traditionally braided into an oval loaf.

cheddar   The ubiquitous hard cow's milk cheese with a rich, buttery flavor that ranges from mellow to sharp. Originally produced in England, cheddar is now produced worldwide.

chevre   French for goat's milk cheese, chevre is a typically creamy-salty soft cheese delicious by itself or paired with fruits or chutney. Chevres vary in style from mild and creamy to aged, firm, and flavorful. *Artisanal* chevres are usually more expensive and sold in smaller quantities; these are often delicious by themselves. Other chevres produced in quantity are less expensive and often more appropriate for combining with fruit or herbs.

chickpeas (also **garbanzo beans**)   A yellow-gold, roundish bean that's the base ingredient in hummus. Chickpeas are high in fiber and low in fat, making this a delicious and healthful component of many appetizers and main dishes.

chiffonade   Vegetables such as lettuces that are cut into very thin strips.

chilies (also **chiles**)   Any one of many different "hot" peppers, ranging in intensity from the relatively mild ancho pepper to the blisteringly hot habañero.

chili powder   A seasoning blend that includes chili pepper, cumin, garlic, and oregano. Proportions vary among different versions, but they all offer a warm, rich flavor.

Chinese five-spice powder   A seasoning blend of cinnamon, anise, ginger, fennel, and pepper.

chipotle chilies   Smoked jalapeño chilies, packed in a hot red pepper sauce with herbs and vinegar.

chives   A member of the onion family, chives grow in bunches of long leaves that resemble tall grass or the green tops of onions. Chives provide a light onion flavor to any dish. They're very easy to grow and are often grown in gardens.

chop   To cut into pieces, usually qualified by an adverb such as "*coarsely* chopped," or by a size measurement, such as "chopped into ½-inch pieces." "Finely chopped" is much closer to "minced."

chorizo   A spiced pork sausage eaten alone and used as a component in many recipes.

chutney   A thick condiment often served with Indian curries made with fruits and/or vegetables with vinegar, sugar, and spices.

cider vinegar   Vinegar produced from apple cider, popular in North America.

cilantro   A member of the parsley family and used in Mexican cooking and some Asian dishes. Cilantro is what gives some salsas their unique flavor. Use in moderation, as the flavor can overwhelm. The seed of the cilantro is the spice coriander.

cinnamon   A sweet, rich, aromatic spice commonly used in baking or desserts. Cinnamon can also be used for delicious and interesting entrées.

clafouti   A French fruit dessert made with a batter that is baked.

clove   A sweet, strong, almost wintergreen-flavor spice used in baking and with meats such as ham.

cobbler   A deep-dish fruit pie with a pie crust or biscuit topping.

collard greens   A member of the cabbage family that grows on tall stems with floppy leaves and is very high in iron.

coriander seed   A rich, warm, spicy seed used in all types of recipes, from African to South American, from entrées to desserts.

cornstarch   A powdery substance used as a thickening agent, made from grinding the endosperm of corn kernels.

count   In terms of seafood or other foods that come in small sizes, the number of that item that compose 1 pound. For example, 31 to 40 count shrimp are large appetizer shrimp often served with cocktail sauce; 51 to 60 are much smaller.

couscous   Granular semolina (durum wheat) that is cooked and used in many Mediterranean and North African dishes.

cream   To cream is to mix ingredients to form a homogenous mixture, such as butter and sugar as the basis for a dough or batter.

crème fraîche   A thickened cream with a slightly tangy flavor that does not curdle if boiled.

crimini mushrooms   A relative of the white button mushroom, but brown in color and with a richer flavor. The larger, fully grown version is the portobello. *See also* portobello mushrooms.

crimping (or **fluting**)   To pinch pastry edges together in a decorative way to seal an unbaked pie.

croutons   Pieces of bread, usually between ¼ and ½ inch in size, that are sometimes seasoned and baked, broiled, or fried to a crisp texture. Popular in soups and salads.

cumin   A fiery, smoky-tasting spice popular in Southwestern, Middle Eastern, and Indian dishes. Cumin is a seed; ground cumin seed is the most common form of the spice used in cooking.

curry   A general term referring to rich, spicy, Indian-style sauces and the dishes prepared with them. A curry will use curry powder as its base seasoning.

curry powder   A ground blend of spices used as a basis for curry and a huge range of other Indian-influenced dishes. All blends are rich and flavorful. Some, such as Vindaloo and Madras, are notably hotter than others. Common ingredients include hot pepper, nutmeg, cumin, cinnamon, pepper, and turmeric. Some curry can also be found in paste form.

custard   A cooked mixture of eggs and milk. Custards are a popular base for desserts.

dash   A few drops, usually of a liquid, released by a quick shake of, for example, a bottle of hot sauce.

deglaze   To scrape up the bits of meat and seasoning left in a pan or skillet after cooking by adding a liquid such as wine or broth and creating a flavorful stock that can be used to create sauces.

devein   The removal of the dark intestinal vein from the back of a large shrimp with a sharp knife. The vein can contain grit, especially in large shrimp.

dice   To cut into small cubes about ¼-inch square.

Dijon mustard   Hearty, spicy mustard made in the style of the Dijon region of France.

dill   A unique herb with a fresh aroma that is perfect for eggs, salmon, cheese dishes, and, of course, vegetables (pickles!).

dollop   A spoonful of something creamy and thick, like sour cream or whipped cream.

dredge   To cover a piece of food with a dry substance, such as flour or corn meal.

drizzle   To lightly sprinkle drops of a liquid over food. Drizzling is often the finishing touch to a dish.

dry-pack   Frozen fruits packed without any additional sugar or syrup.

emulsion   A combination of liquid ingredients that would normally separate beaten together to create a thick liquid, such as a fat or oil with water. Classic examples are salad dressings and mayonnaise. Creation of an emulsion must be done carefully and rapidly to ensure that particles of one ingredient are suspended in the other.

entrée   The main dish in a meal. In France, however, the entrée is considered the first course.

extra-virgin olive oil   *See* olive oil.

fennel   In seed form, a fragrant, licorice-tasting spice. The bulbs have a much milder flavor and a celerylike crunch and are used as a vegetable in salads or cooked recipes.

fermented black beans   Small Chinese black soy beans with a pungent flavor that are preserved in salt before being packaged.

feta   This white, crumbly, salty cheese is popular in Greek cooking, on salads, and on its own. Traditional feta is usually made with sheep's milk, but feta-style cheese can be made from sheep's, cow's, or goat's milk. Its sharp flavor is especially nice with bitter, cured black olives.

fillet   A piece of meat or seafood with the bones removed.

flake   To break into thin sections, as with fish.

floret   The flower or bud end of broccoli or cauliflower.

fold   To combine a dense and light mixture with a circular action from the middle of the bowl.

fricassee   A dish, usually chicken, cut into pieces and cooked in a liquid or sauce.

frittata   A skillet and oven-cooked mixture of eggs and other ingredients that is not stirred but is cooked slowly and then removed from the pan after baking.

fry   *See* sauté.

fusion   To blend two or more styles of cooking, such as Chinese and French.

garlic   A member of the onion family, a pungent and flavorful element in many savory dishes. A garlic bulb, the form in which garlic is often sold, contains multiple cloves. Each clove, when chopped, provides about 1 teaspoon garlic. Most recipes call for cloves or chopped garlic by the teaspoon.

garnish   An embellishment not vital to the dish, but added to enhance visual appeal.

ginger   Technically a rhizome, ginger is available in fresh root or dried, ground and crystallized forms. Ginger adds a pungent, sweet, and spicy quality to both savory dishes and desserts. It is a very popular element of many Asian and Indian dishes, among others.

goulash   A rich, Hungarian-style meat-and-vegetable stew seasoned with paprika, as well as other spices.

grate   To shave into tiny pieces using a sharp rasp or grater.

gratin   Any cheese- and/or breadcrumb-topped dish that is cooked in a low pan to achieve a crispy, brown crust.

grind   To reduce a large, hard substance, often a seasoning such as peppercorns, to the consistency of sand.

grits   Coarsely ground grains, usually corn.

Gruyère   A rich, sharp cow's milk cheese made in Switzerland. It has a nutty flavor.

handful   An unscientific measurement term that refers to the amount of an ingredient you can hold in your hand.

hash   Food that is finely chopped and is frequently made from leftovers.

hazelnuts (also **filberts**)   A sweet nut popular in desserts and, to a lesser degree, in savory dishes.

herbes de Provence   A seasoning mix including basil, fennel, marjoram, rosemary, sage, and thyme, common in the south of France.

hoisin sauce   A sweet Asian condiment similar to ketchup, made with soybeans, sesame, chili peppers, and sugar.

infusion   A liquid in which flavorful ingredients such as herbs have been soaked or steeped to extract that flavor into the liquid.

Italian breadcrumbs   Breadcrumbs seasoned with parsley, other herbs, garlic, and Parmesan cheese.

Italian seasoning (also **spaghetti sauce seasoning**)   The ubiquitous grocery store blend of dried herbs, which includes basil, oregano, rosemary, and thyme, is a useful seasoning for quick flavor that evokes the "old country" in sauces, meatballs, soups, and vegetable dishes.

julienne   A French word meaning "to slice into very thin pieces."

kalamata olives   Traditionally from Greece, these medium-small long black olives have a smoky rich flavor, very different from run-of-the-mill canned black olives.

kasha   Roasted buckwheat groats popular in traditional Eastern European cooking.

knead   To work dough to make it pliable so it will hold gas bubbles as it bakes. Kneading is fundamental in the process of making yeast breads.

kosher salt   A coarse-grained salt made without any additives or iodine, used by many cooks because it does not impart a chemical flavor.

lentils   Tiny lens-shape pulses used in European, Middle Eastern, and Indian cuisines.

marbling   Thin streaks of fat that run through pieces of red meat such as beef and lamb. The veins enhance the flavor and tenderness.

marinate   To soak meat, seafood, or other food in a seasoned sauce, called a marinade, which is high in acid content. The acids break down the muscle of the meat, making it tender and adding flavor.

marjoram   A sweet herb, a cousin of and similar to oregano, popular in Greek, Spanish, and Italian dishes.

mesclun   Mixed salad greens, usually containing lettuce and assorted greens such as arugula, cress, endive, and others.

mince   To cut into very small pieces smaller than diced pieces, about ⅛ inch or smaller.

mold   A decorative, shaped metal pan in which contents, such as mousse or gelatin, set up and take the shape of the pan.

nam pla   A salty, fermented fish sauce with a pungent aroma used in Thai cooking.

nutmeg   A sweet, fragrant, musky spice used primarily in baking.

olive oil   A fragrant liquid produced by crushing or pressing olives. Extra-virgin olive oil is the oil produced from the first pressing of a batch of olives; oil is also produced from other pressings after the first. Extra-virgin olive oil is generally considered the most flavorful and highest quality and is the type you want to use when your focus is on the oil itself.

olives   The fruit of the olive tree commonly grown on all sides of the Mediterranean. There are many varieties of olives but two general types: green and black. Black olives are also called ripe olives. Green olives are immature, although they are also widely eaten. *See also* kalamata olives.

oregano   A fragrant, slightly astringent herb used in Greek, Spanish, and Italian dishes.

orzo   A rice-shape pasta used in Greek cooking.

oxidation   The browning of fruit flesh that happens over time and with exposure to air. If you need to cut apples in advance, minimize oxidation by rubbing the cut surfaces with a lemon half. Oxidation also affects wine, which is why the taste changes over time after a bottle is opened.

oyster sauce   A thick Asian sauce made from ground oysters, salt, and water with a slightly sweet taste.

paella   A grand Spanish dish of rice, shellfish, onion, meats, rich broth, and herbs.

paprika   A rich, red, warm, earthy spice that also lends a rich red color to many dishes.

parboil   To partially cook in boiling water or broth. Parboiling is similar to blanching, although blanched foods are quickly cooled with cold water.

Parmesan   A hard, dry, flavorful cheese primarily used grated or shredded as a seasoning for Italian-style dishes.

parsley   A fresh-tasting green leafy herb used to add flavor, color, and interest to just about any savory dish. Often used as a garnish just before serving.

pecans   Rich, buttery nuts native to North America. Their flavor, a terrific addition to appetizers, is at least partially due to their high unsaturated fat content.

peppercorns   Large, round, dried berries that are ground to produce pepper.

Pernod   A light green, licorice-flavored liqueur popular in France.

pesto   A thick spread or sauce made with fresh basil leaves, garlic, olive oil, pine nuts, and Parmesan cheese. Some newer versions are made with other herbs. Pesto can be made at home or purchased in a grocery store and used on anything from appetizers to pasta and other main dishes.

pickle   A food, usually a vegetable such as a cucumber, that has been pickled in brine.

pilaf   A rice dish in which the rice is browned in butter or oil, then cooked in a flavorful liquid such as a broth, often with the addition of meats or vegetables. The rice absorbs the broth, resulting in a savory dish.

pinch   An unscientific measurement term that refers to the amount of an ingredient—typically a dry, granular substance such as an herb or seasoning—you can hold between your finger and thumb.

pine nuts (also **pignoli** or **piñon**)   Nuts grown on pine trees that are rich (read: high fat), flavorful, and a bit pine-y. Pine nuts are a traditional component of pesto and add a wonderful hearty crunch to many other recipes.

plantain   A relative of the banana, a plantain is larger, milder in flavor, and used as a staple in many Latin American dishes.

poach   To cook a food in simmering liquid, such as water, wine, or broth.

porcini mushrooms   Rich and flavorful mushrooms used in rice and Italian-style dishes.

portobello mushrooms   A mature and larger form of the smaller crimini mushroom, portobellos are brownish, chewy, and flavorful. They are trendy served as whole caps, grilled, and as thin sautéed slices. *See also* crimini mushrooms.

preheat   To turn on an oven, broiler, or other cooking appliance in advance of cooking so the temperature will be at the desired level when the assembled dish is ready for cooking.

prosciutto   Dry, salt-cured ham that originated in Italy. Prosciutto is popular in many simple dishes in which its unique flavor is allowed to shine.

purée   To reduce a food to a thick, creamy texture, usually using a blender or food processor.

radicchio   Part of the chicory family, radicchio is a brightly colored burgundy lettuce with white ribs.

ragout   A thick stew made with a number of ingredients in a richly flavored sauce.

reduce   To boil or simmer a broth or sauce to remove some of the water content, resulting in smaller volume, as well as more concentrated flavor and color.

reserve   To hold a specified ingredient for another use later in the recipe.

rice vinegar   Vinegar produced from fermented rice or rice wine, popular in Asian-style dishes. Different from rice wine vinegar.

risotto   A popular Italian rice dish made by browning arborio rice in butter or oil, then slowly adding liquid to cook the rice, resulting in a creamy texture from releasing the starch from the rice by stirring.

roast   To cook something uncovered in an oven, usually without additional liquid.

Roquefort   A world-famous (French) creamy but sharp sheep's milk cheese containing blue lines of mold, making it a "blue cheese."

rosemary   A pungent, sweet herb used with chicken, pork, fish, and especially lamb. A little of it goes a long way.

roux   A mixture of butter or another fat and flour, used to thicken sauces and soups.

rutabaga   A root vegetable similar in appearance to a turnip, but with a sweeter flavor.

saffron   A famous spice made from the stamens of crocus flowers. Saffron lends a dramatic yellow color and distinctive flavor to a dish. Only a tiny amount needs to be used, which is good because saffron is very expensive.

sage   An herb with a musty yet fruity, lemon-rind scent and "sunny" flavor. It is a terrific addition to many dishes.

salsa   A style of mixing fresh vegetables and/or fresh fruit in a coarse chop. Salsa can be spicy or not, fruit-based or not, and served as a starter on its own (with chips, for example) or as a companion to a main course.

sauté   The French term for pan-frying with very little fat by keeping the food moving around in the pan so that it does not stick.

savory   A popular herb with a fresh, woody taste.

sear   To quickly brown the exterior of a food over high heat to preserve interior moisture (that's why many meat recipes involve searing).

sesame oil   An oil, made from pressing sesame seeds, that is tasteless if clear and aromatic and flavorful if brown.

shallot   A member of the onion family that grows in a bulb somewhat like garlic and has a milder onion flavor that grows both as single and double bulbs.

shanks   The lowest part of the front leg of lambs, cattle, veal calves, and pigs. Lamb and pork shanks are sold whole, while beef and veal shanks are sold in crosswise sections.

shellfish   A broad range of seafood, including mollusks such as clams, mussels, and oysters, as well as crabs, shrimp, and lobster, which are classified as crustaceans. Some people are allergic to shellfish, so care should be taken with its inclusion in recipes.

shiitake mushrooms   Large, dark brown mushrooms originally from Asia with a hearty, meaty flavor that can be grilled or used as a component in other recipes and as a flavoring source for broth. They can be used either fresh or dried.

short-grain rice   A starchy rice popular for Asian-style dishes because it readily clumps for eating with chopsticks.

shred   To cut into many long, thin slices.

simmer   To boil gently so the liquid barely bubbles.

skillet (also **frying pan**)   A generally heavy, flat-bottomed metal pan with a handle designed to cook food over heat on a stovetop or campfire. Ones with metal handles can also be placed in the oven.

skim   To remove fat or other material from the top of liquid.

slice   To cut into thin pieces.

spaghetti squash   A hard-skinned winter squash shaped like a watermelon that, once cooked and combed with the tines of a fork, forms distinct, spaghettilike strands.

steam   To suspend a food over boiling water and allow the heat of the steam (water vapor) to cook the food. Steaming is a very quick cooking method that preserves the flavor and texture of a food.

steep   To let sit in hot water, as in steeping tea in hot water for 10 minutes.

stew   To slowly cook pieces of food submerged in a liquid. Also, a dish that has been prepared by this method.

sticky rice (or **glutinous rice**)   *See* short-grain rice.

Stilton The famous English blue-veined cheese, delicious with toasted nuts and renowned for its pairing with Port wine.

stir-fry To cook small pieces of food in a wok or skillet over high heat, moving and turning the food quickly to cook all sides.

stock A flavorful broth made by cooking meats and/or vegetables with seasonings until the liquid absorbs these flavors. This liquid is then strained and the solids discarded. Stock can be eaten by itself or used as a base for soups, stews, sauces, risotto, or many other recipes.

strata A savory bread pudding made with eggs and cheese.

Swiss chard A member of the beet family with crinkly green leaves and silver, celerylike stalks.

tamari A dark sauce made from soy beans with a more mellow, and less salty, flavor than soy sauce.

tarragon A sweet, rich-smelling herb perfect with seafood, vegetables (especially asparagus), chicken, and pork.

thyme A minty, zesty herb whose leaves are used in a wide range of recipes.

toast To heat something, usually bread, so it is browned and crisp.

tofu A cheeselike substance made from soybeans and soy milk. Flavorful and nutritious, tofu is an important component of foods across the globe, especially from East Asia.

tomatillo A small, round fruit with a distinctive spicy flavor. Tomatillos are a traditional component of many south-of-the-border dishes. To use, remove the papery outer skin, rinse off any sticky residue, and chop like a tomato.

turmeric A spicy, pungent yellow rhizome used in many dishes, especially in Indian cuisine, for color and flavor. Turmeric is the source of the brilliant yellow color in many prepared mustards.

veal Meat from a calf, generally characterized by mild flavor and tenderness. Certain cuts of veal, such as cutlets and scaloppini, are well suited to quick-cooking.

vinegar An acidic liquid widely used as dressing and seasoning. Many cuisines use vinegars made from different source materials such as fermented grapes, apples, and rice. *See also* balsamic vinegar; cider vinegar; rice vinegar; white vinegar; wine vinegar.

walnuts Grown worldwide, walnuts bring a rich, slightly woody flavor to all types of food. For the quick cook, walnuts are available chopped and ready to go at your grocery store. They are delicious toasted and make fine accompaniments to cheeses.

water chestnuts Actually a tuber, water chestnuts are a popular element in many types of Asian-style cooking. The flesh is white, crunchy, and juicy, and the vegetable holds its texture whether cool or hot.

whisk To rapidly mix, introducing air to the mixture.

white mushrooms Ubiquitous button mushrooms. When fresh, they will have an earthy smell and an appealing "soft crunch." White mushrooms are delicious raw in salads, marinated, sautéed, and as component ingredients in many recipes.

white vinegar The most common type of vinegar found on grocery store shelves. It is produced from grain.

whole-wheat flour   Wheat flour that contains the entire grain.

wild rice   Actually a grass with a rich, nutty flavor, popular as a nutritious side dish and also used for stuffings.

wine vinegar   Vinegar produced from red or white wine.

wok   A wonderful tool for quick-cooking.

Worcestershire sauce   Originally developed in India and containing tamarind, this spicy sauce is used as a seasoning for many meats and other dishes.

zest   Small slivers of peel, usually from a citrus fruit such as lemon, lime, or orange.

zester   A small kitchen tool used to scrape zest off a fruit. A small grater also works well.

Metric Conversion and Common Measurement Tables

The scientifically precise calculations needed for baking are not necessary when cooking conventionally, and the tables in this appendix are designed for general cooking. If you're making conversions for baking, grab your calculator and compute the exact figure.

Converting Ounces to Grams

Ounces	Grams	Ounces	Grams
1 oz.	30 g	9 oz.	250 g
2 oz.	60 g	10 oz.	285 g
3 oz.	85 g	11 oz.	300 g
4 oz.	115 g	12 oz.	340 g
5 oz.	140 g	13 oz.	370 g
6 oz.	180 g	14 oz.	400 g
7 oz.	200 g	15 oz.	425 g
8 oz.	225 g	16 oz.	450 g

The numbers in this table are approximate. To reach the exact amount of grams, multiply the number of ounces by 28.35.

Converting Quarts to Liters

Quarts	Liter	Quarts	Liter
1 cup (¼ qt.)	¼ L	4 qt.	3¾ L
1 pt. (½ qt.)	½ L	5 qt.	4¾ L
1 qt.	1 L	6 qt.	5½ L
2 qt.	2 L	7 qt.	6½ L
2½ qt.	2½ L	8 qt.	7½ L
3 qt.	2¾ L		

The numbers in this table are approximate. To reach the exact amount of liters, multiply the number of quarts by 0.95.

Converting Pounds to Grams and Kilograms

Pounds	Grams; Kilograms	Pounds	Grams; Kilograms
1 lb.	450 g	5 lb.	2¼ kg
1½ lb.	675 g	5½ lb.	2½ kg
2 lb.	900 g	6 lb.	2¾ kg
2½ lb.	1,125 g; 1¼ kg	6½ lb.	3 kg
3 lb.	1,350 g	7 lb.	3¼ kg
3½ lb.	1,500 g; 1½ kg	7½ lb.	3½ kg
4 lb.	1,800 g	8 lb.	3¾ kg
4½ lb.	2 kg		

The numbers in this table are approximate. To reach the exact amount of kilograms, multiply the number of pounds by 453.6.

Converting Fahrenheit to Celsius

Fahrenheit	Celsius	Fahrenheit	Celsius
170°F	77°C	350°F	180°C
180°F	82°C	375°F	190°C
190°F	88°C	400°F	205°C
200°F	95°C	425°F	220°C
225°F	110°C	450°F	230°C
250°F	120°C	475°F	245°C
300°F	150°C	500°F	260°C
325°F	165°C		

The numbers in this table are approximate. To reach the exact temperature, subtract 32 from the Fahrenheit reading, multiply the number by 5, and then divide by 9.

Converting Inches to Centimeters

Inches	Centimeters	Inches	Centimeters
½ in.	1.5 cm	7 in.	18 cm
1 in.	2.5 cm	8 in.	20 cm
2 in.	5 cm	9 in.	23 cm
3 in.	8 cm	10 in.	25 cm
4 in.	10 cm	11 in.	28 cm
5 in.	13 cm	12 in.	30 cm
6 in.	15 cm		

The numbers in this table are approximate. To reach the exact number of centimeters, multiply the number of inches by 2.54.

Americans measure foods by both weight and volume, and it can be confusing to make the correlation between the two. Ingredients are usually sold by weight, but are specified by volume in recipes. In this chapter are the weights and measures of some more commonly used foods.

When multiplying or dividing a recipe, it's also important to know liquid measures. That's why these tables will come in handy not only for the recipes in this book, but in all your general cooking.

Weights and Measures of Common Ingredients

Food	Quantity	Yield
Apples	1 lb.	2½ to 3 cups, sliced
Bananas	1 medium	1 cup, sliced
Blueberries	1 lb.	3⅓ cups
Butter	¼ lb. (1 stick)	8 TB.
Chocolate, bulk	1 oz.	3 TB., grated
Chocolate, morsels	12 oz.	2 cups
Cocoa powder	1 oz.	¼ cup
Coconut, flaked	7 oz.	2½ cups
Cream	½ pt.	1 cup; 2 cups, whipped
Cream cheese	8 oz.	1 cup
Flour	1 lb.	4 cups
Lemons	1 medium	3 TB. juice
Milk	1 qt.	4 cups
Molasses	12 oz.	1½ cups

continues

Weights and Measures of Common Ingredients   (continued)

Food	Quantity	Yield
Pecans	6 oz.	1½ cups
Raisins	1 lb.	3 cups
Strawberries	1 pt.	1½ cups, sliced
Sugar, brown	1 lb.	2¼ cups, packed
Sugar, confectioners'	1 lb.	4 cups
Sugar, granulated	1 lb.	2¼ cups

Liquid Measurements		
Pinch	=	less than ⅛ tsp.
3 tsp.	=	1 TB.
2 TB.	=	1 oz.
8 TB.	=	½ cup
2 cups	=	1 pt.
1 qt.	=	2 pt.

Index

W-X-Y-Z